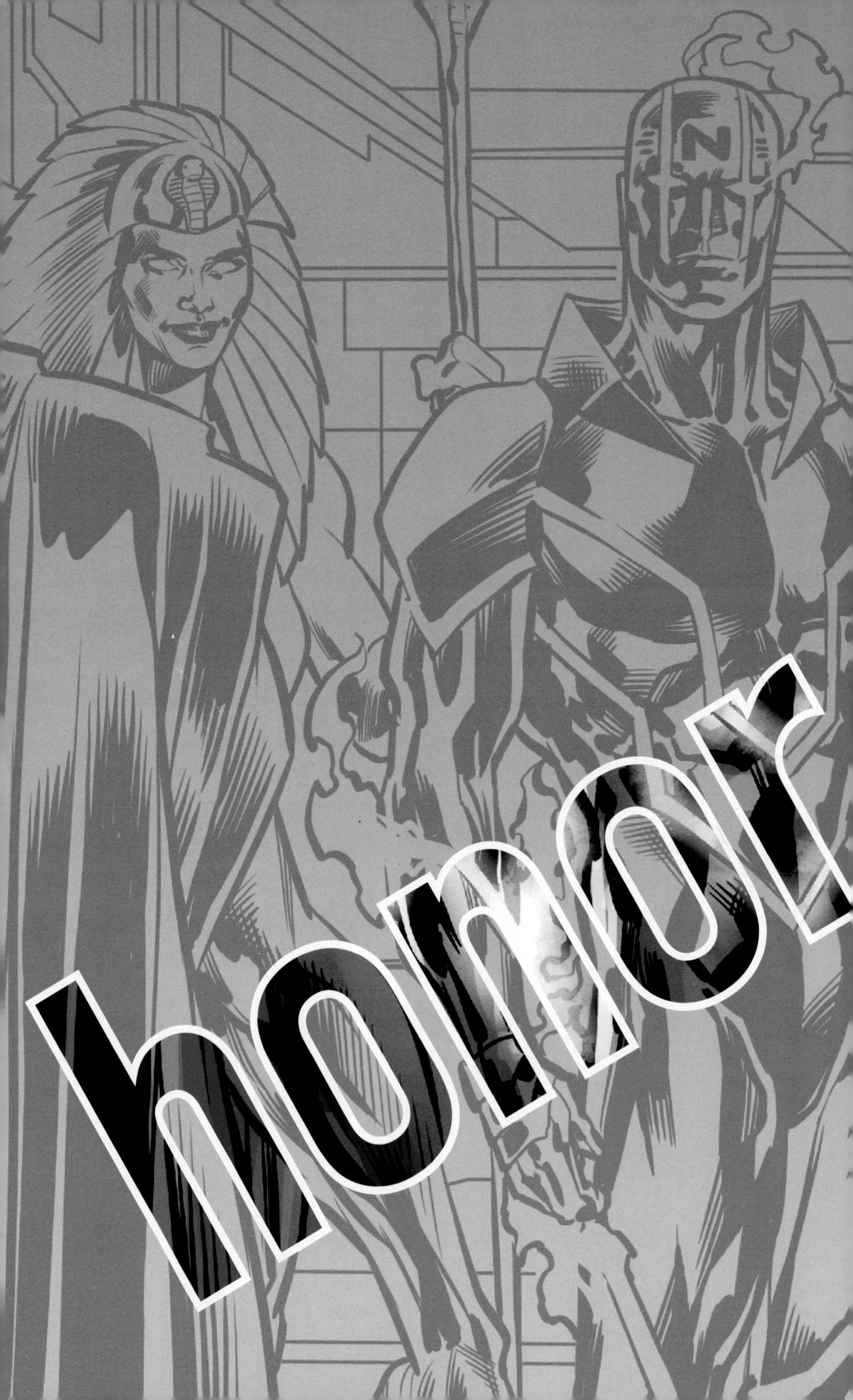
honor

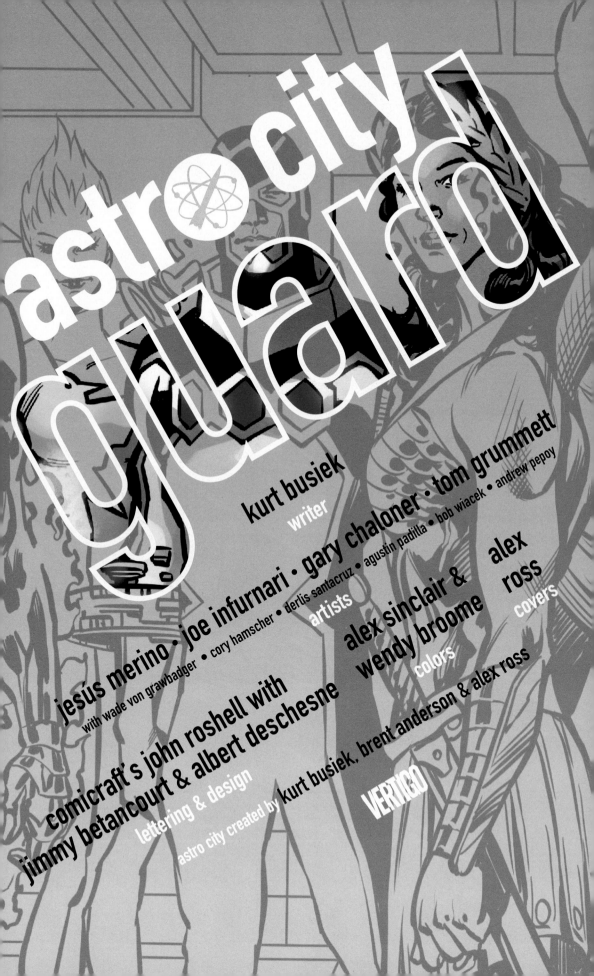

astro city guard

kurt busiek
writer

jesús merino · joe infurnari · gary chaloner · tom grummett
with wade von grawbadger · cory hamscher · derlis santacruz · agustin padilla · bob wiacek · andrew pepoy
artists

alex sinclair & wendy broome
colors

alex ross
covers

comicraft's john roshell with jimmy betancourt & albert deschesne
lettering & design

astro city created by kurt busiek, brent anderson & alex ross

VERTIGO

VERTIGO

Kristy Quinn — Editors – Original Series
Molly Mahan — Assistant Editor – Original Series
Jessica Chen — Group Editor – Vertigo
Jamie Rich — Group Editor – Collected Edition
Jeb Woodard — Editor – Collected Editions
Liz Erickson — Design Director – Books
Steve Cook

Diane Nelson — President
Dan DiDio — Publisher
Jim Lee — Publisher
Geoff Johns — President & Chief Creative Officer
Amit Desai — Executive VP – Business & Marketing Strategy, Direct to Consumer & Global Franchise Management
— Senior VP – Direct to Consumer

Sam Ades — VP – Talent Development
Bobbie Chase — Senior VP – Art, Design & Collected Editions
Mark Chiarello — Senior VP – Sales & Trade Marketing
John Cunningham — Senior VP – Business Strategy, Finance & Administration
Anne DePies — VP – Business Operations
Don Falletti — VP – Manufacturing Operations
Lawrence Ganem — VP – Editorial Administration & Talent Relations
Alison Gill — Senior VP – Manufacturing & Operations
Hank Kanalz — Senior VP – Editorial Strategy & Administration
Jay Kogan — VP – Legal Affairs
Thomas Loftus — VP – Business Affairs
Jack Mahan — VP – Business Affairs
Nick J. Napolitano — VP – Manufacturing Administration
Eddie Scannell — VP – Consumer Marketing
Courtney Simmons — VP – Publicity & Communications
Jim (Ski) Sokolowski — Senior VP – Comic Book Specialty Sales & Trade Marketing
Nancy Spears — VP – Mass, Book, Digital Sales & Trade Marketing

Juke Box PRODUCTIONS

COMICRAFT SINCE 1992

RICHARD STARKINGS
Art Director

ASTRO CITY VOL. 13: HONOR GUARD

Published by DC Comics. Compilation, cover and all new material
Copyright © 2017 Juke Box Productions. All Rights Reserved.

Originally published in single magazine form as ASTRO CITY 17, 22,
25, 27-28, 31 © 2014, 2015, 2016 Juke Box Productions. All Rights
Reserved. Astro City, its logos, symbols, prominent characters
featured in this volume and the distinctive likenesses thereof are
trademarks of Juke Box Productions. VERTIGO is a trademark of
DC Comics. The stories, characters and incidents featured in this
publication are entirely fictional. DC Comics does not read or accept
unsolicited submissions of ideas, stories or artwork.

DC Comics, 2900 West Alameda Ave., Burbank, CA 91505
Printed by LSC Communications, Salem, VA. 2/3/17. First Pr
ISBN: 978-1-4012-6828-2

Library of Congress Cataloging-in-Publication Data

Names: Busiek, Kurt, author. | Ross, Alex, 1970- illustrator. | Merino,
Jesus, illustrator.
Title: Astro City : honor guard / Kurt Busiek, writer ; Alex Ross, Jesus
Merino, artists.
Description: Burbank, CA : DC Comics/Vertigo, [2016]
Identifiers: LCCN 2016013380 | ISBN 9-781401-268282
Subjects: LCSH: Comic books, strips, etc. | BISAC: COMICS & GRAPHIC NOVELS /
Superheroes.
Classification: LCC PN6728.A79 B75 2016 | DDC 741.5/973—dc23
LC record available at https://lccn.loc.gov/2016013380

Contents

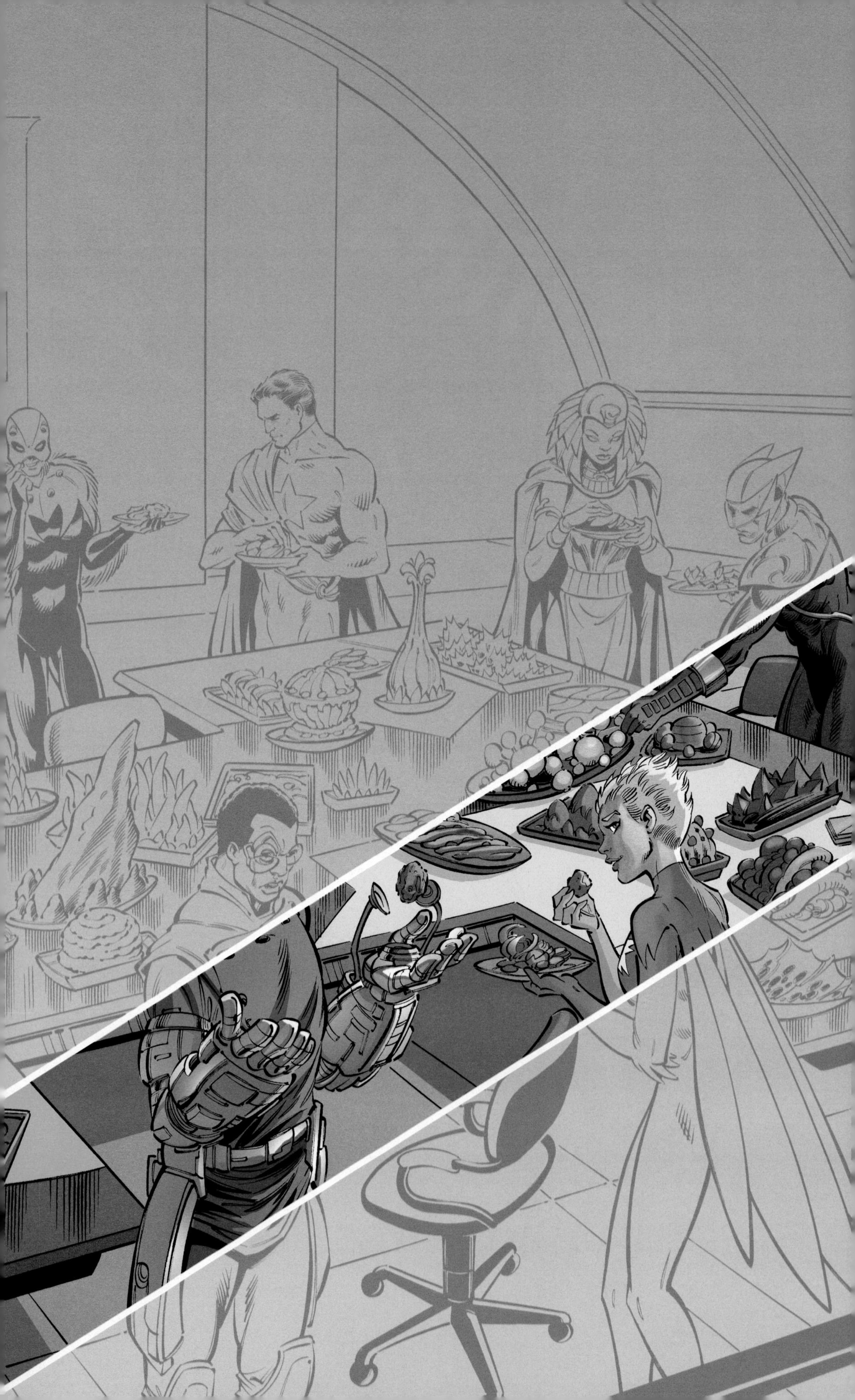

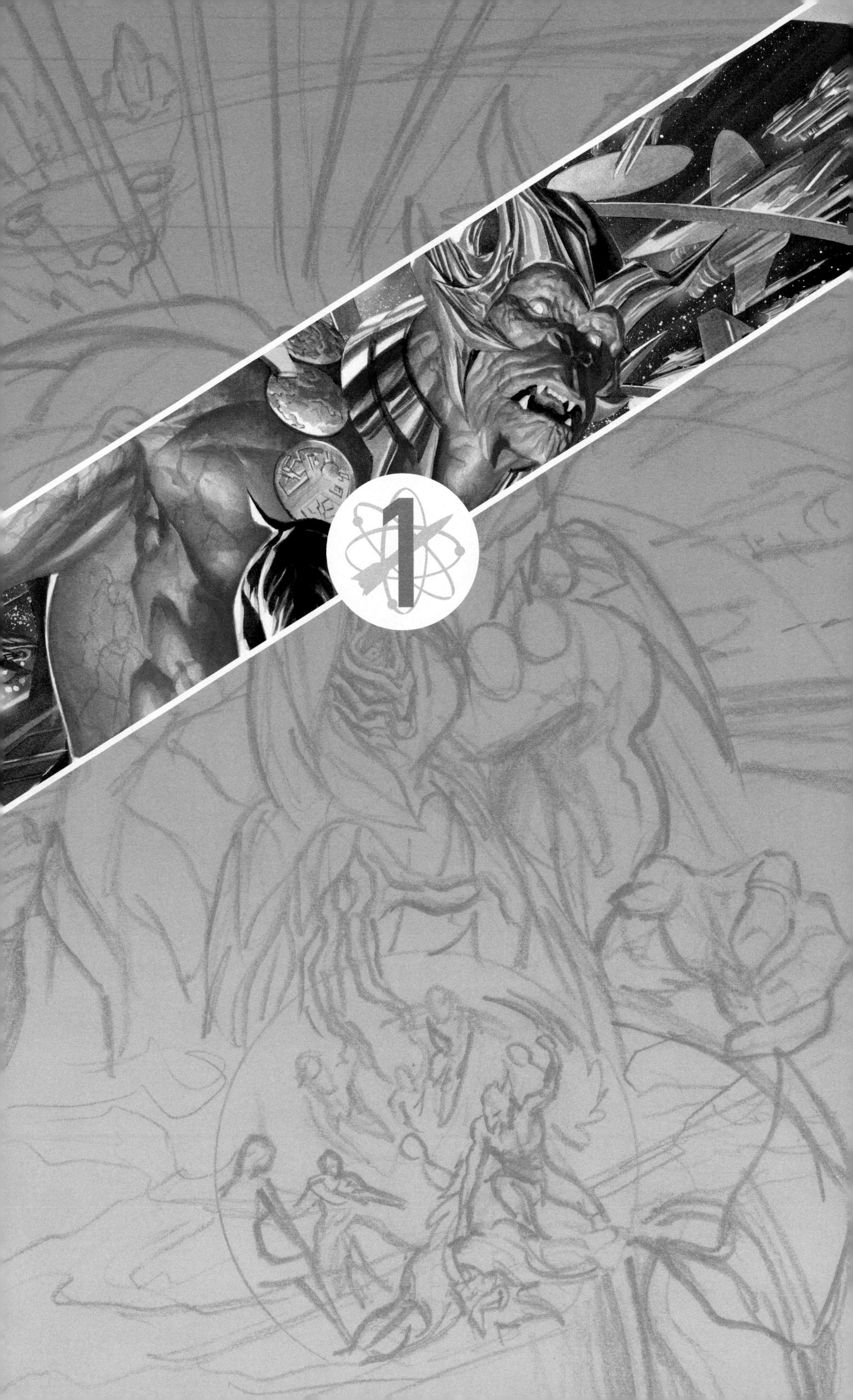
1

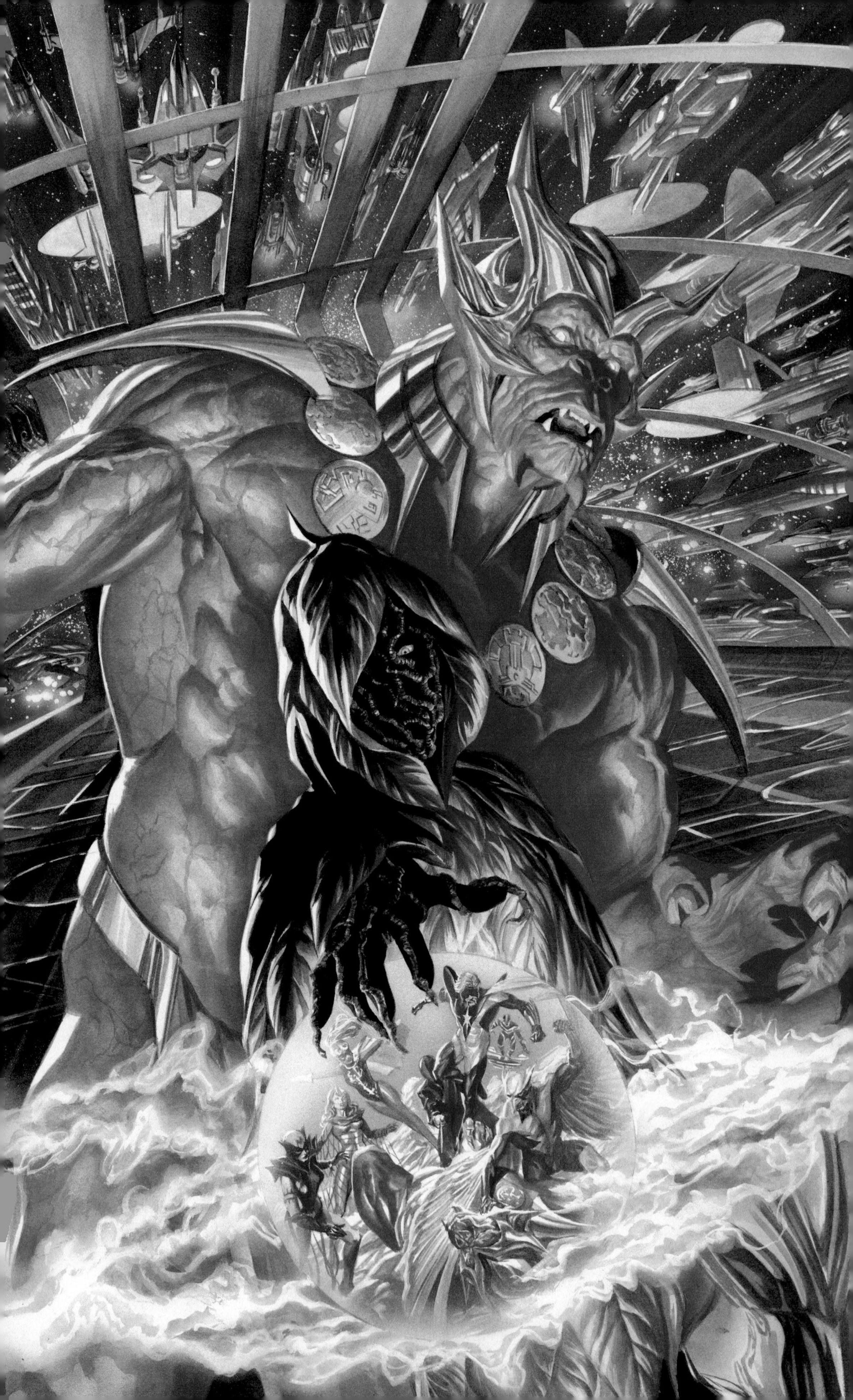

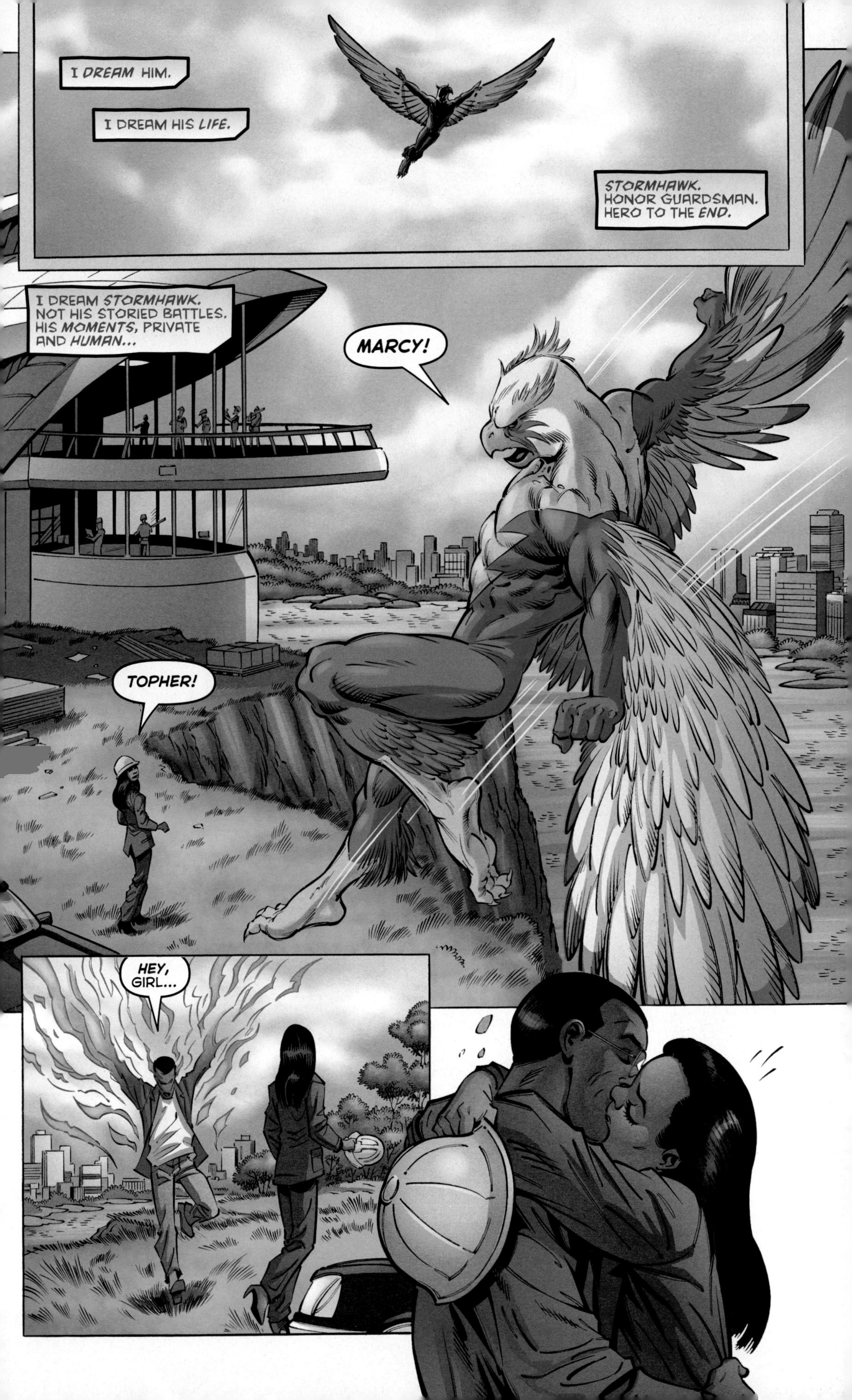
I DREAM HIM.
I DREAM HIS LIFE.
STORMHAWK. HONOR GUARDSMAN. HERO TO THE END.
I DREAM STORMHAWK. NOT HIS STORIED BATTLES. HIS MOMENTS, PRIVATE AND HUMAN...
MARCY!
TOPHER!
HEY, GIRL...

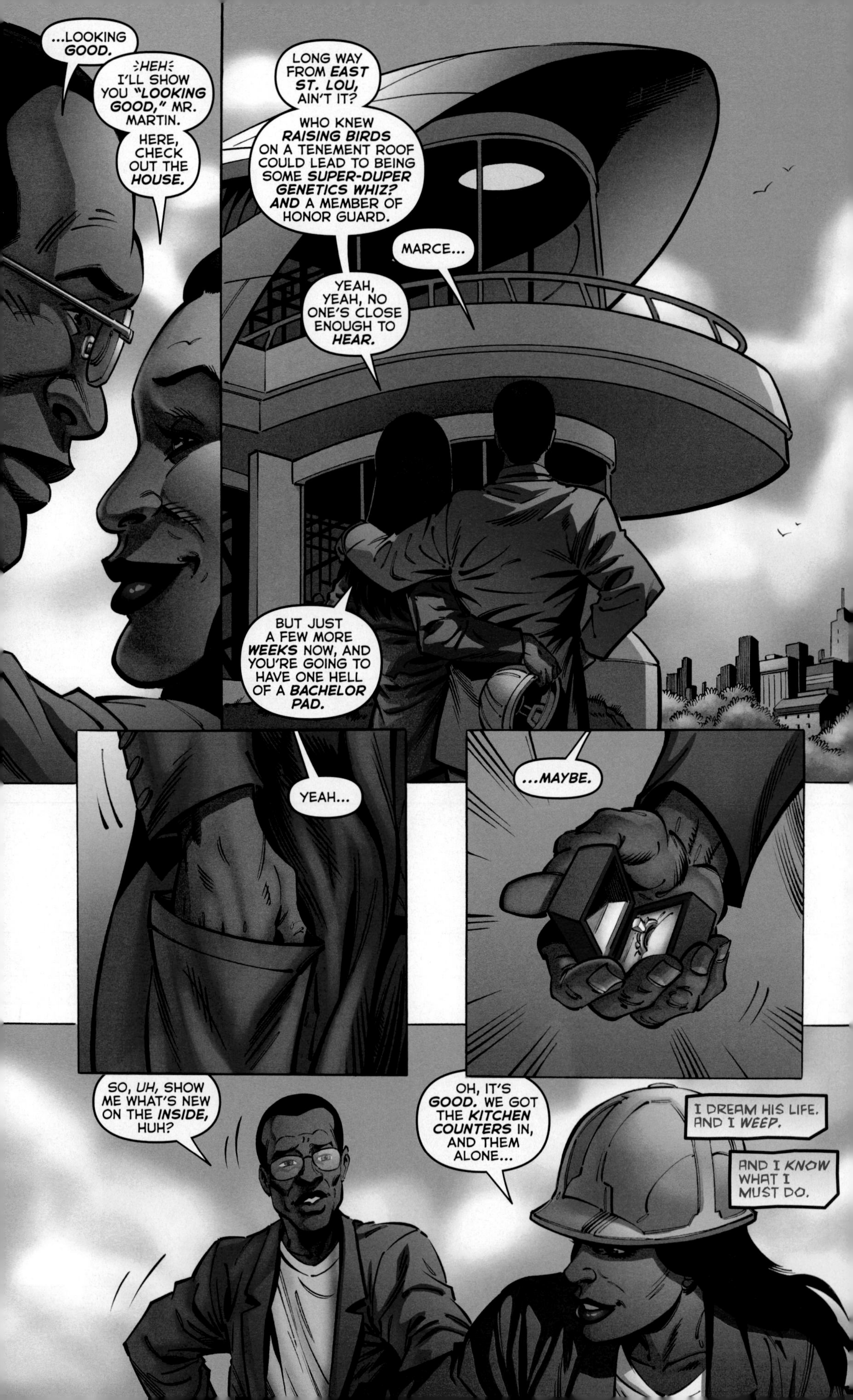
...LOOKING GOOD.
HEH I'LL SHOW YOU "LOOKING GOOD," MR. MARTIN.
HERE, CHECK OUT THE HOUSE.
LONG WAY FROM EAST ST. LOU, AIN'T IT?
WHO KNEW RAISING BIRDS ON A TENEMENT ROOF COULD LEAD TO BEING SOME SUPER-DUPER GENETICS WHIZ? AND A MEMBER OF HONOR GUARD.
MARCE...
YEAH, YEAH, NO ONE'S CLOSE ENOUGH TO HEAR.
BUT JUST A FEW MORE WEEKS NOW, AND YOU'RE GOING TO HAVE ONE HELL OF A BACHELOR PAD.
YEAH...
...MAYBE.
SO, UH, SHOW ME WHAT'S NEW ON THE INSIDE, HUH?
OH, IT'S GOOD. WE GOT THE KITCHEN COUNTERS IN, AND THEM ALONE...
I DREAM HIS LIFE. AND I WEEP.
AND I KNOW WHAT I MUST DO.

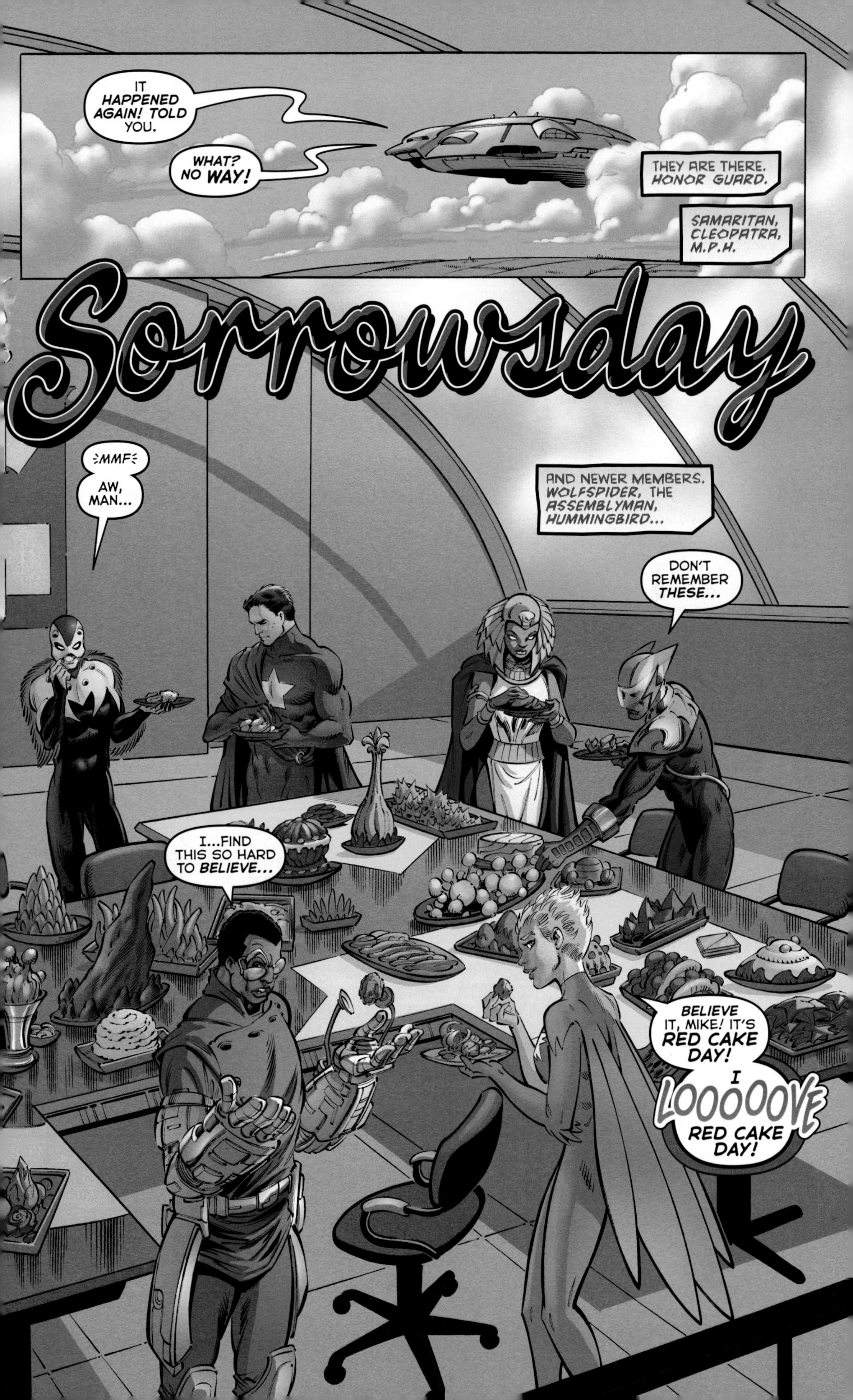
IT HAPPENED AGAIN! TOLD YOU.
WHAT? NO WAY!
THEY ARE THERE. HONOR GUARD.
SAMARITAN, CLEOPATRA, M.P.H.
Sorrowsday
MMF
AW, MAN...
AND NEWER MEMBERS. WOLFSPIDER, THE ASSEMBLYMAN, HUMMINGBIRD...
DON'T REMEMBER THESE...
I...FIND THIS SO HARD TO BELIEVE...
BELIEVE IT, MIKE! IT'S RED CAKE DAY!
I LOOOOOVE RED CAKE DAY!

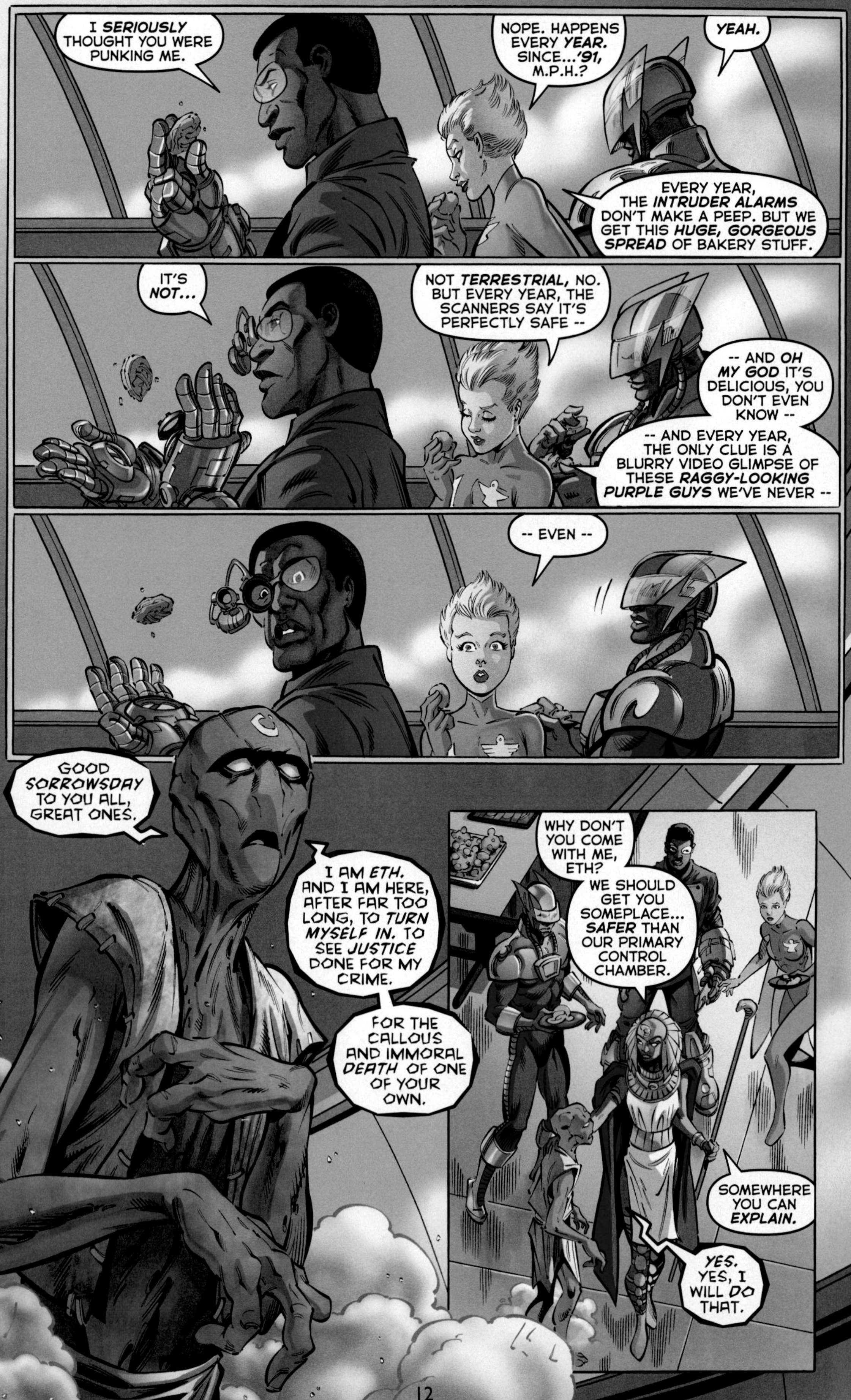

I SERIOUSLY THOUGHT YOU WERE PUNKING ME.
NOPE. HAPPENS EVERY YEAR. SINCE...'91, M.P.H.?
YEAH.
EVERY YEAR, THE INTRUDER ALARMS DON'T MAKE A PEEP. BUT WE GET THIS HUGE, GORGEOUS SPREAD OF BAKERY STUFF.
IT'S NOT...
NOT TERRESTRIAL, NO. BUT EVERY YEAR, THE SCANNERS SAY IT'S PERFECTLY SAFE --
-- AND OH MY GOD IT'S DELICIOUS, YOU DON'T EVEN KNOW --
-- AND EVERY YEAR, THE ONLY CLUE IS A BLURRY VIDEO GLIMPSE OF THESE RAGGY-LOOKING PURPLE GUYS WE'VE NEVER --
-- EVEN --
GOOD SORROWSDAY TO YOU ALL, GREAT ONES.
I AM ETH. AND I AM HERE, AFTER FAR TOO LONG, TO TURN MYSELF IN. TO SEE JUSTICE DONE FOR MY CRIME.
FOR THE CALLOUS AND IMMORAL DEATH OF ONE OF YOUR OWN.
WHY DON'T YOU COME WITH ME, ETH?
WE SHOULD GET YOU SOMEPLACE... SAFER THAN OUR PRIMARY CONTROL CHAMBER.
SOMEWHERE YOU CAN EXPLAIN.
YES. YES, I WILL DO THAT.

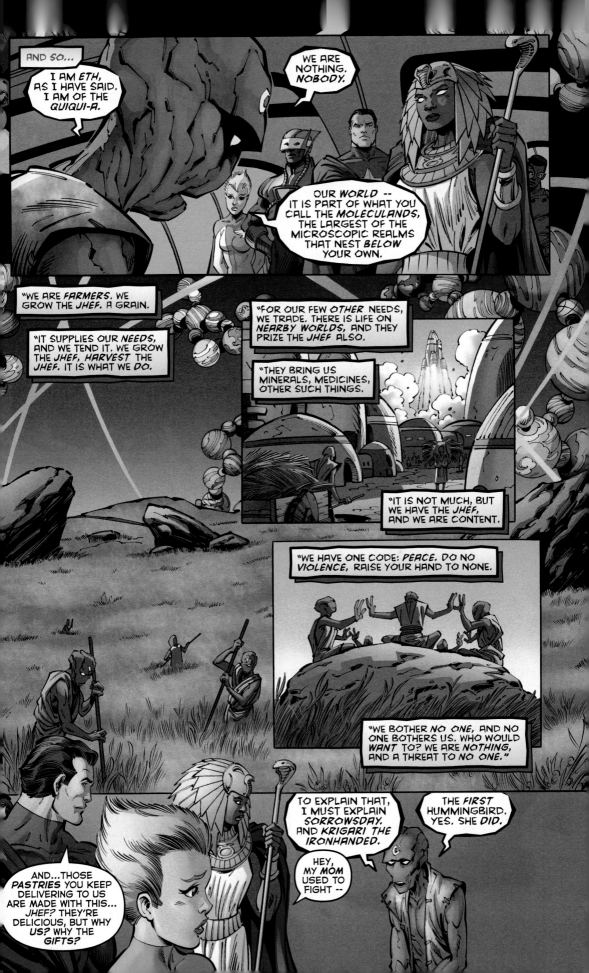

AND SO... I AM *ETH*, AS I HAVE SAID. I AM OF THE *QUIQUI-A*.

WE ARE NOTHING. *NOBODY.*

OUR *WORLD* -- IT IS PART OF WHAT YOU CALL THE *MOLECULANDS,* THE LARGEST OF THE MICROSCOPIC REALMS THAT NEST *BELOW* YOUR OWN.

"WE ARE *FARMERS.* WE GROW THE *JHEF.* A GRAIN.

"IT SUPPLIES OUR *NEEDS,* AND WE TEND IT. WE GROW THE *JHEF, HARVEST* THE *JHEF.* IT IS WHAT WE *DO.*

"FOR OUR FEW *OTHER* NEEDS, WE TRADE. THERE IS LIFE ON *NEARBY WORLDS,* AND THEY PRIZE THE *JHEF* ALSO.

"THEY BRING US MINERALS, MEDICINES, OTHER SUCH THINGS.

"IT IS NOT MUCH, BUT WE HAVE THE *JHEF,* AND WE ARE CONTENT.

"WE HAVE ONE CODE: *PEACE.* DO NO *VIOLENCE,* RAISE YOUR HAND TO NONE.

"WE BOTHER *NO ONE,* AND NO ONE BOTHERS US. WHO WOULD *WANT* TO? WE ARE *NOTHING,* AND A THREAT TO *NO ONE.*"

TO EXPLAIN THAT, I MUST EXPLAIN *SORROWSDAY.* AND *KRIGARI THE IRONHANDED.*

THE *FIRST* HUMMINGBIRD. YES. SHE *DID.*

HEY, MY *MOM* USED TO FIGHT --

AND...THOSE *PASTRIES* YOU KEEP DELIVERING TO US ARE MADE WITH THIS... *JHEF?* THEY'RE DELICIOUS, BUT WHY *US?* WHY THE *GIFTS?*

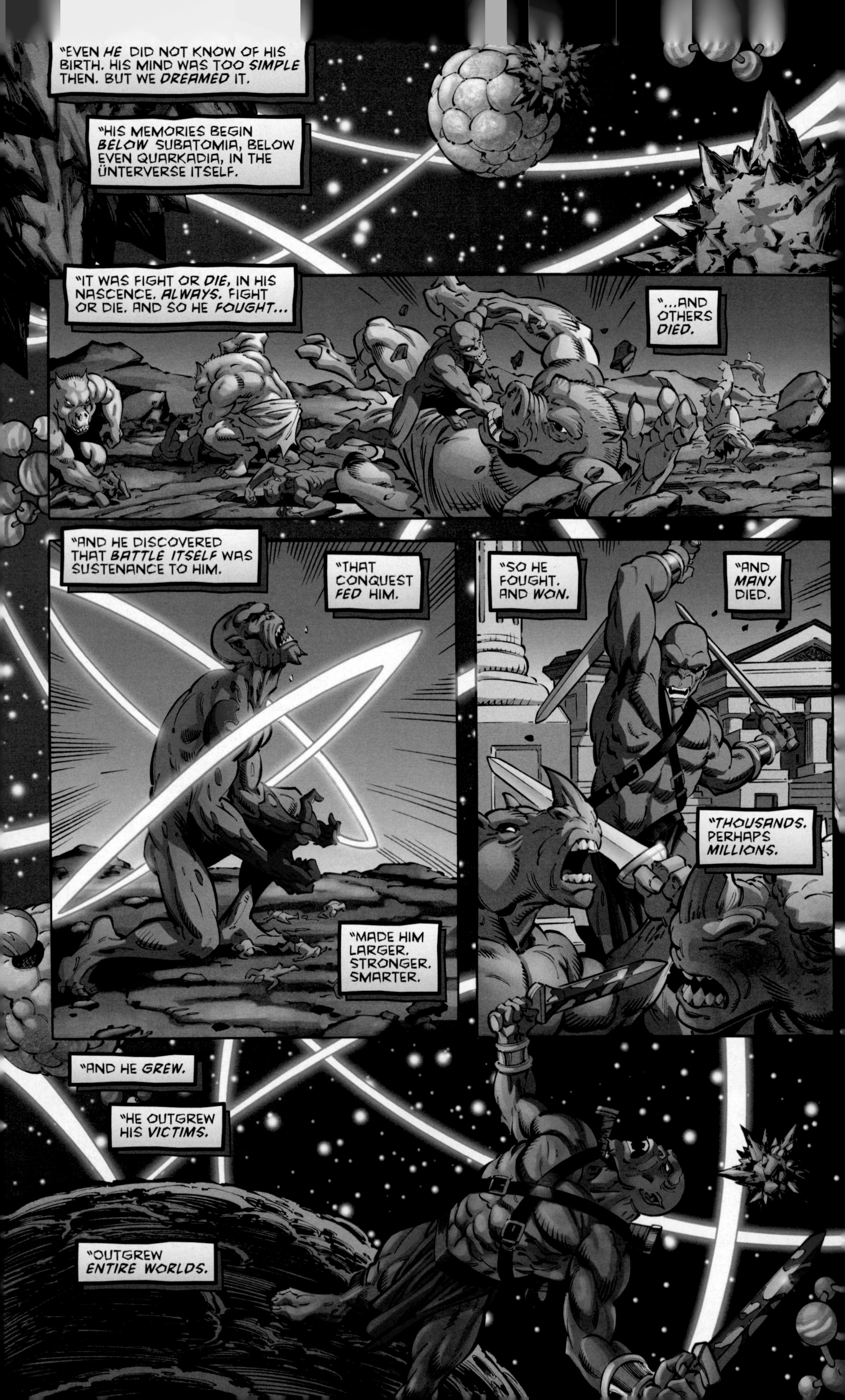
"EVEN HE DID NOT KNOW OF HIS BIRTH. HIS MIND WAS TOO SIMPLE THEN. BUT WE DREAMED IT.
"HIS MEMORIES BEGIN BELOW SUBATOMIA, BELOW EVEN QUARKADIA, IN THE ÜNTERVERSE ITSELF.
"IT WAS FIGHT OR DIE, IN HIS NASCENCE. ALWAYS. FIGHT OR DIE. AND SO HE FOUGHT...
"...AND OTHERS DIED.
"AND HE DISCOVERED THAT BATTLE ITSELF WAS SUSTENANCE TO HIM.
"THAT CONQUEST FED HIM.
"MADE HIM LARGER. STRONGER. SMARTER.
"SO HE FOUGHT. AND WON.
"AND MANY DIED.
"THOUSANDS. PERHAPS MILLIONS.
"AND HE GREW.
"HE OUTGREW HIS VICTIMS.
"OUTGREW ENTIRE WORLDS.

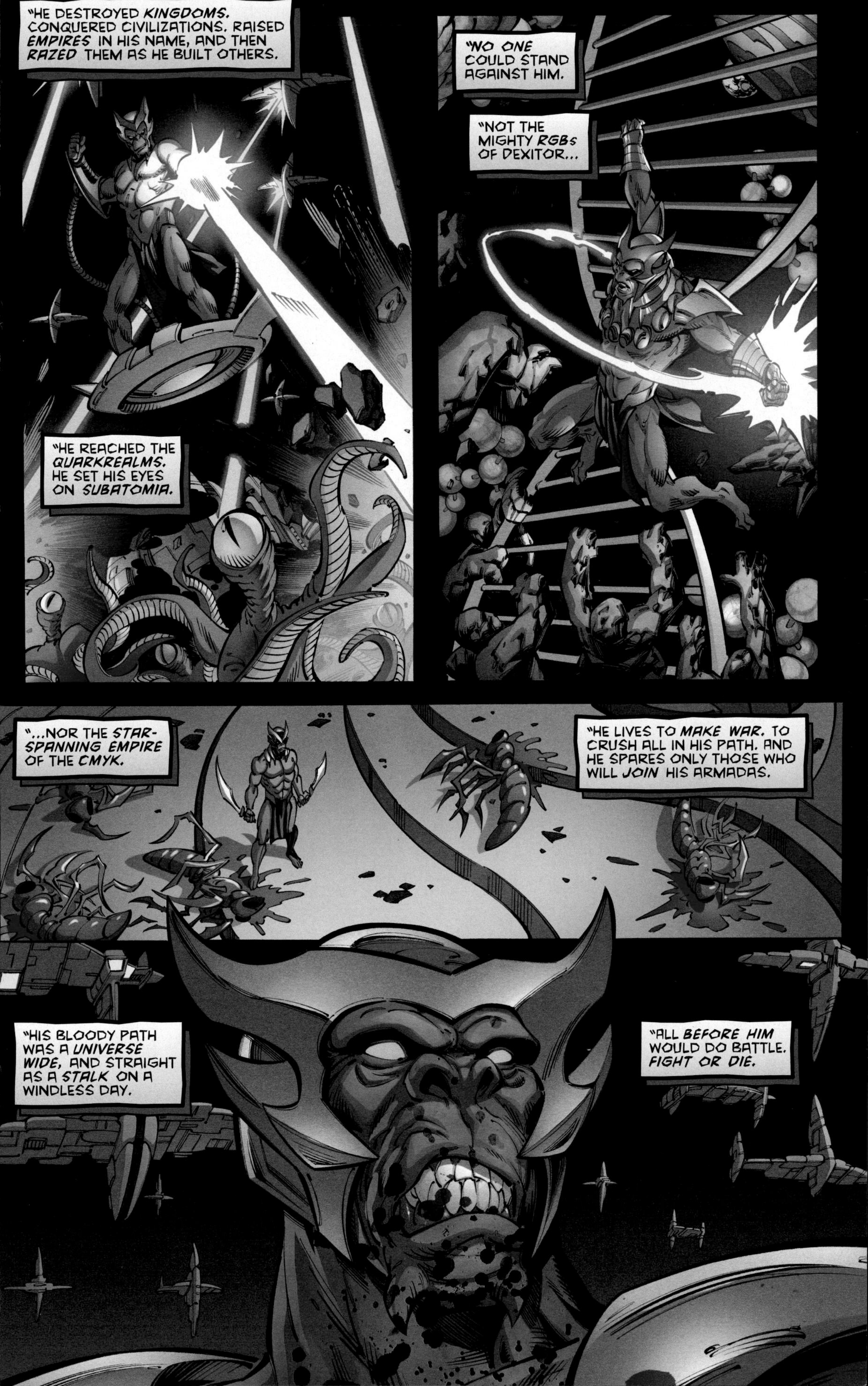
"HE DESTROYED KINGDOMS. CONQUERED CIVILIZATIONS. RAISED EMPIRES IN HIS NAME, AND THEN RAZED THEM AS HE BUILT OTHERS.
"HE REACHED THE QUARKREALMS. HE SET HIS EYES ON SUBATOMIA.
"NO ONE COULD STAND AGAINST HIM.
"NOT THE MIGHTY RGBs OF DEXITOR...
"...NOR THE STAR-SPANNING EMPIRE OF THE CMYK.
"HE LIVES TO MAKE WAR. TO CRUSH ALL IN HIS PATH. AND HE SPARES ONLY THOSE WHO WILL JOIN HIS ARMADAS.
"HIS BLOODY PATH WAS A UNIVERSE WIDE, AND STRAIGHT AS A STALK ON A WINDLESS DAY.
"ALL BEFORE HIM WOULD DO BATTLE. FIGHT OR DIE.

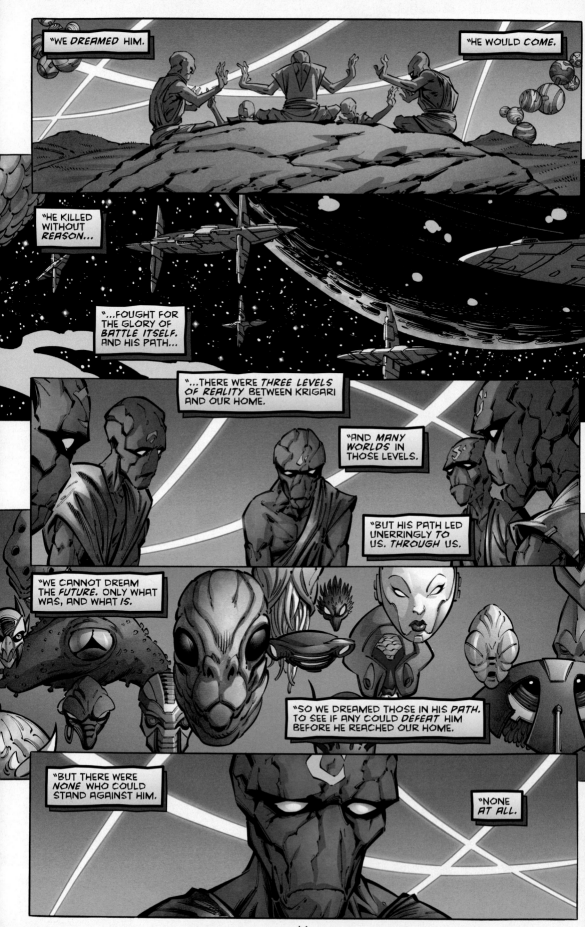

"WE *DREAMED* HIM.

"HE WOULD *COME*.

"HE KILLED WITHOUT *REASON*...

"...FOUGHT FOR THE GLORY OF *BATTLE ITSELF*. AND HIS PATH...

"...THERE WERE *THREE LEVELS* OF *REALITY* BETWEEN KRIGARI AND OUR HOME.

"AND *MANY WORLDS* IN THOSE LEVELS.

"BUT HIS PATH LED UNERRINGLY *TO* US. *THROUGH* US.

"WE CANNOT DREAM THE *FUTURE*. ONLY WHAT WAS, AND WHAT *IS*.

"SO WE DREAMED THOSE IN HIS *PATH*. TO SEE IF ANY COULD *DEFEAT* HIM BEFORE HE REACHED OUR HOME.

"BUT THERE WERE *NONE* WHO COULD STAND AGAINST HIM.

"NONE *AT ALL*.

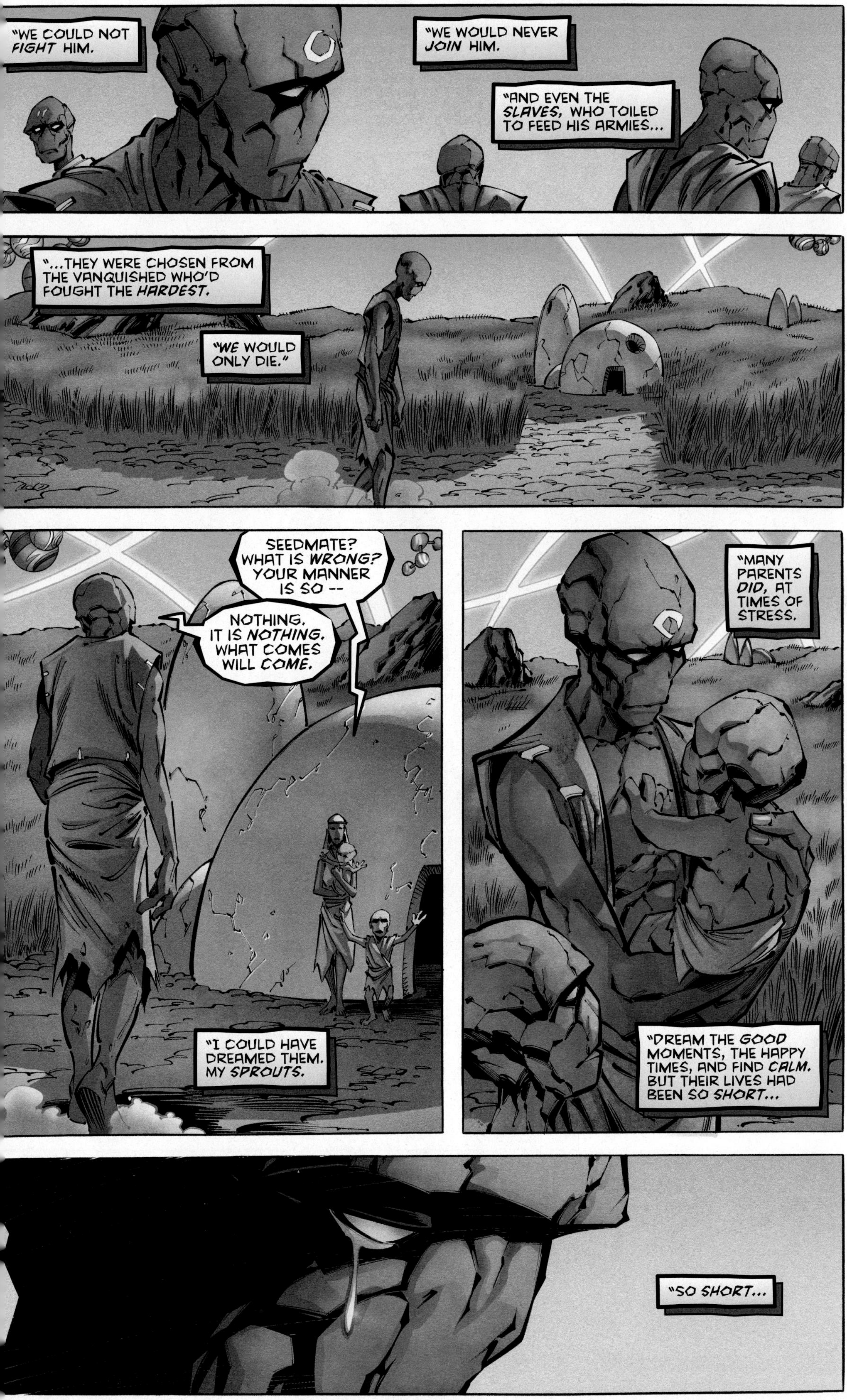
"WE COULD NOT FIGHT HIM.
"WE WOULD NEVER JOIN HIM.
"AND EVEN THE SLAVES, WHO TOILED TO FEED HIS ARMIES...
"...THEY WERE CHOSEN FROM THE VANQUISHED WHO'D FOUGHT THE HARDEST.
"WE WOULD ONLY DIE."
SEEDMATE? WHAT IS WRONG? YOUR MANNER IS SO --
NOTHING. IT IS NOTHING. WHAT COMES WILL COME.
"I COULD HAVE DREAMED THEM. MY SPROUTS.
"MANY PARENTS DID, AT TIMES OF STRESS.
"DREAM THE GOOD MOMENTS, THE HAPPY TIMES, AND FIND CALM. BUT THEIR LIVES HAD BEEN SO SHORT...
"SO SHORT...

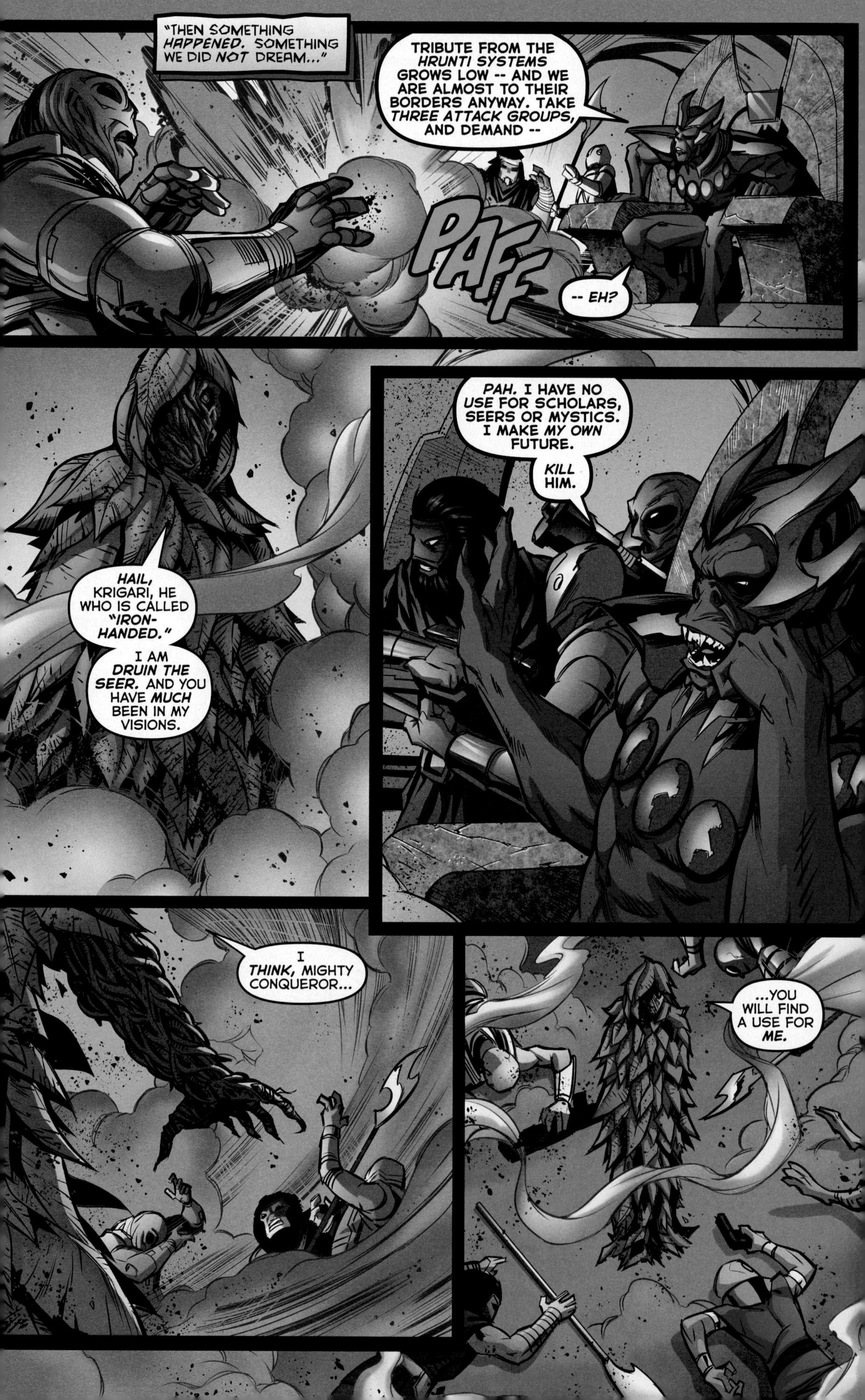
"THEN SOMETHING HAPPENED. SOMETHING WE DID NOT DREAM..."
TRIBUTE FROM THE HRUNTI SYSTEMS GROWS LOW -- AND WE ARE ALMOST TO THEIR BORDERS ANYWAY. TAKE THREE ATTACK GROUPS, AND DEMAND --
PAFF
-- EH?
HAIL, KRIGARI, HE WHO IS CALLED "IRON-HANDED."
I AM DRUIN THE SEER. AND YOU HAVE MUCH BEEN IN MY VISIONS.
PAH. I HAVE NO USE FOR SCHOLARS, SEERS OR MYSTICS. I MAKE MY OWN FUTURE.
KILL HIM.
I THINK, MIGHTY CONQUEROR...
...YOU WILL FIND A USE FOR ME.

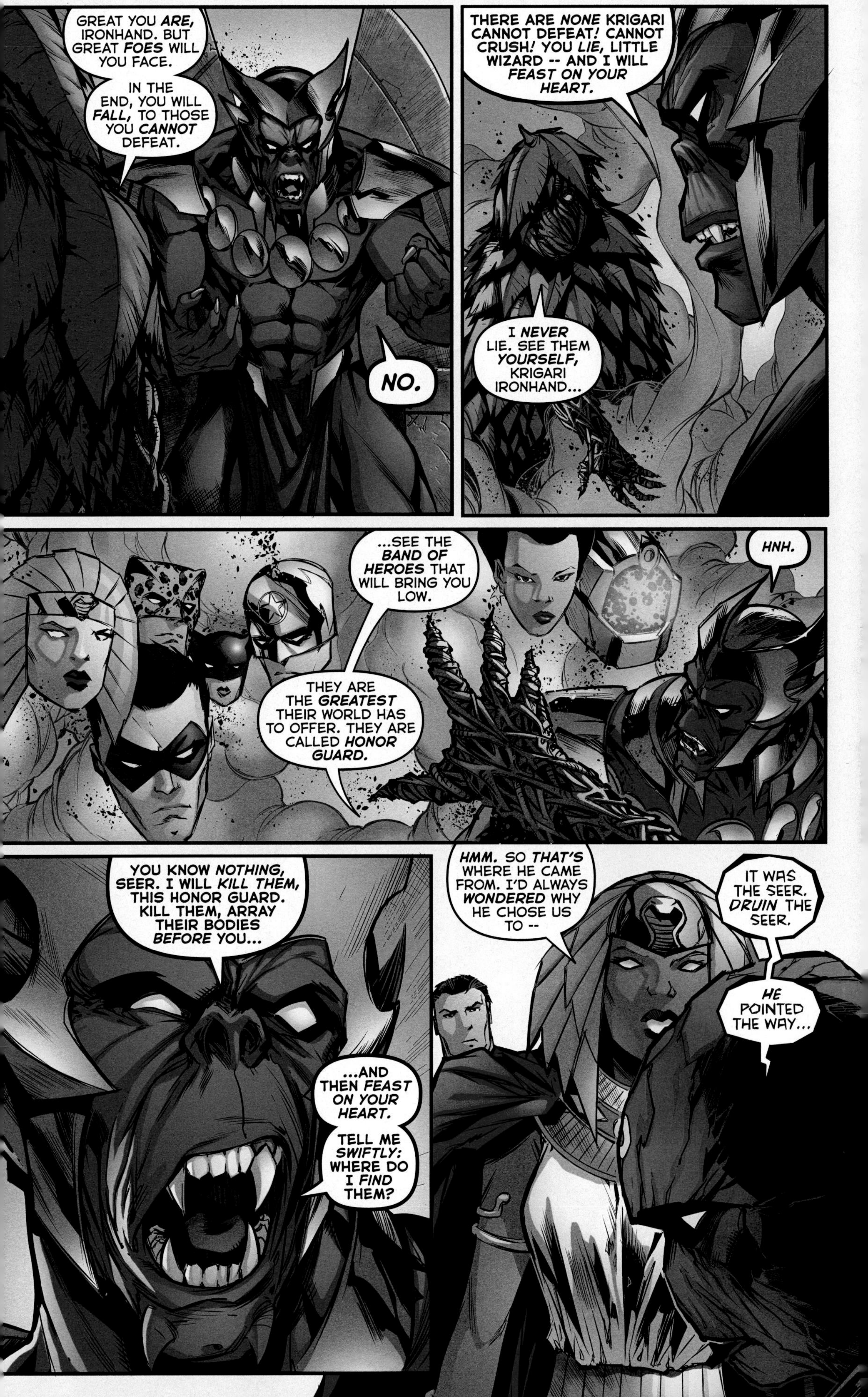
GREAT YOU ARE, IRONHAND. BUT GREAT FOES WILL YOU FACE.
IN THE END, YOU WILL FALL, TO THOSE YOU CANNOT DEFEAT.
NO.
THERE ARE NONE KRIGARI CANNOT DEFEAT! CANNOT CRUSH! YOU LIE, LITTLE WIZARD -- AND I WILL FEAST ON YOUR HEART.
I NEVER LIE. SEE THEM YOURSELF, KRIGARI IRONHAND...
...SEE THE BAND OF HEROES THAT WILL BRING YOU LOW.
THEY ARE THE GREATEST THEIR WORLD HAS TO OFFER. THEY ARE CALLED HONOR GUARD.
HNH.
YOU KNOW NOTHING, SEER. I WILL KILL THEM, THIS HONOR GUARD. KILL THEM, ARRAY THEIR BODIES BEFORE YOU...
...AND THEN FEAST ON YOUR HEART.
TELL ME SWIFTLY: WHERE DO I FIND THEM?
HMM. SO THAT'S WHERE HE CAME FROM. I'D ALWAYS WONDERED WHY HE CHOSE US TO --
IT WAS THE SEER. DRUIN THE SEER.
HE POINTED THE WAY...

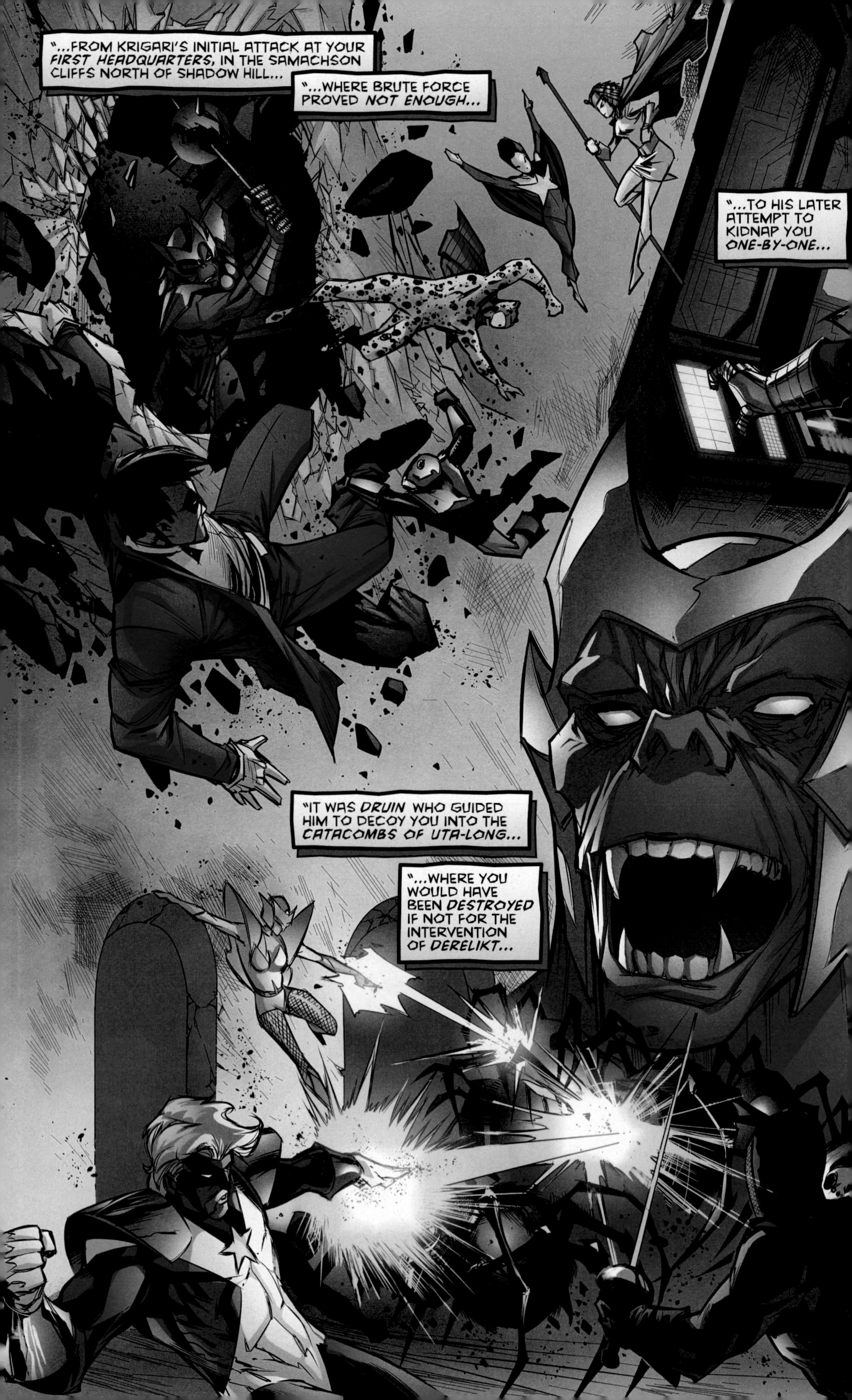
"...FROM KRIGARI'S INITIAL ATTACK AT YOUR *FIRST HEADQUARTERS*, IN THE SAMACHSON CLIFFS NORTH OF SHADOW HILL...
"...WHERE BRUTE FORCE PROVED *NOT ENOUGH*...
"...TO HIS LATER ATTEMPT TO KIDNAP YOU *ONE-BY-ONE*...
"IT WAS *DRUIN* WHO GUIDED HIM TO DECOY YOU INTO THE *CATACOMBS OF UTA-LONG*...
"...WHERE YOU WOULD HAVE BEEN *DESTROYED* IF NOT FOR THE INTERVENTION OF *DERELIKT*...

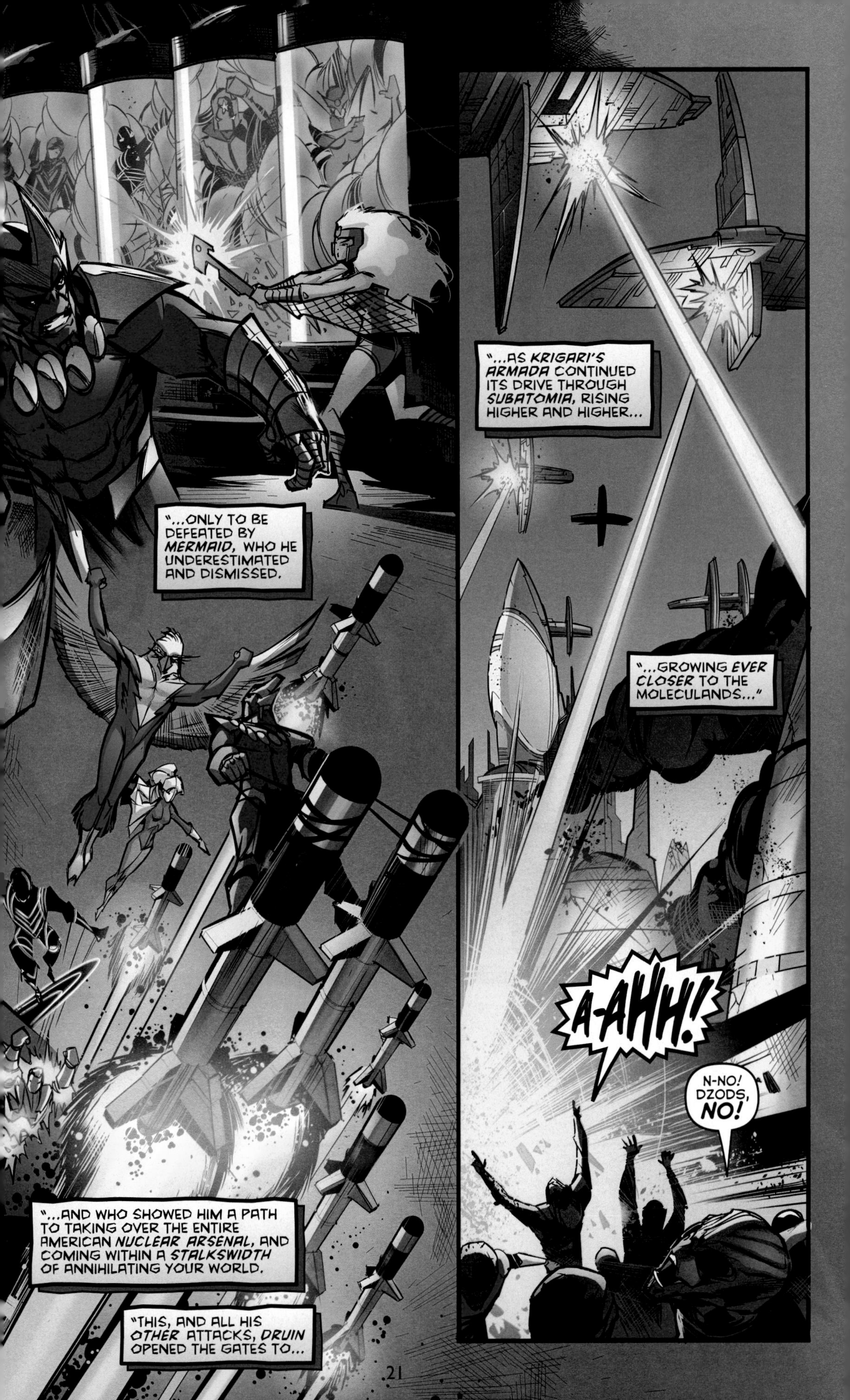
"...ONLY TO BE DEFEATED BY MERMAID, WHO HE UNDERESTIMATED AND DISMISSED.
"...AND WHO SHOWED HIM A PATH TO TAKING OVER THE ENTIRE AMERICAN NUCLEAR ARSENAL, AND COMING WITHIN A STALKSWIDTH OF ANNIHILATING YOUR WORLD.
"THIS, AND ALL HIS OTHER ATTACKS, DRUIN OPENED THE GATES TO...
"...AS KRIGARI'S ARMADA CONTINUED ITS DRIVE THROUGH SUBATOMIA, RISING HIGHER AND HIGHER...
"...GROWING EVER CLOSER TO THE MOLECULANDS..."
A-AHH!
N-NO! DZODS, NO!

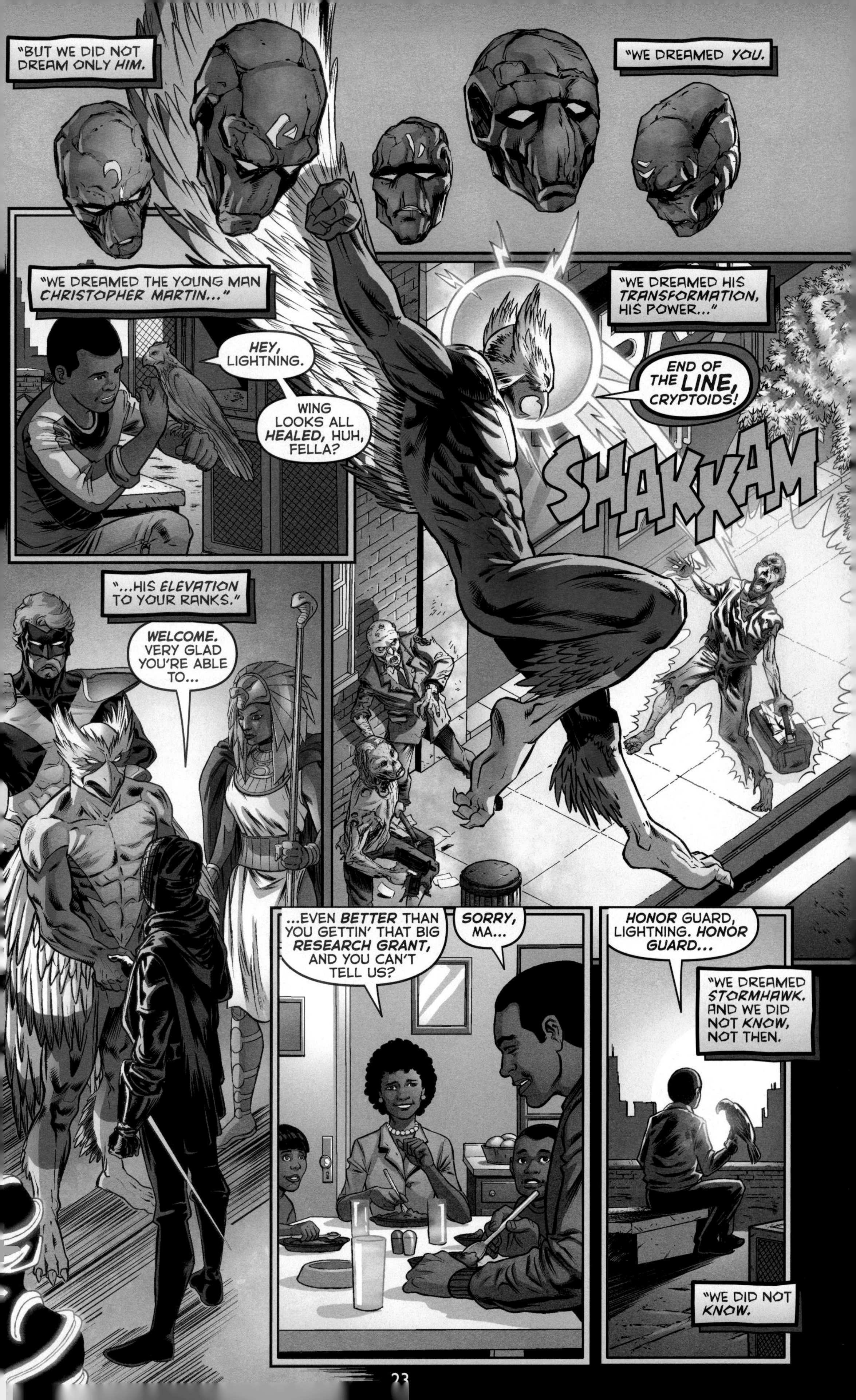
"BUT WE DID NOT DREAM ONLY HIM.
"WE DREAMED YOU.
"WE DREAMED THE YOUNG MAN CHRISTOPHER MARTIN..."
HEY, LIGHTNING.
WING LOOKS ALL HEALED, HUH, FELLA?
"WE DREAMED HIS TRANSFORMATION, HIS POWER..."
END OF THE LINE, CRYPTOIDS!
SHAKKAM
"...HIS ELEVATION TO YOUR RANKS."
WELCOME. VERY GLAD YOU'RE ABLE TO...
...EVEN BETTER THAN YOU GETTIN' THAT BIG RESEARCH GRANT, AND YOU CAN'T TELL US?
SORRY, MA...
HONOR GUARD, LIGHTNING. HONOR GUARD...
"WE DREAMED STORMHAWK. AND WE DID NOT KNOW, NOT THEN.
"WE DID NOT KNOW.

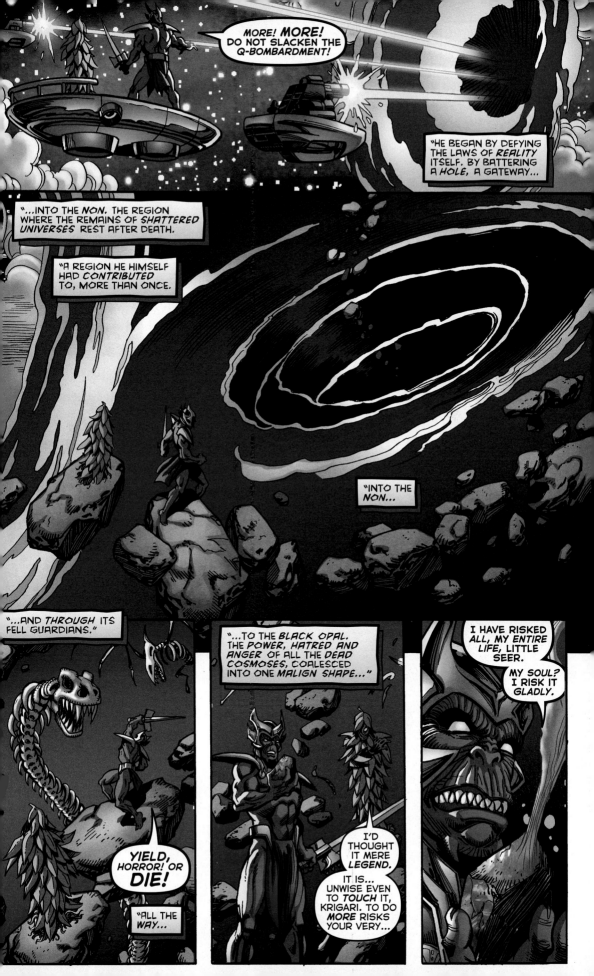

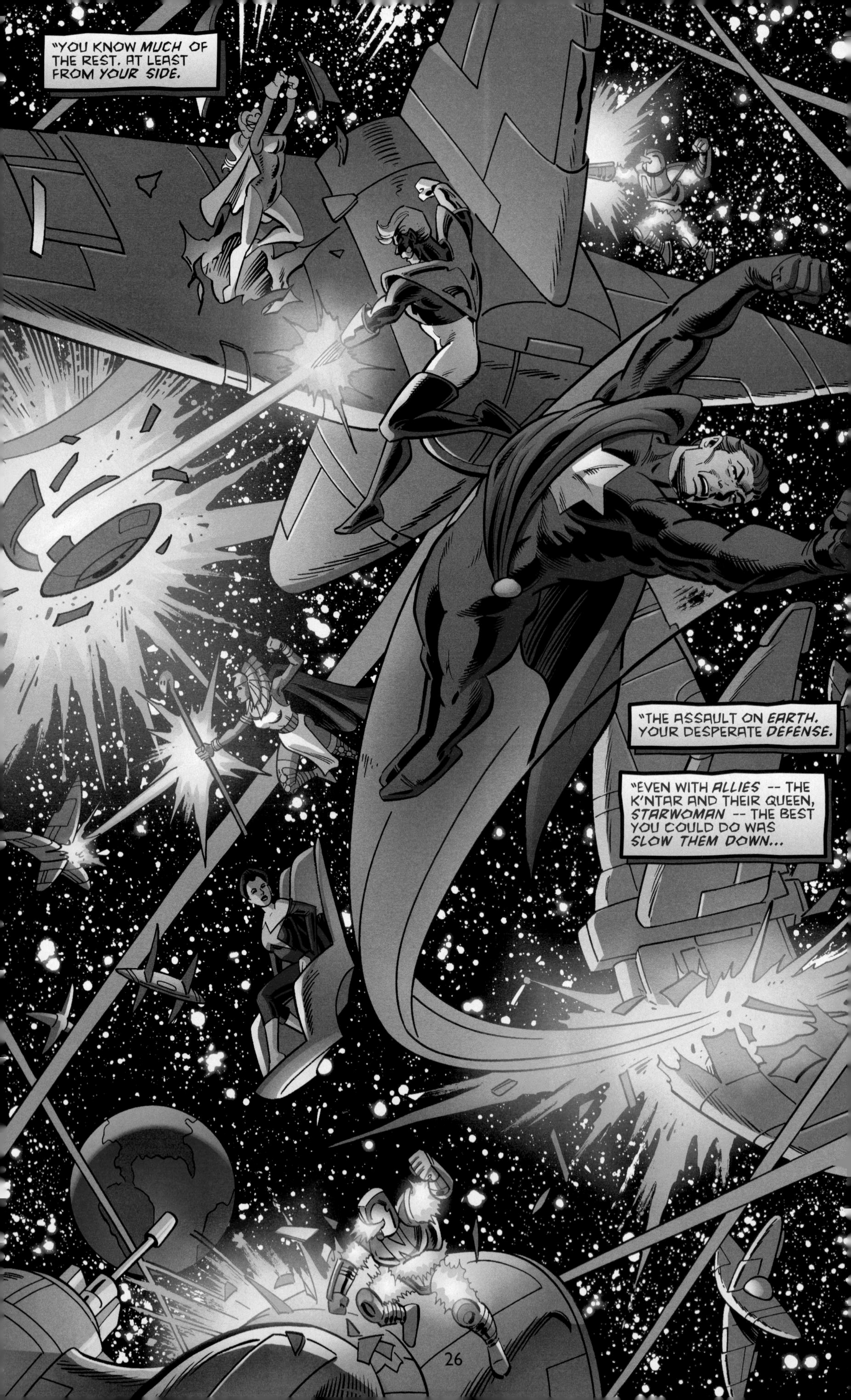
"YOU KNOW MUCH OF THE REST. AT LEAST FROM YOUR SIDE.
"THE ASSAULT ON EARTH. YOUR DESPERATE DEFENSE.
"EVEN WITH ALLIES -- THE K'NTAR AND THEIR QUEEN, STARWOMAN -- THE BEST YOU COULD DO WAS SLOW THEM DOWN...

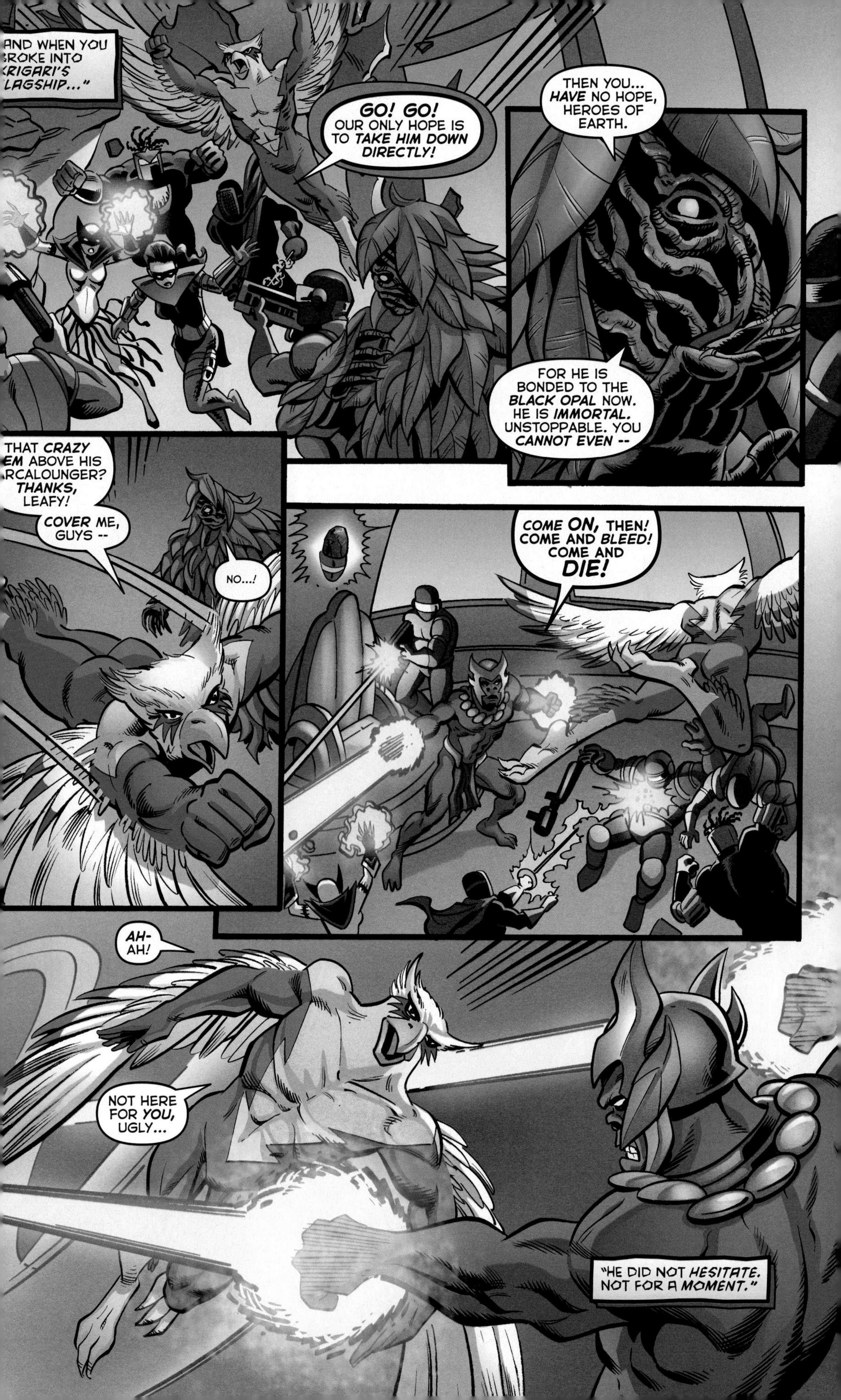
AND WHEN YOU BROKE INTO KRIGARI'S FLAGSHIP..."
GO! GO! OUR ONLY HOPE IS TO TAKE HIM DOWN DIRECTLY!
THEN YOU... HAVE NO HOPE, HEROES OF EARTH.
FOR HE IS BONDED TO THE BLACK OPAL NOW. HE IS IMMORTAL. UNSTOPPABLE. YOU CANNOT EVEN --
THAT CRAZY GEM ABOVE HIS ARCALOUNGER? THANKS, LEAFY!
COVER ME, GUYS --
NO...!
COME ON, THEN! COME AND BLEED! COME AND DIE!
AH-AH!
NOT HERE FOR YOU, UGLY...
"HE DID NOT HESITATE. NOT FOR A MOMENT."

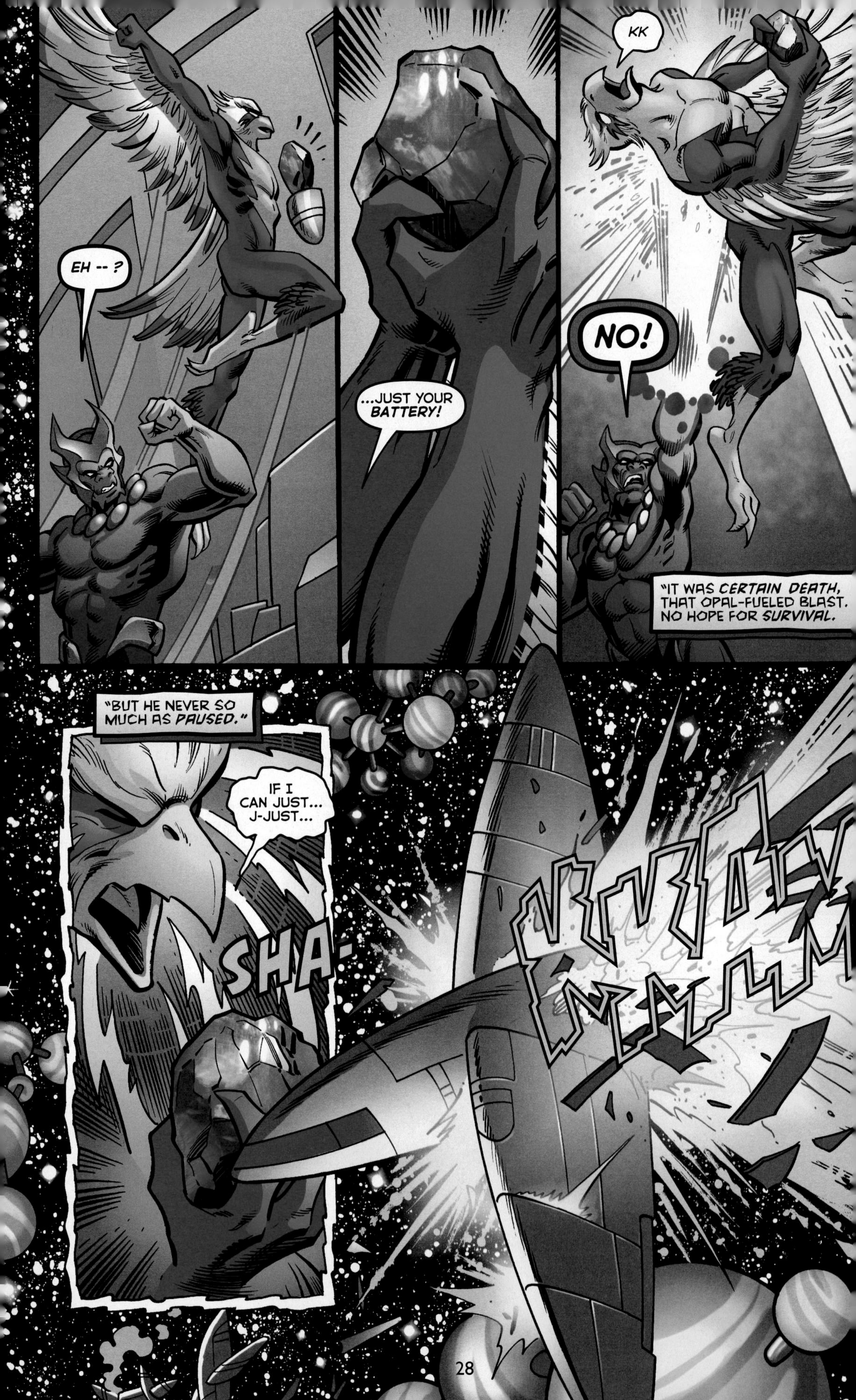
EH -- ?
...JUST YOUR BATTERY!
KK
NO!
"IT WAS CERTAIN DEATH, THAT OPAL-FUELED BLAST. NO HOPE FOR SURVIVAL.
"BUT HE NEVER SO MUCH AS PAUSED."
IF I CAN JUST... J-JUST...
SHA-

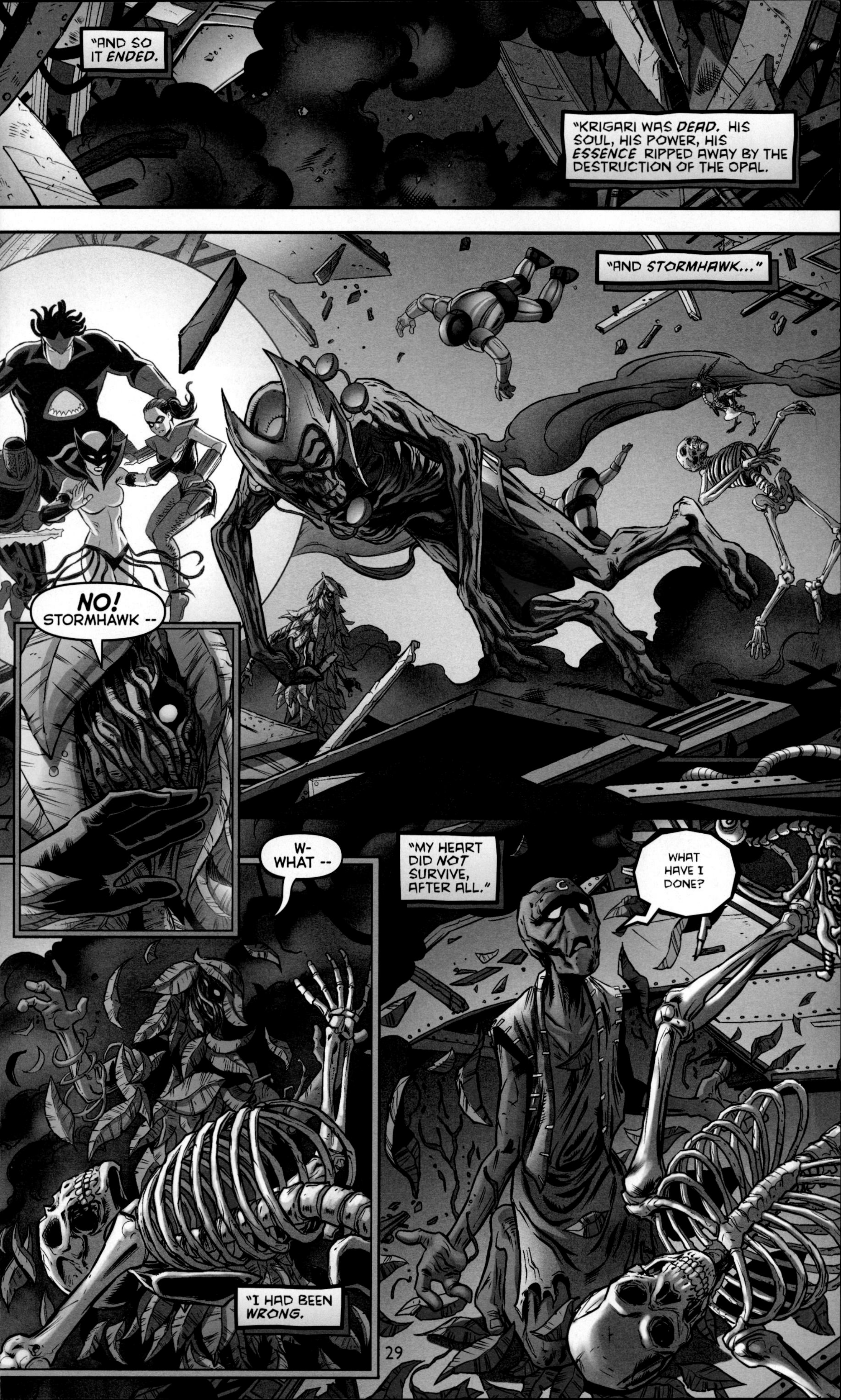
"AND SO IT ENDED.
"KRIGARI WAS DEAD. HIS SOUL, HIS POWER, HIS ESSENCE RIPPED AWAY BY THE DESTRUCTION OF THE OPAL.
"AND STORMHAWK..."
NO! STORMHAWK --
W- WHAT --
"I HAD BEEN WRONG.
"MY HEART DID NOT SURVIVE, AFTER ALL."
WHAT HAVE I DONE?

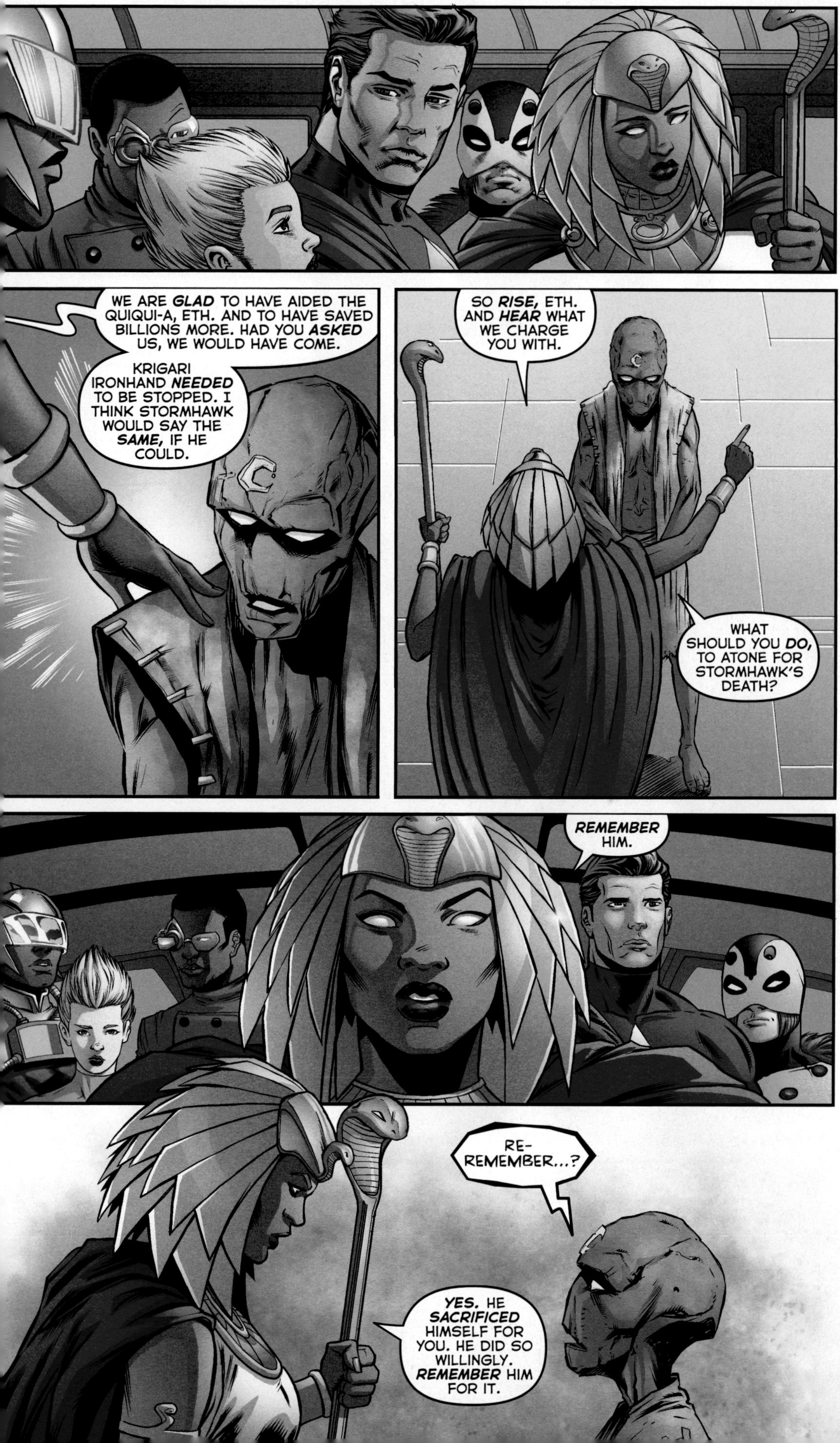
WE ARE GLAD TO HAVE AIDED THE QUIQUI-A, ETH. AND TO HAVE SAVED BILLIONS MORE. HAD YOU ASKED US, WE WOULD HAVE COME.
KRIGARI IRONHAND NEEDED TO BE STOPPED. I THINK STORMHAWK WOULD SAY THE SAME, IF HE COULD.
SO RISE, ETH. AND HEAR WHAT WE CHARGE YOU WITH.
WHAT SHOULD YOU DO, TO ATONE FOR STORMHAWK'S DEATH?
REMEMBER HIM.
RE-REMEMBER...?
YES. HE SACRIFICED HIMSELF FOR YOU. HE DID SO WILLINGLY. REMEMBER HIM FOR IT.

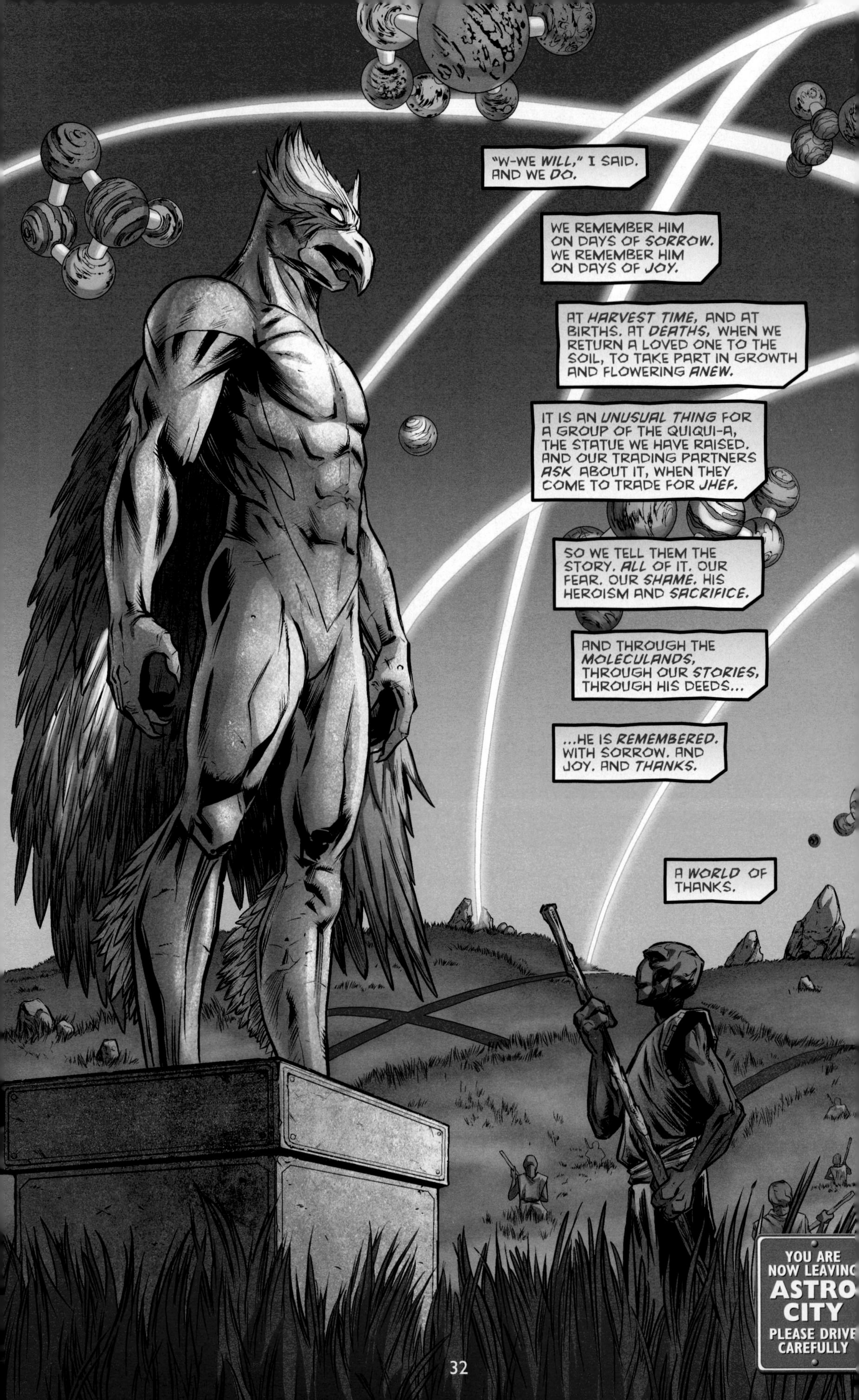
"W-WE WILL," I SAID. AND WE DO.
WE REMEMBER HIM ON DAYS OF SORROW. WE REMEMBER HIM ON DAYS OF JOY.
AT HARVEST TIME, AND AT BIRTHS. AT DEATHS, WHEN WE RETURN A LOVED ONE TO THE SOIL, TO TAKE PART IN GROWTH AND FLOWERING ANEW.
IT IS AN UNUSUAL THING FOR A GROUP OF THE QUIQUI-A, THE STATUE WE HAVE RAISED. AND OUR TRADING PARTNERS ASK ABOUT IT, WHEN THEY COME TO TRADE FOR JHEF.
SO WE TELL THEM THE STORY. ALL OF IT. OUR FEAR. OUR SHAME. HIS HEROISM AND SACRIFICE.
AND THROUGH THE MOLECULANDS, THROUGH OUR STORIES, THROUGH HIS DEEDS...
...HE IS REMEMBERED. WITH SORROW. AND JOY. AND THANKS.
A WORLD OF THANKS.
YOU ARE NOW LEAVING ASTRO CITY PLEASE DRIVE CAREFULLY

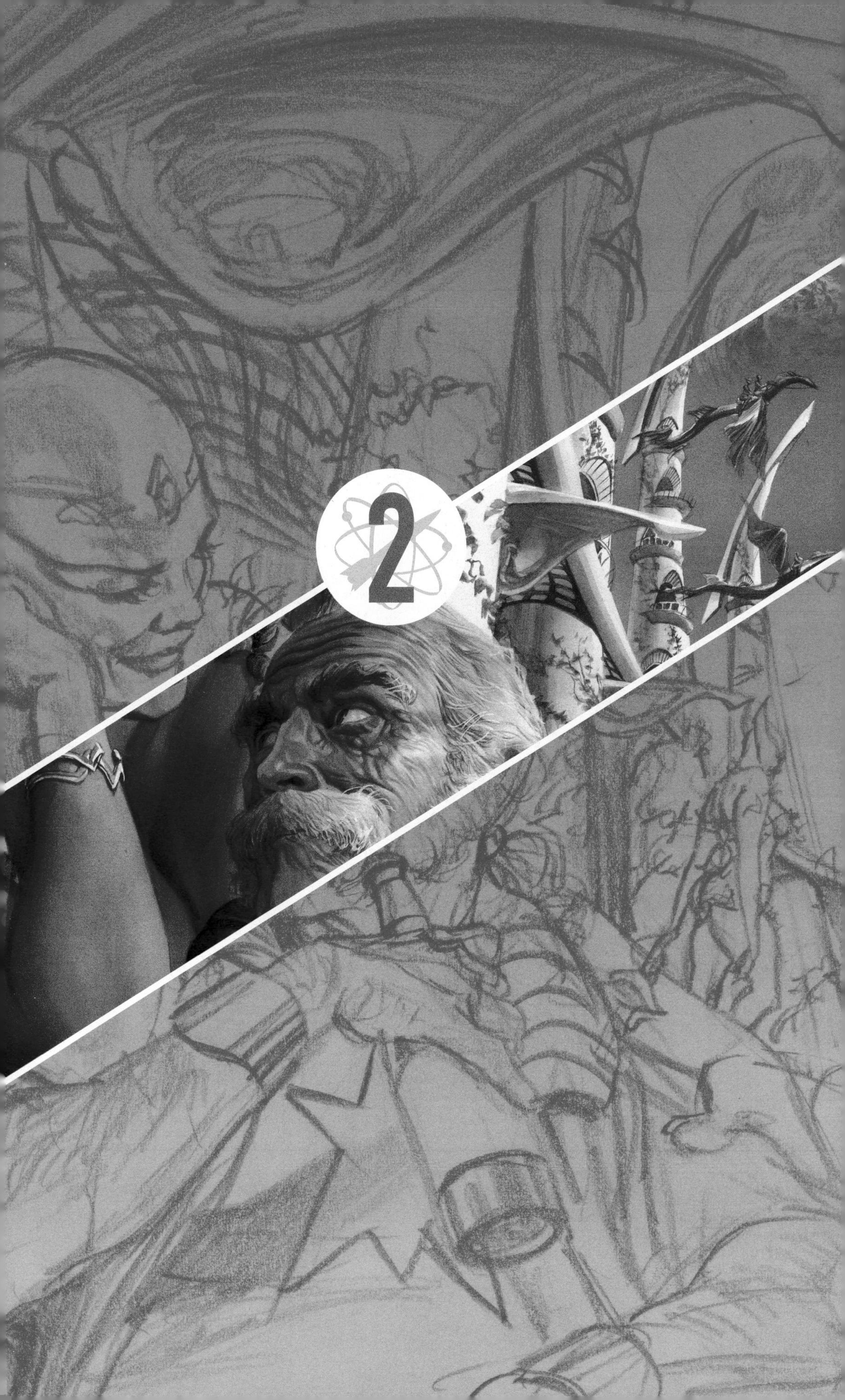
2

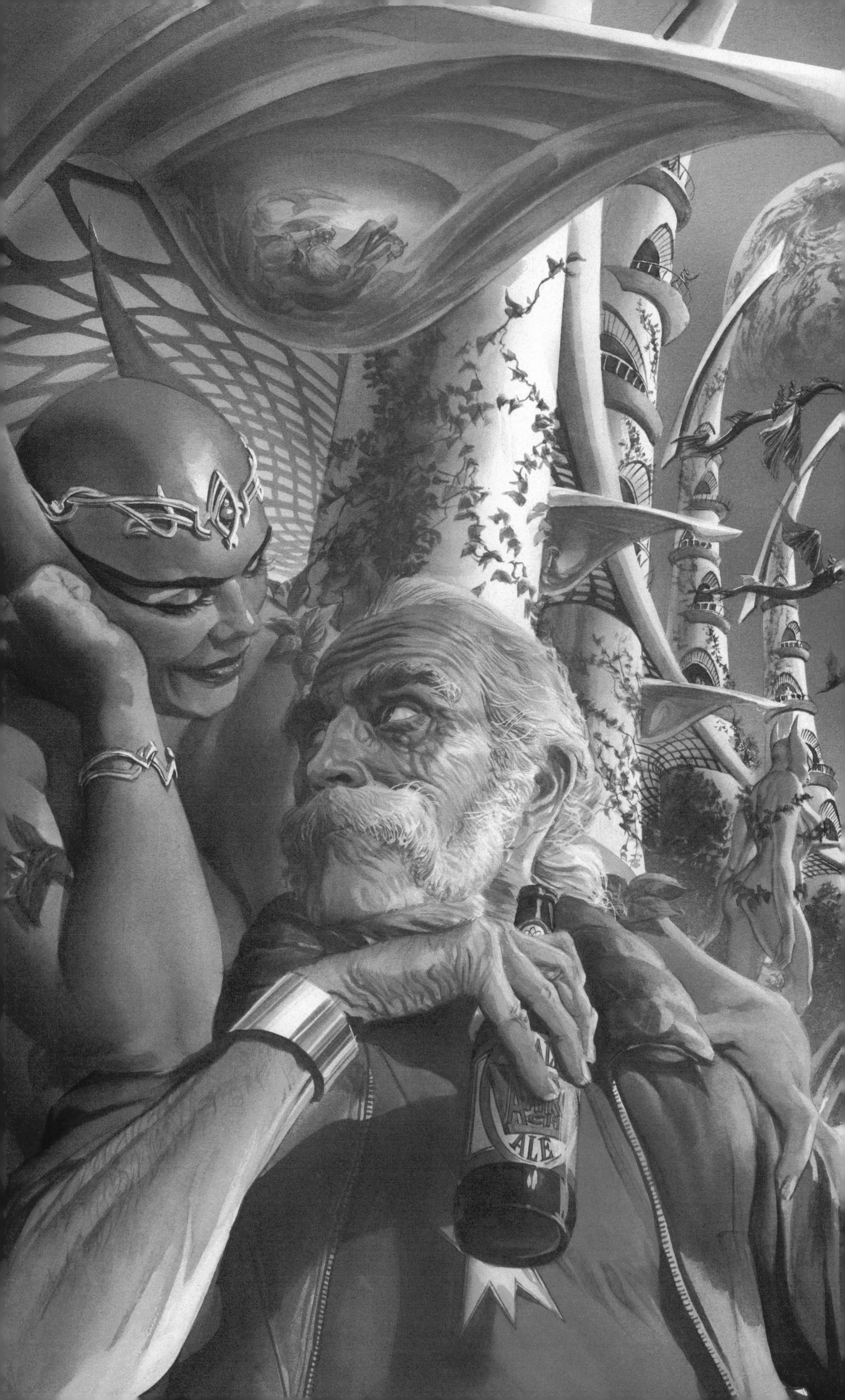
ALE

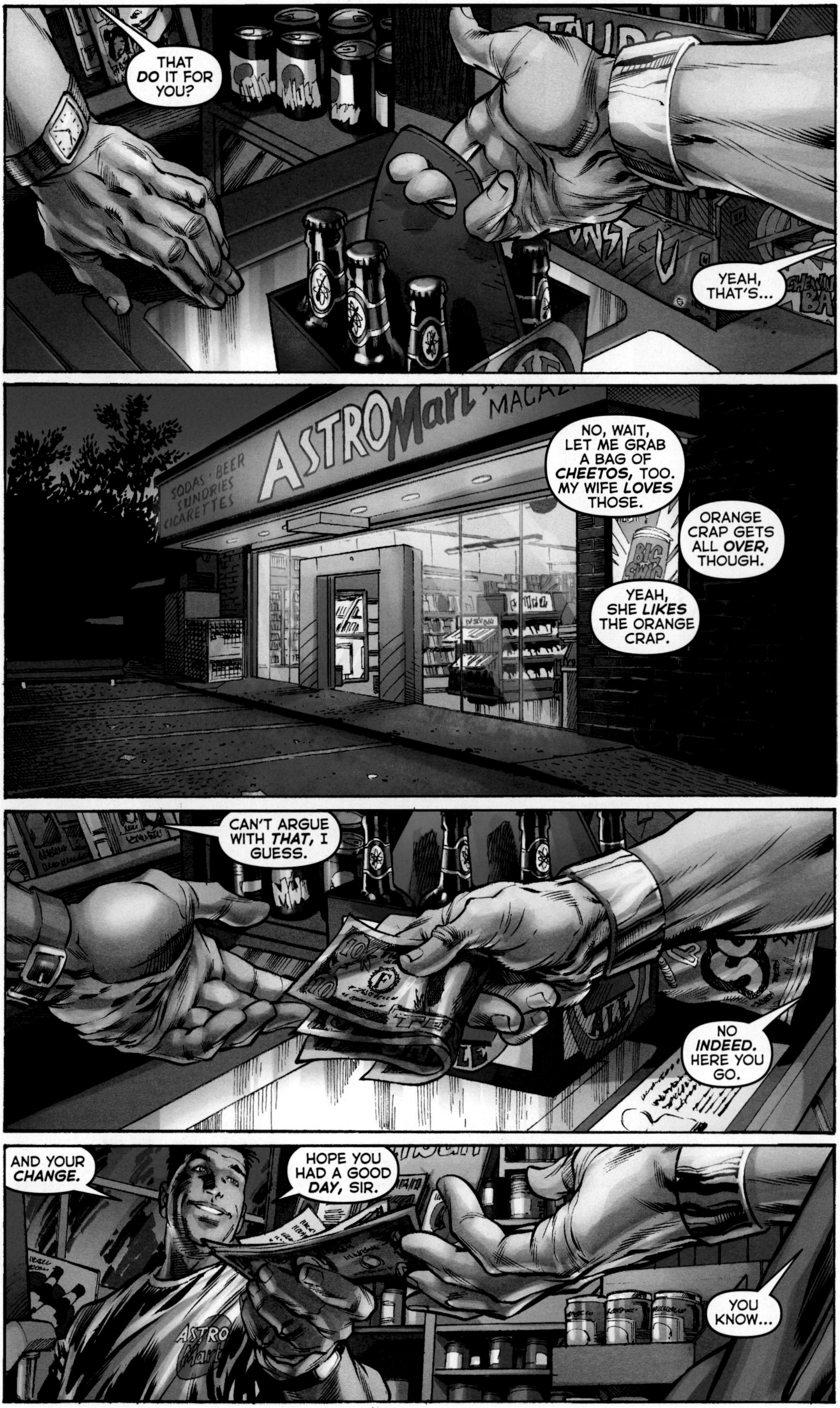
THAT DO IT FOR YOU?
YEAH, THAT'S...
ASTRO Mart
SODAS · BEER
SUNDRIES
CIGARETTES
NO, WAIT, LET ME GRAB A BAG OF CHEETOS, TOO. MY WIFE LOVES THOSE.
BIG SWIG
ORANGE CRAP GETS ALL OVER, THOUGH.
YEAH, SHE LIKES THE ORANGE CRAP.
CAN'T ARGUE WITH THAT, I GUESS.
NO INDEED. HERE YOU GO.
AND YOUR CHANGE.
HOPE YOU HAD A GOOD DAY, SIR.
ASTRO Mart
YOU KNOW...

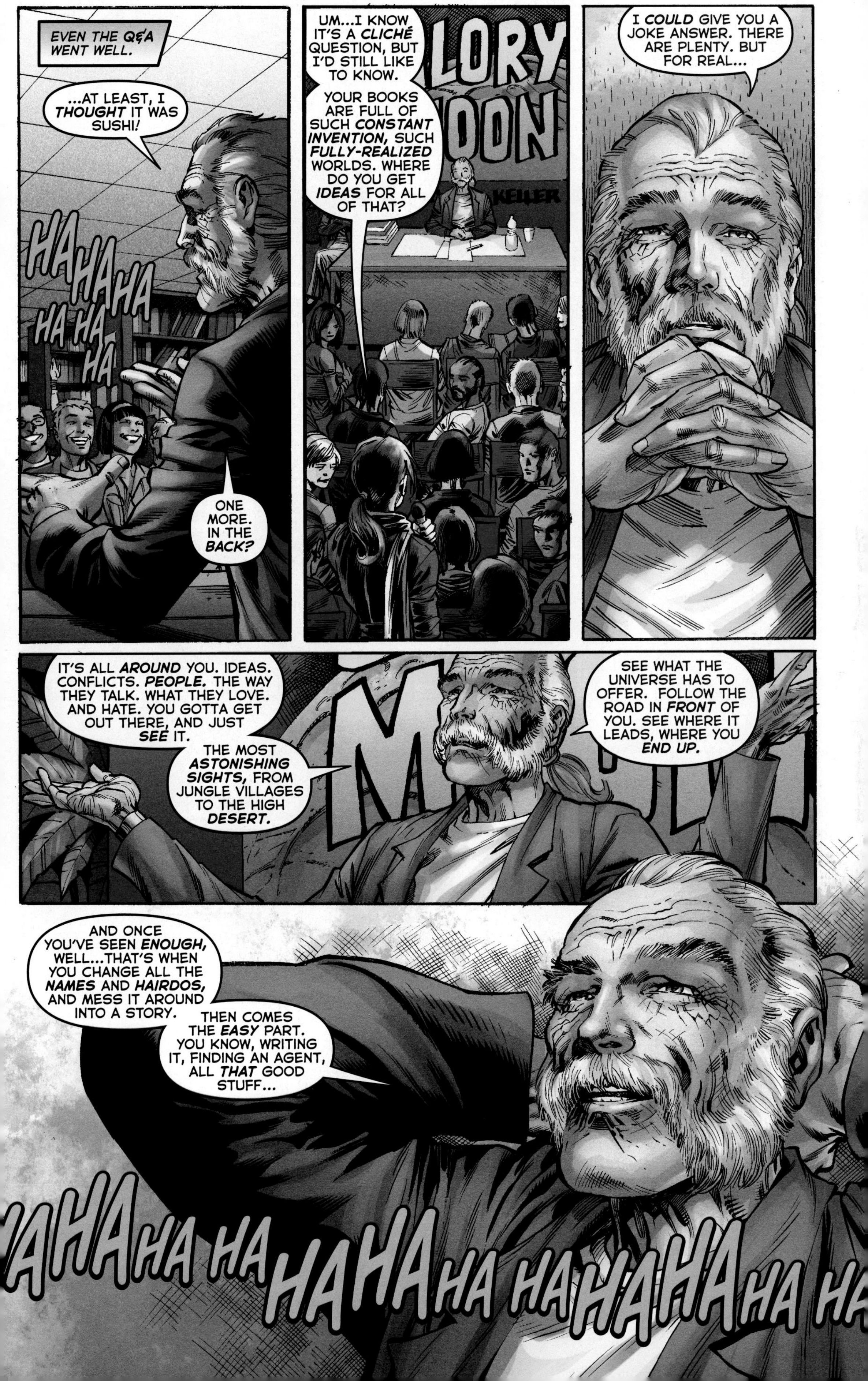

EVEN THE Q&A WENT WELL.
...AT LEAST, I THOUGHT IT WAS SUSHI!
HA HA HA HA HA HA HA HA
ONE MORE. IN THE BACK?
LORY OON
KELLER
UM...I KNOW IT'S A CLICHÉ QUESTION, BUT I'D STILL LIKE TO KNOW.
YOUR BOOKS ARE FULL OF SUCH CONSTANT INVENTION, SUCH FULLY-REALIZED WORLDS. WHERE DO YOU GET IDEAS FOR ALL OF THAT?
I COULD GIVE YOU A JOKE ANSWER. THERE ARE PLENTY. BUT FOR REAL...
IT'S ALL AROUND YOU. IDEAS. CONFLICTS. PEOPLE. THE WAY THEY TALK. WHAT THEY LOVE. AND HATE. YOU GOTTA GET OUT THERE, AND JUST SEE IT.
THE MOST ASTONISHING SIGHTS, FROM JUNGLE VILLAGES TO THE HIGH DESERT.
SEE WHAT THE UNIVERSE HAS TO OFFER. FOLLOW THE ROAD IN FRONT OF YOU. SEE WHERE IT LEADS, WHERE YOU END UP.
AND ONCE YOU'VE SEEN ENOUGH, WELL...THAT'S WHEN YOU CHANGE ALL THE NAMES AND HAIRDOS, AND MESS IT AROUND INTO A STORY.
THEN COMES THE EASY PART. YOU KNOW, WRITING IT, FINDING AN AGENT, ALL THAT GOOD STUFF...
HAHA HA HA HAHA HA HA HAHA HA HA

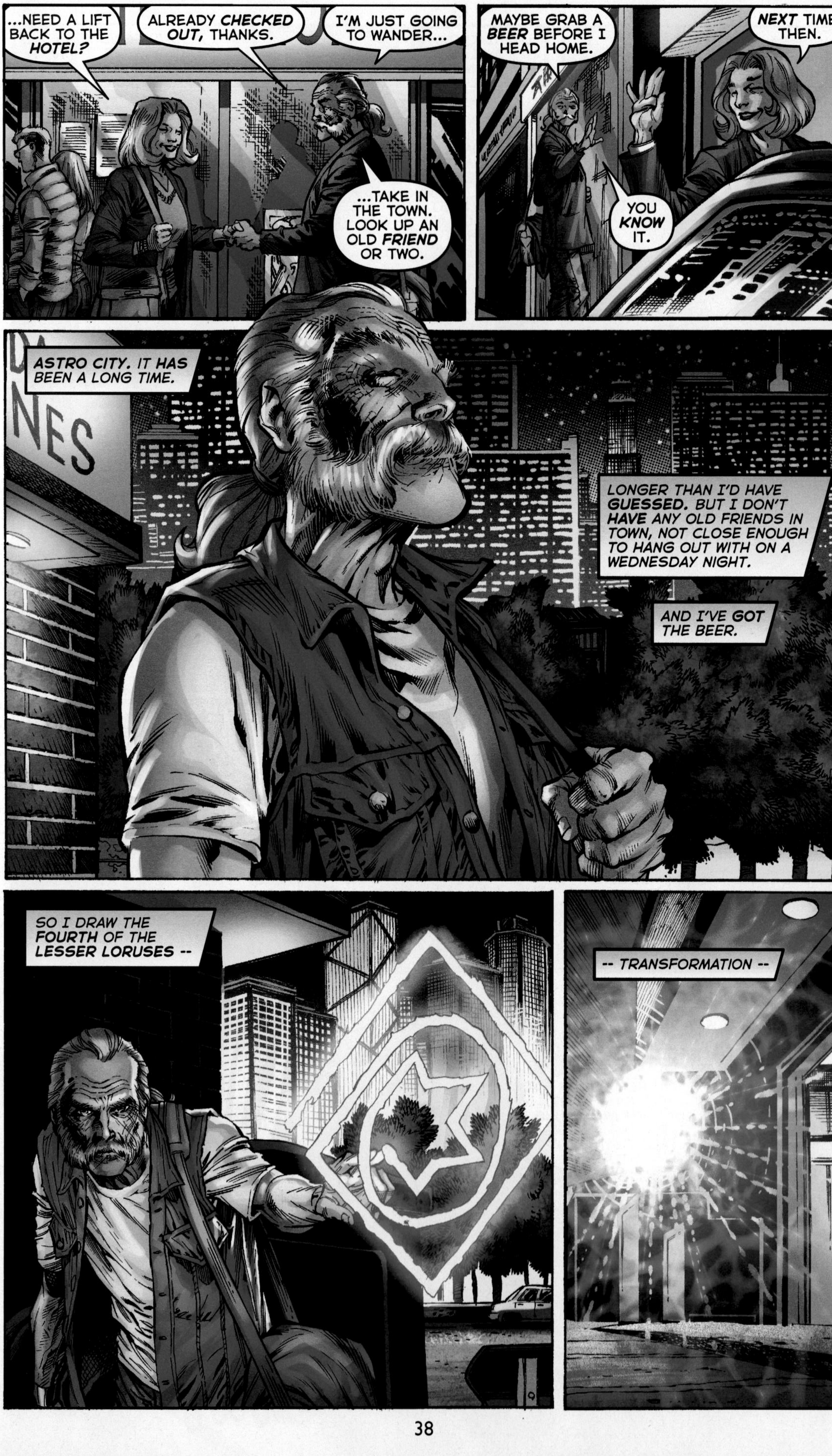
...NEED A LIFT BACK TO THE HOTEL?
ALREADY CHECKED OUT, THANKS.
I'M JUST GOING TO WANDER...
...TAKE IN THE TOWN. LOOK UP AN OLD FRIEND OR TWO.
MAYBE GRAB A BEER BEFORE I HEAD HOME.
NEXT TIME, THEN.
YOU KNOW IT.
ASTRO CITY. IT HAS BEEN A LONG TIME.
NES
LONGER THAN I'D HAVE GUESSED. BUT I DON'T HAVE ANY OLD FRIENDS IN TOWN, NOT CLOSE ENOUGH TO HANG OUT WITH ON A WEDNESDAY NIGHT.
AND I'VE GOT THE BEER.
SO I DRAW THE FOURTH OF THE LESSER LORUSES --
-- TRANSFORMATION --

SO I FLY UP THE WILDENBERG, UP TO THE CLIFFS ON THE WEST FACE OF MOUNT KIRBY --

-- AND I DRAW THE SEVENTEETH GREAT LORUS --

-- TRANSPORTATION --

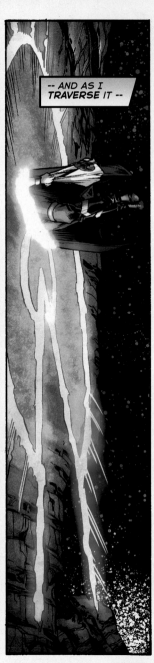

-- AND AS I TRAVERSE IT --

-- I FEEL THAT SENSATION --

-- THAT ODD SENSATION I'VE BEEN FEELING MORE AND MORE, LATELY --

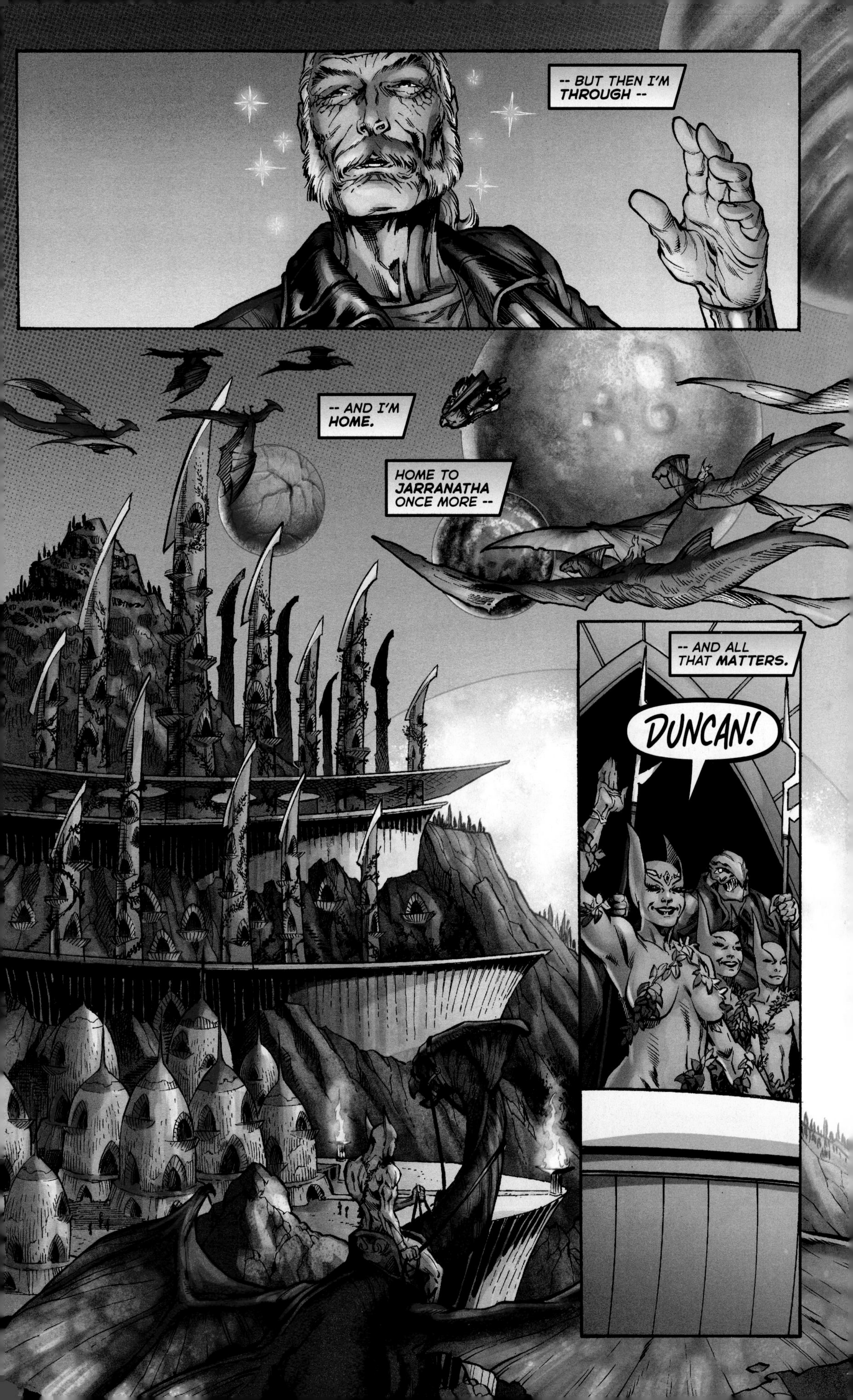

-- BUT THEN I'M THROUGH --
-- AND I'M HOME.
HOME TO JARRANATHA ONCE MORE --
-- AND ALL THAT MATTERS.
DUNCAN!

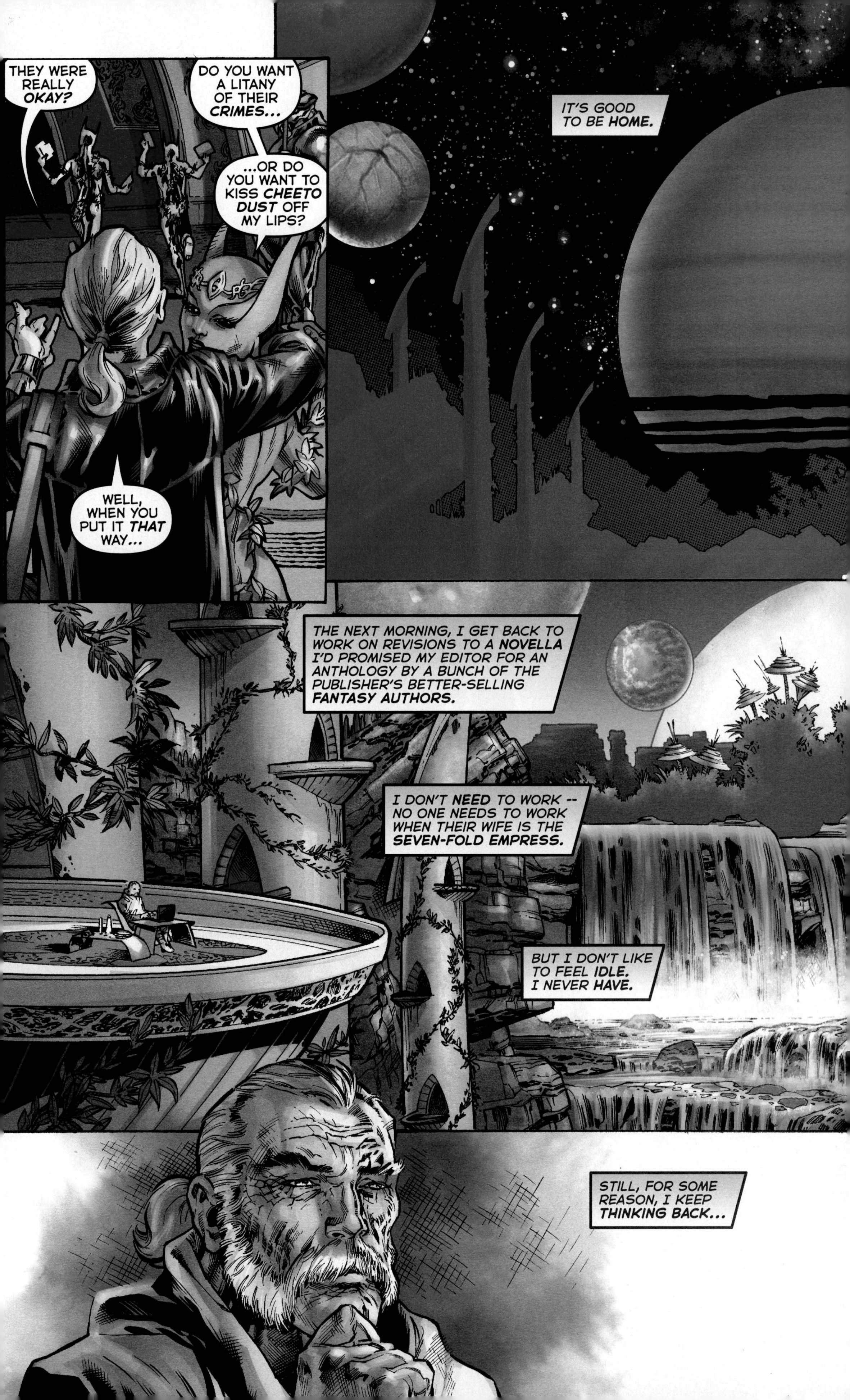
THEY WERE REALLY OKAY?
DO YOU WANT A LITANY OF THEIR CRIMES...
...OR DO YOU WANT TO KISS CHEETO DUST OFF MY LIPS?
WELL, WHEN YOU PUT IT THAT WAY...
IT'S GOOD TO BE HOME.
THE NEXT MORNING, I GET BACK TO WORK ON REVISIONS TO A NOVELLA I'D PROMISED MY EDITOR FOR AN ANTHOLOGY BY A BUNCH OF THE PUBLISHER'S BETTER-SELLING FANTASY AUTHORS.
I DON'T NEED TO WORK -- NO ONE NEEDS TO WORK WHEN THEIR WIFE IS THE SEVEN-FOLD EMPRESS.
BUT I DON'T LIKE TO FEEL IDLE. I NEVER HAVE.
STILL, FOR SOME REASON, I KEEP THINKING BACK...

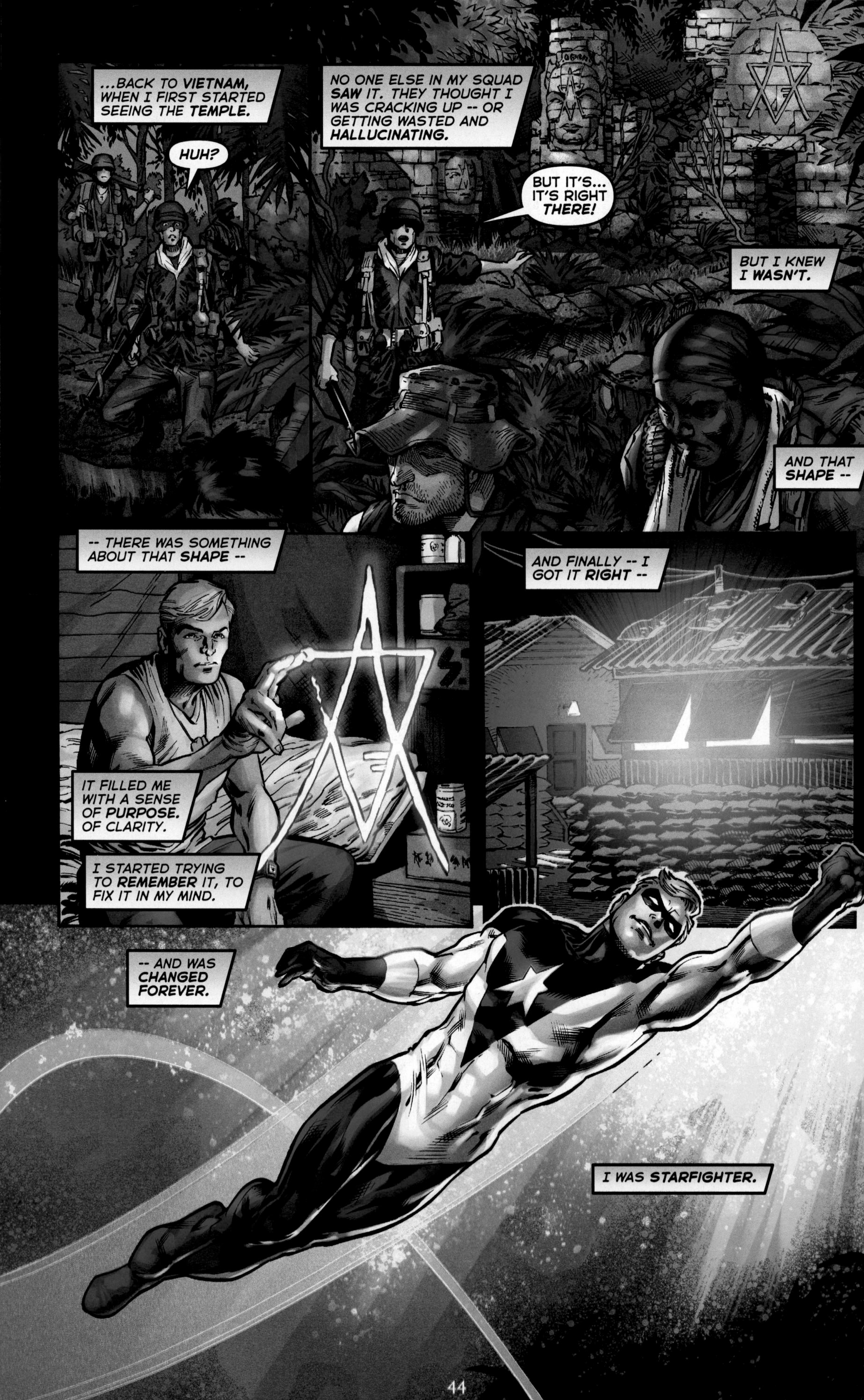
...BACK TO VIETNAM, WHEN I FIRST STARTED SEEING THE TEMPLE.
HUH?
NO ONE ELSE IN MY SQUAD SAW IT. THEY THOUGHT I WAS CRACKING UP -- OR GETTING WASTED AND HALLUCINATING.
BUT IT'S... IT'S RIGHT THERE!
BUT I KNEW I WASN'T.
AND THAT SHAPE --
-- THERE WAS SOMETHING ABOUT THAT SHAPE --
IT FILLED ME WITH A SENSE OF PURPOSE. OF CLARITY.
I STARTED TRYING TO REMEMBER IT, TO FIX IT IN MY MIND.
AND FINALLY -- I GOT IT RIGHT --
-- AND WAS CHANGED FOREVER.
I WAS STARFIGHTER.

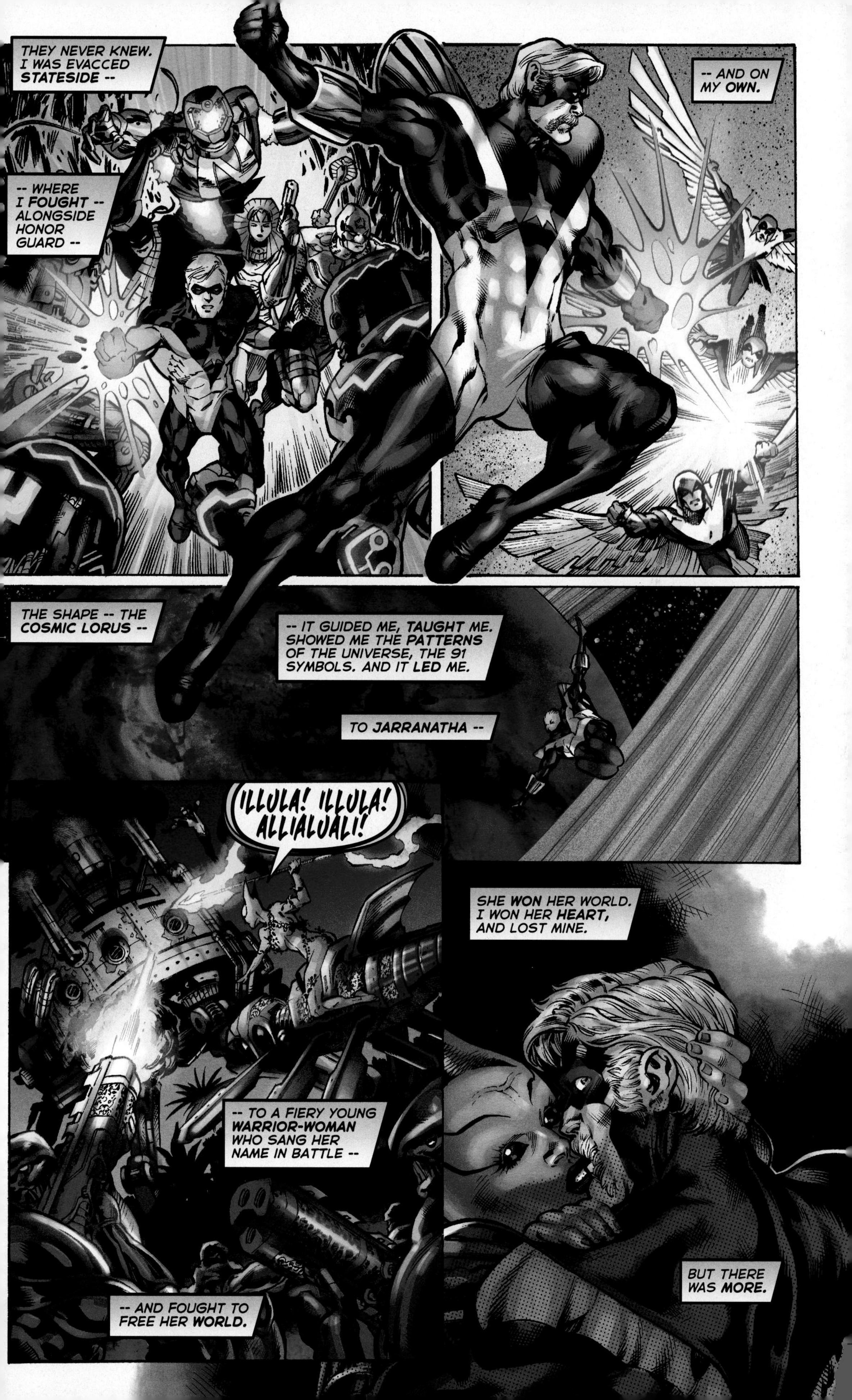
THEY NEVER KNEW. I WAS EVACCED STATESIDE --
-- AND ON MY OWN.
-- WHERE I FOUGHT -- ALONGSIDE HONOR GUARD --
THE SHAPE -- THE COSMIC LORUS --
-- IT GUIDED ME, TAUGHT ME. SHOWED ME THE PATTERNS OF THE UNIVERSE, THE 91 SYMBOLS. AND IT LED ME.
TO JARRANATHA --
ILLULA! ILLULA! ALLIALUALI!
-- TO A FIERY YOUNG WARRIOR-WOMAN WHO SANG HER NAME IN BATTLE --
-- AND FOUGHT TO FREE HER WORLD.
SHE WON HER WORLD. I WON HER HEART, AND LOST MINE.
BUT THERE WAS MORE.

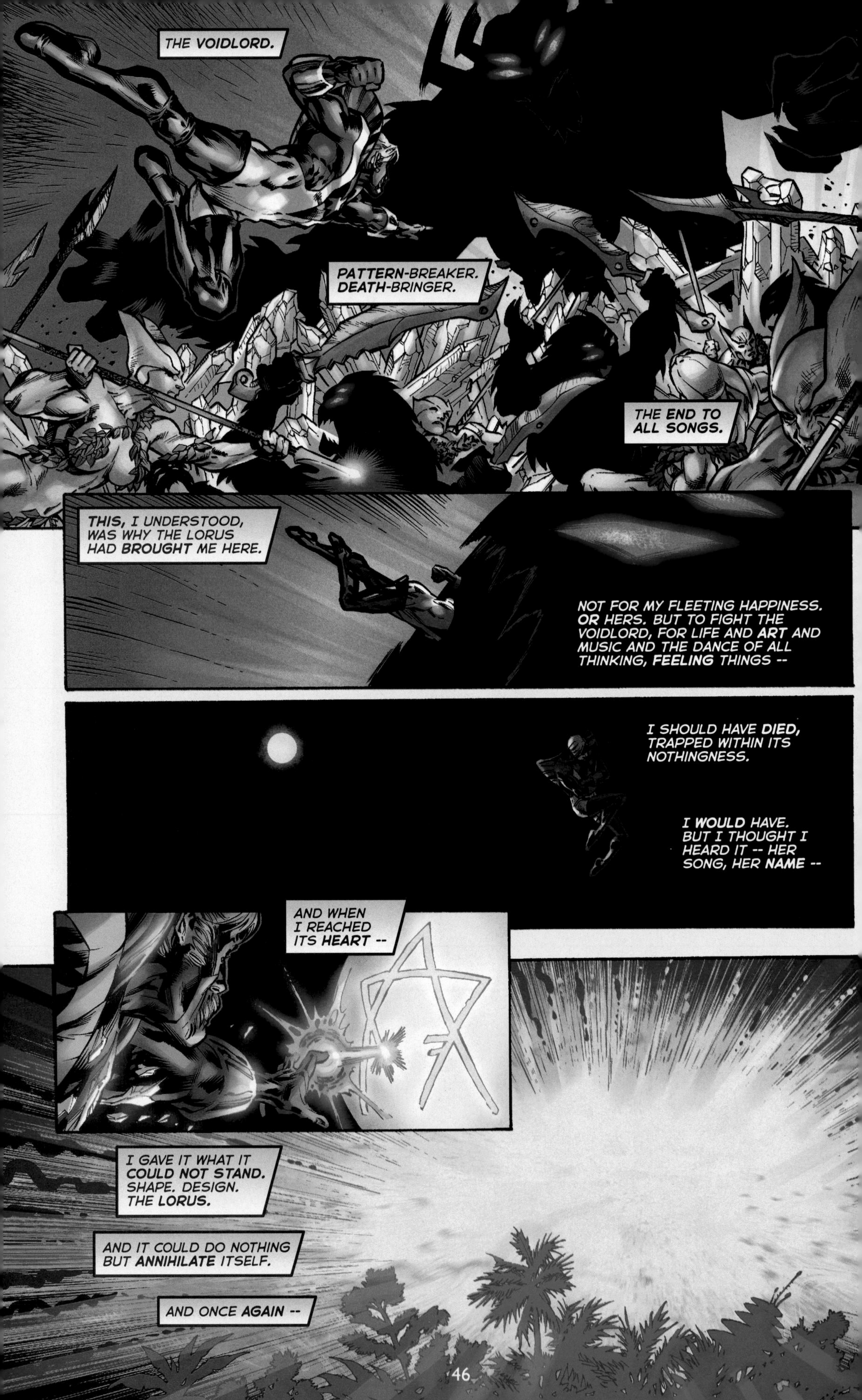
THE VOIDLORD.
PATTERN-BREAKER. DEATH-BRINGER.
THE END TO ALL SONGS.
THIS, I UNDERSTOOD, WAS WHY THE LORUS HAD BROUGHT ME HERE.
NOT FOR MY FLEETING HAPPINESS. OR HERS. BUT TO FIGHT THE VOIDLORD, FOR LIFE AND ART AND MUSIC AND THE DANCE OF ALL THINKING, FEELING THINGS --
I SHOULD HAVE DIED, TRAPPED WITHIN ITS NOTHINGNESS.
I WOULD HAVE. BUT I THOUGHT I HEARD IT -- HER SONG, HER NAME --
AND WHEN I REACHED ITS HEART --
I GAVE IT WHAT IT COULD NOT STAND. SHAPE. DESIGN. THE LORUS.
AND IT COULD DO NOTHING BUT ANNIHILATE ITSELF.
AND ONCE AGAIN --

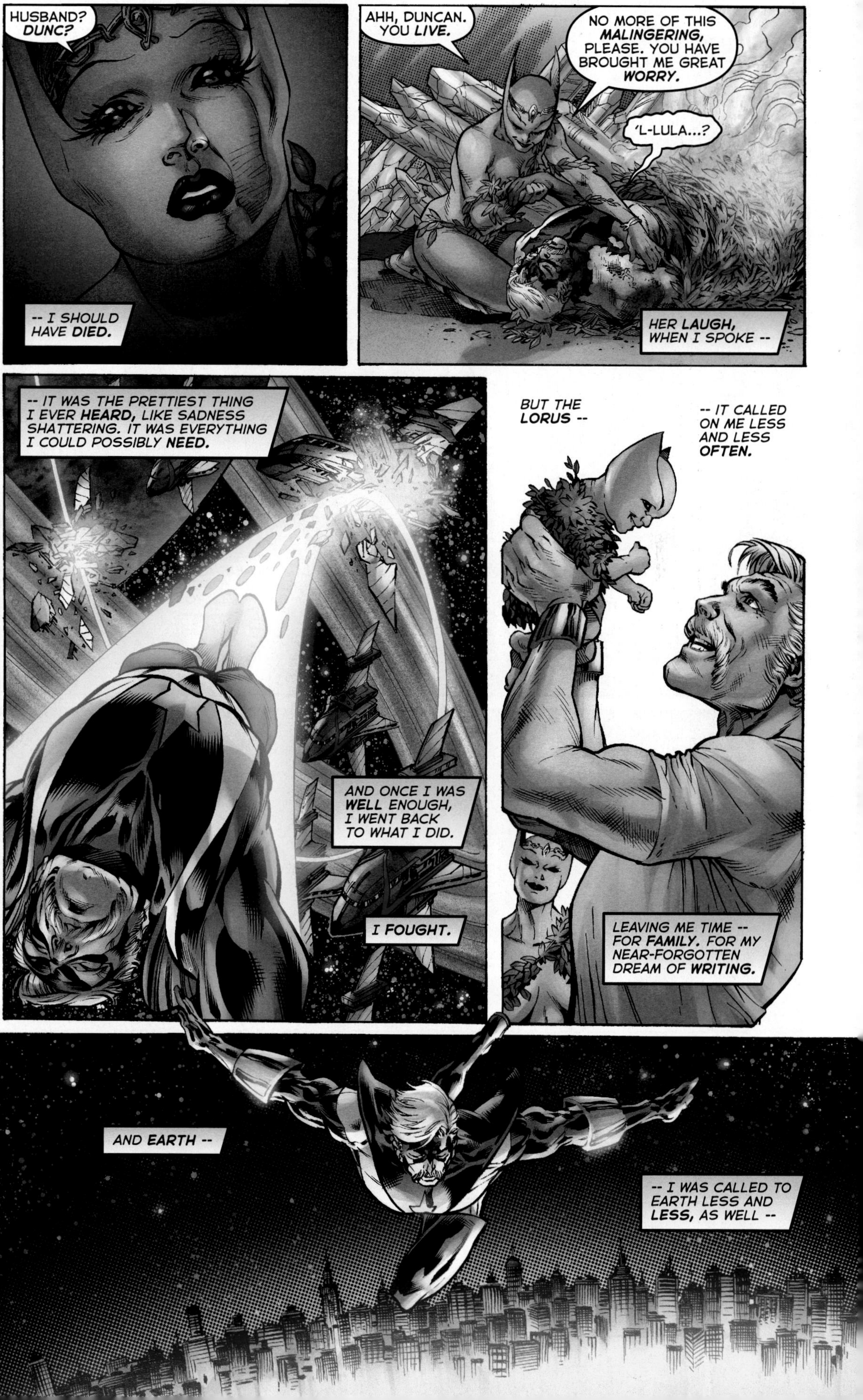
HUSBAND? DUNC?
-- I SHOULD HAVE DIED.
AHH, DUNCAN. YOU LIVE.
NO MORE OF THIS MALINGERING, PLEASE. YOU HAVE BROUGHT ME GREAT WORRY.
'L-LULA...?
HER LAUGH, WHEN I SPOKE --
-- IT WAS THE PRETTIEST THING I EVER HEARD, LIKE SADNESS SHATTERING. IT WAS EVERYTHING I COULD POSSIBLY NEED.
AND ONCE I WAS WELL ENOUGH, I WENT BACK TO WHAT I DID.
I FOUGHT.
BUT THE LORUS --
-- IT CALLED ON ME LESS AND LESS OFTEN.
LEAVING ME TIME -- FOR FAMILY. FOR MY NEAR-FORGOTTEN DREAM OF WRITING.
AND EARTH --
-- I WAS CALLED TO EARTH LESS AND LESS, AS WELL --

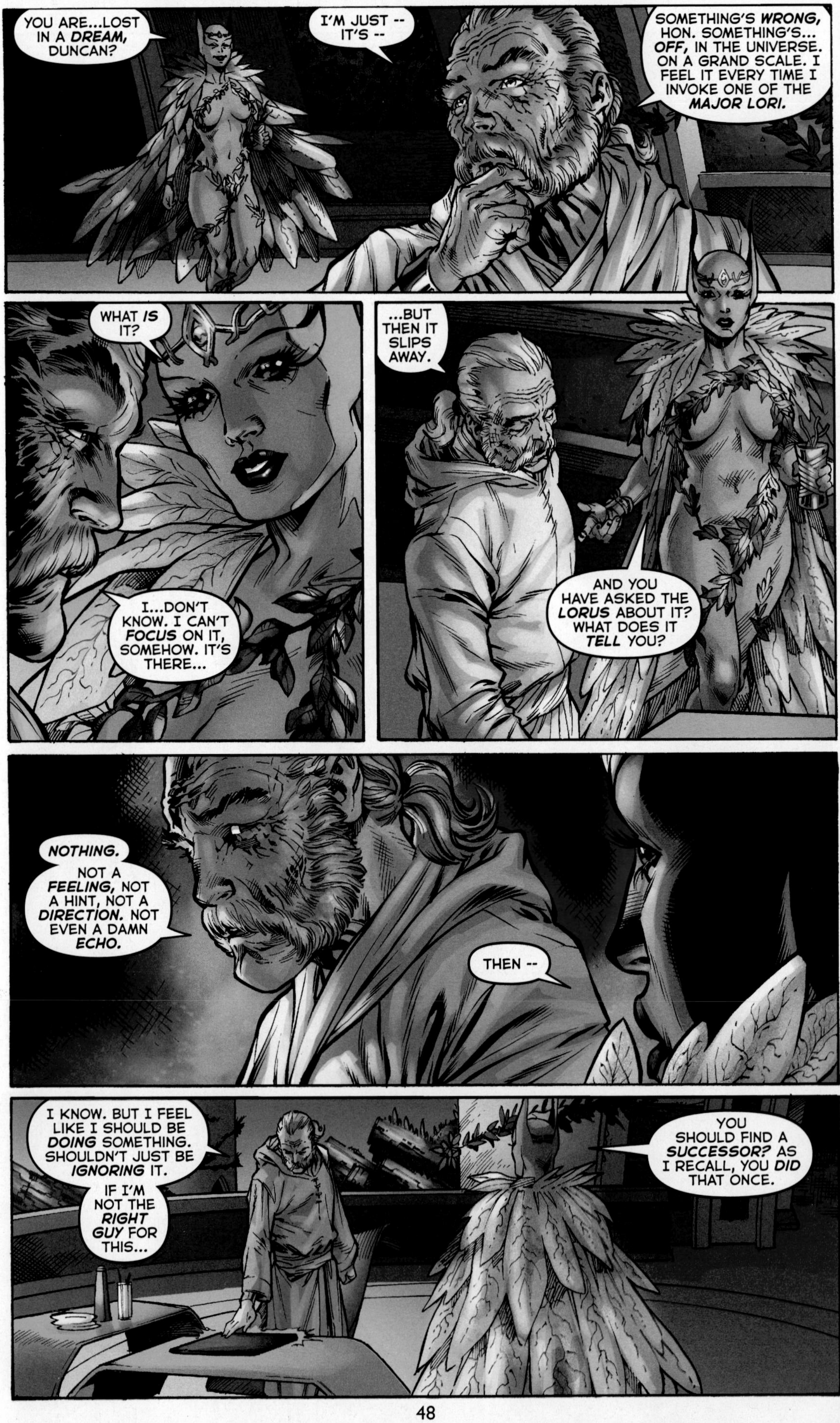

YOU ARE...LOST IN A *DREAM,* DUNCAN?
I'M JUST -- IT'S --
SOMETHING'S *WRONG,* HON. SOMETHING'S... *OFF,* IN THE UNIVERSE. ON A GRAND SCALE. I FEEL IT EVERY TIME I INVOKE ONE OF THE *MAJOR LORI.*
WHAT *IS* IT?
I...DON'T KNOW. I CAN'T *FOCUS* ON IT, SOMEHOW. IT'S THERE...
...BUT THEN IT SLIPS AWAY.
AND YOU HAVE ASKED THE *LORUS* ABOUT IT? WHAT DOES IT *TELL* YOU?
NOTHING.
NOT A *FEELING,* NOT A HINT, NOT A *DIRECTION.* NOT EVEN A DAMN *ECHO.*
THEN --
I KNOW. BUT I FEEL LIKE I SHOULD BE *DOING* SOMETHING. SHOULDN'T JUST BE *IGNORING* IT.
IF I'M NOT THE *RIGHT GUY* FOR THIS...
YOU SHOULD FIND A *SUCCESSOR?* AS I RECALL, YOU *DID* THAT ONCE.

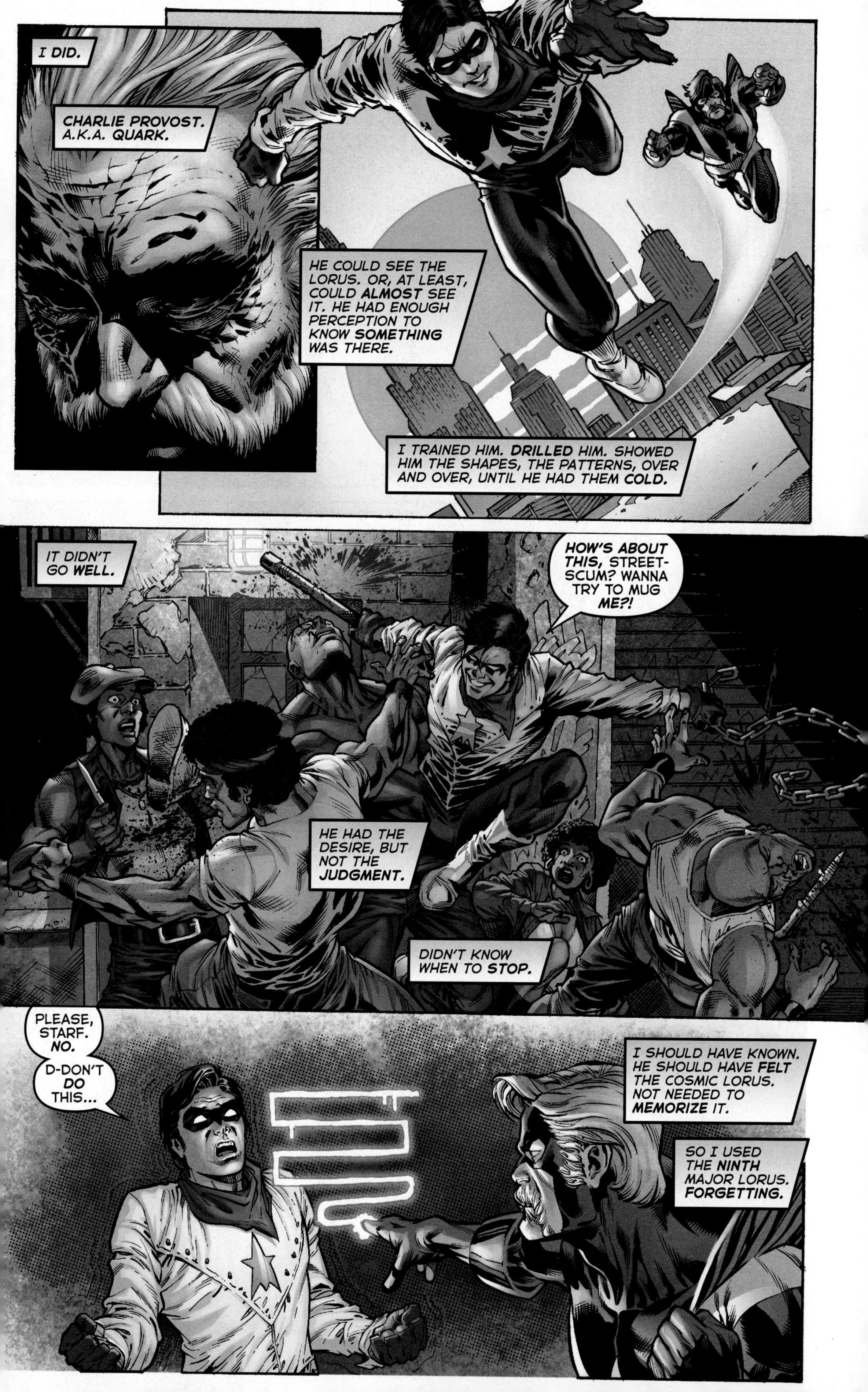
I DID.
CHARLIE PROVOST. A.K.A. QUARK.
HE COULD SEE THE LORUS. OR, AT LEAST, COULD ALMOST SEE IT. HE HAD ENOUGH PERCEPTION TO KNOW SOMETHING WAS THERE.
I TRAINED HIM. DRILLED HIM. SHOWED HIM THE SHAPES, THE PATTERNS, OVER AND OVER, UNTIL HE HAD THEM COLD.
IT DIDN'T GO WELL.
HOW'S ABOUT THIS, STREET-SCUM? WANNA TRY TO MUG ME?!
HE HAD THE DESIRE, BUT NOT THE JUDGMENT.
DIDN'T KNOW WHEN TO STOP.
PLEASE, STARF. NO.
D-DON'T DO THIS...
I SHOULD HAVE KNOWN. HE SHOULD HAVE FELT THE COSMIC LORUS. NOT NEEDED TO MEMORIZE IT.
SO I USED THE NINTH MAJOR LORUS. FORGETTING.

LAST I KNEW OF HIM, HE WAS APPEARING AT *CONVENTIONS*, MAKING A LIVING BY SIGNING *SOUVENIRS*.

I'D LED HIM *INTO* THIS LIFE, THEN SHOVED HIM *OUT* OF IT.

AND HE *COULDN'T* LET GO.

I'LL *REMEMBER!* I'LL REMEMBER -- AN' I'LL BE *BACK!*

DAMN YOU, STARFIGHTER -- I'LL BE *BACK!*

YEAH, I REALLY *CRAPPED THE BED* WITH THAT ONE, HUH? POOR *KID.*

HE SOUNDS LIKE A *HORROR,* TO ME.

YOU FEEL GUILTY FOR NOT HAVING DONE *BETTER* BY HIM? AND NOW YOU FEEL THAT YOU HAVE NOT DONE ENOUGH FOR THE *UNIVERSE?*

I THINK I'VE PROBABLY DONE *ENOUGH* FOR THE UNIVERSE. I THINK THE SCORE'S *PRETTY GOOD* IN MY FAVOR.

BUT JUST BECAUSE I'VE DONE ENOUGH DOESN'T MEAN THERE ISN'T *MORE TO DO.*

THERE'S SOMETHING *OUT THERE...*

I SEE. I *THINK.*

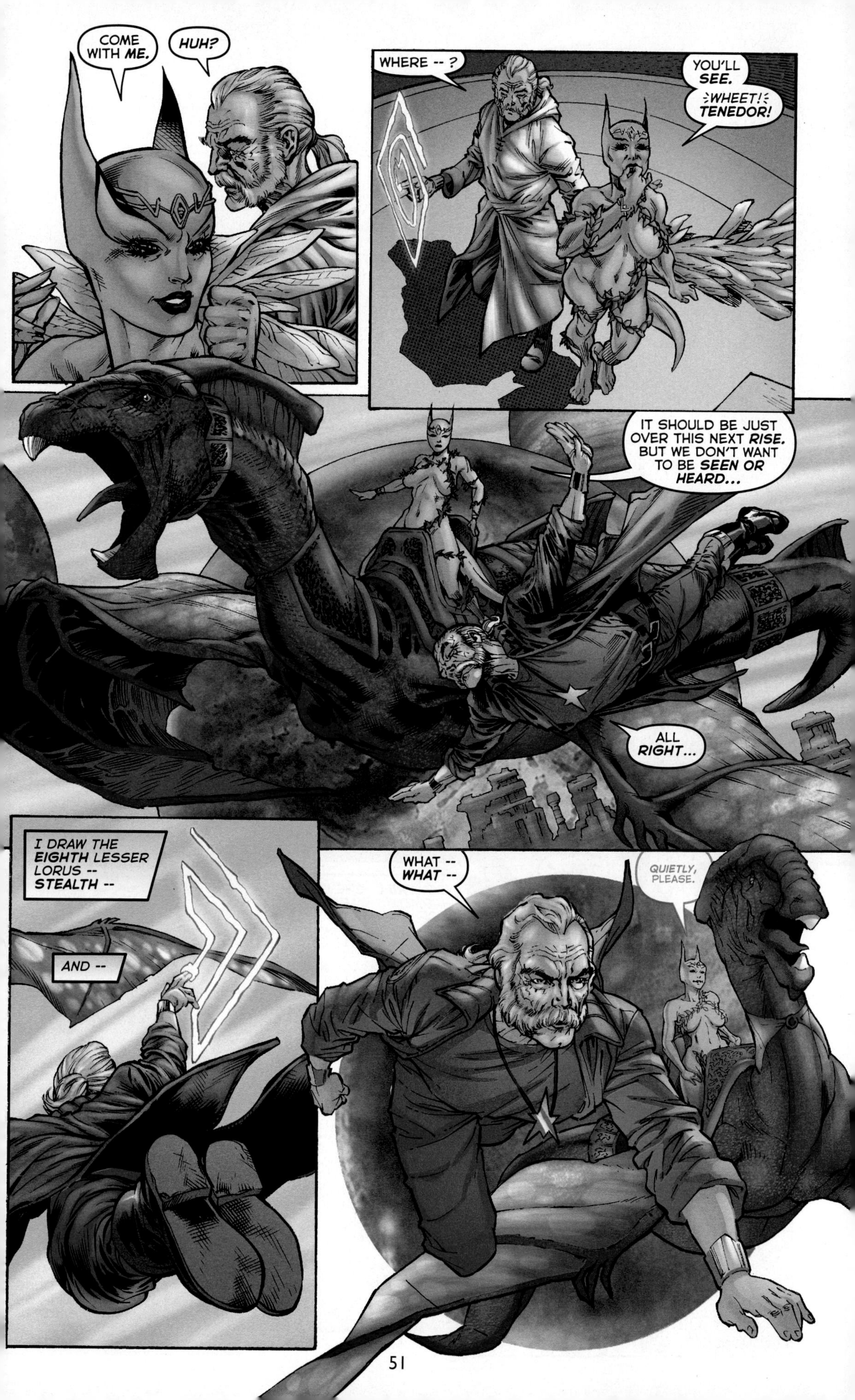
COME WITH ME.
HUH?
WHERE -- ?
YOU'LL SEE.
WHEET!
TENEDOR!
IT SHOULD BE JUST OVER THIS NEXT RISE. BUT WE DON'T WANT TO BE SEEN OR HEARD...
ALL RIGHT...
I DRAW THE EIGHTH LESSER LORUS -- STEALTH --
AND --
WHAT -- WHAT --
QUIETLY, PLEASE.

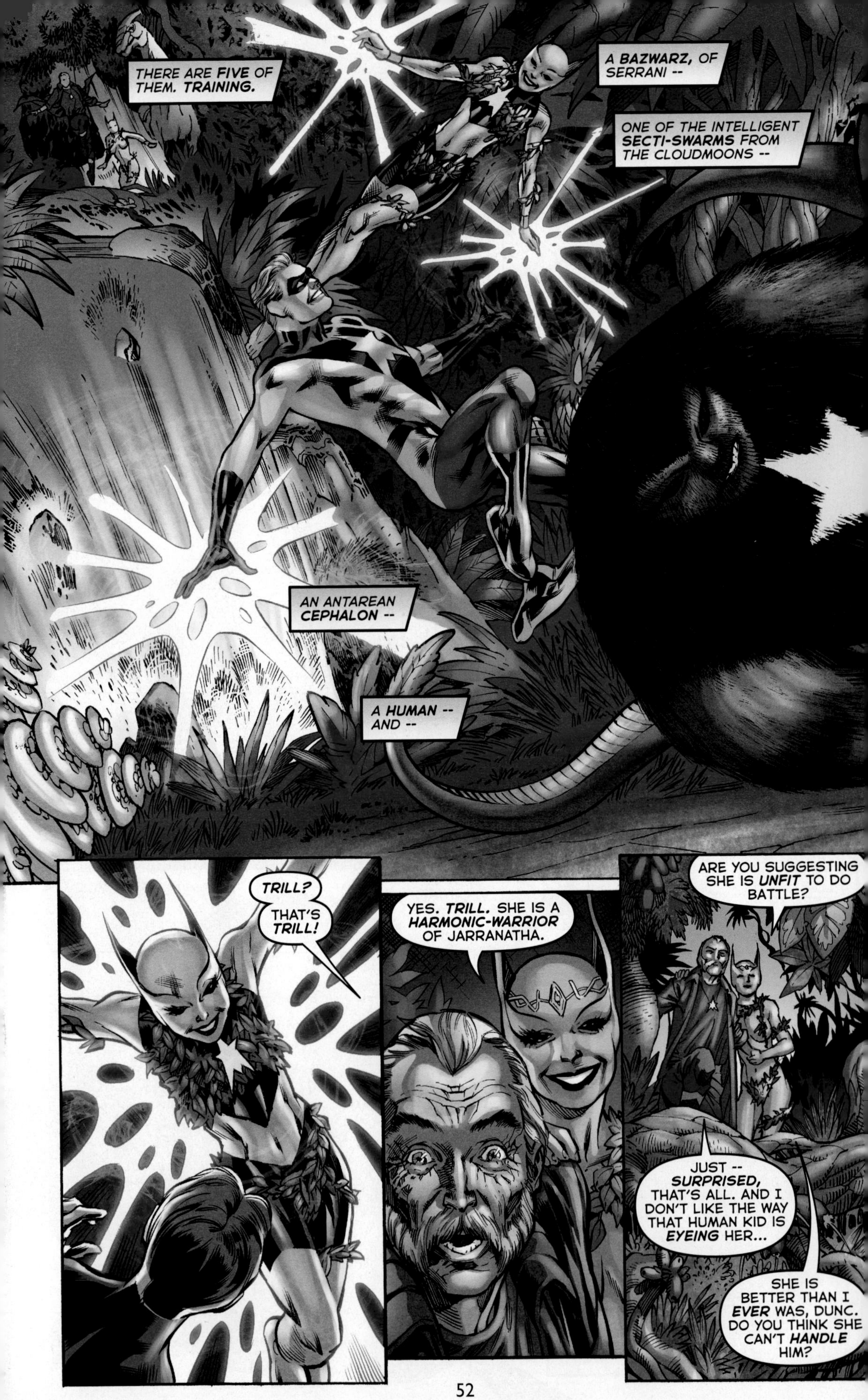
THERE ARE FIVE OF THEM. TRAINING.
A BAZWARZ, OF SERRANI --
ONE OF THE INTELLIGENT SECTI-SWARMS FROM THE CLOUDMOONS --
AN ANTAREAN CEPHALON --
A HUMAN -- AND --
TRILL?
THAT'S TRILL!
YES. TRILL. SHE IS A HARMONIC-WARRIOR OF JARRANATHA.
ARE YOU SUGGESTING SHE IS UNFIT TO DO BATTLE?
JUST -- SURPRISED, THAT'S ALL. AND I DON'T LIKE THE WAY THAT HUMAN KID IS EYEING HER...
SHE IS BETTER THAN I EVER WAS, DUNC. DO YOU THINK SHE CAN'T HANDLE HIM?

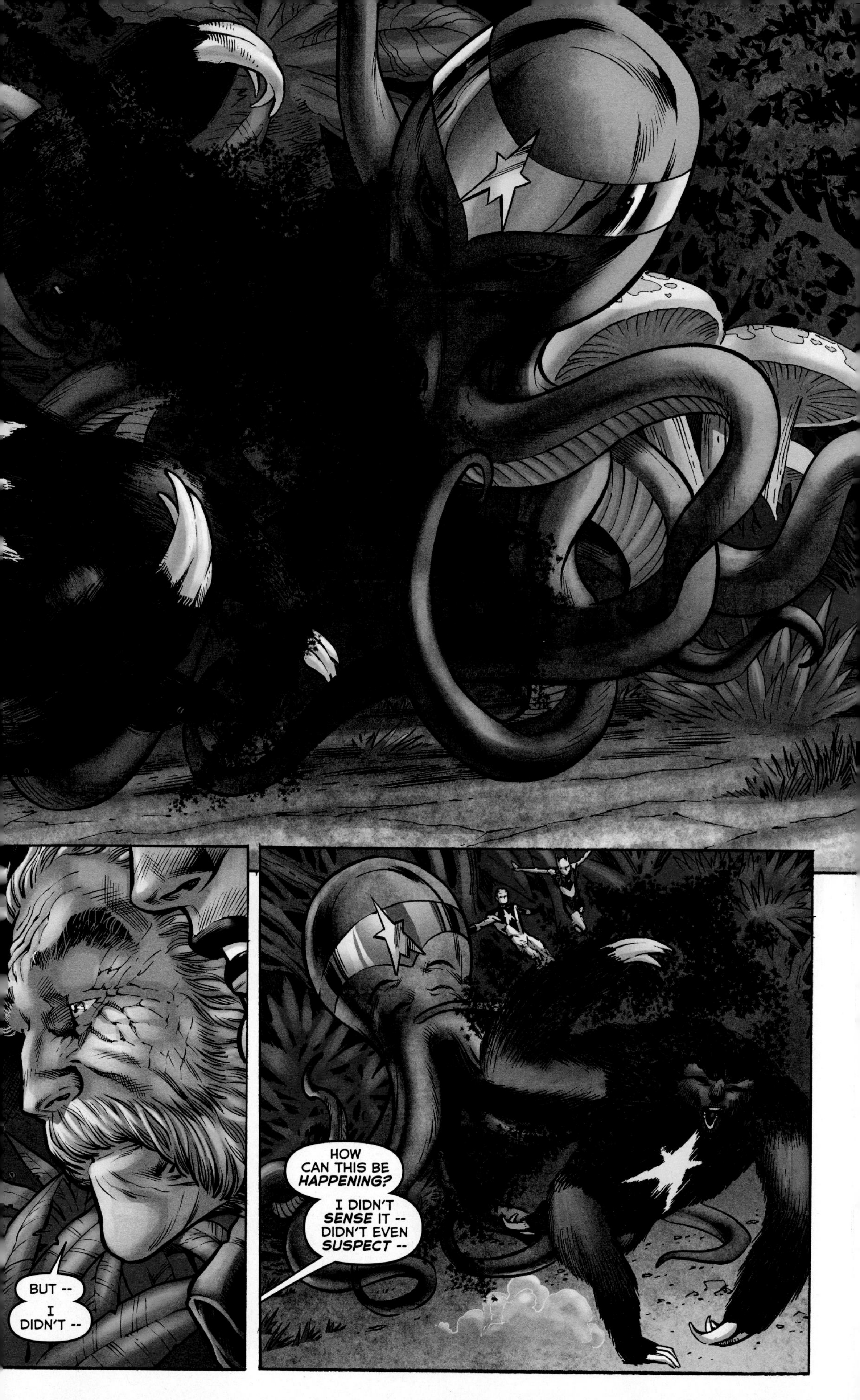

BUT -- I DIDN'T --
HOW CAN THIS BE HAPPENING?
I DIDN'T SENSE IT -- DIDN'T EVEN SUSPECT --

54

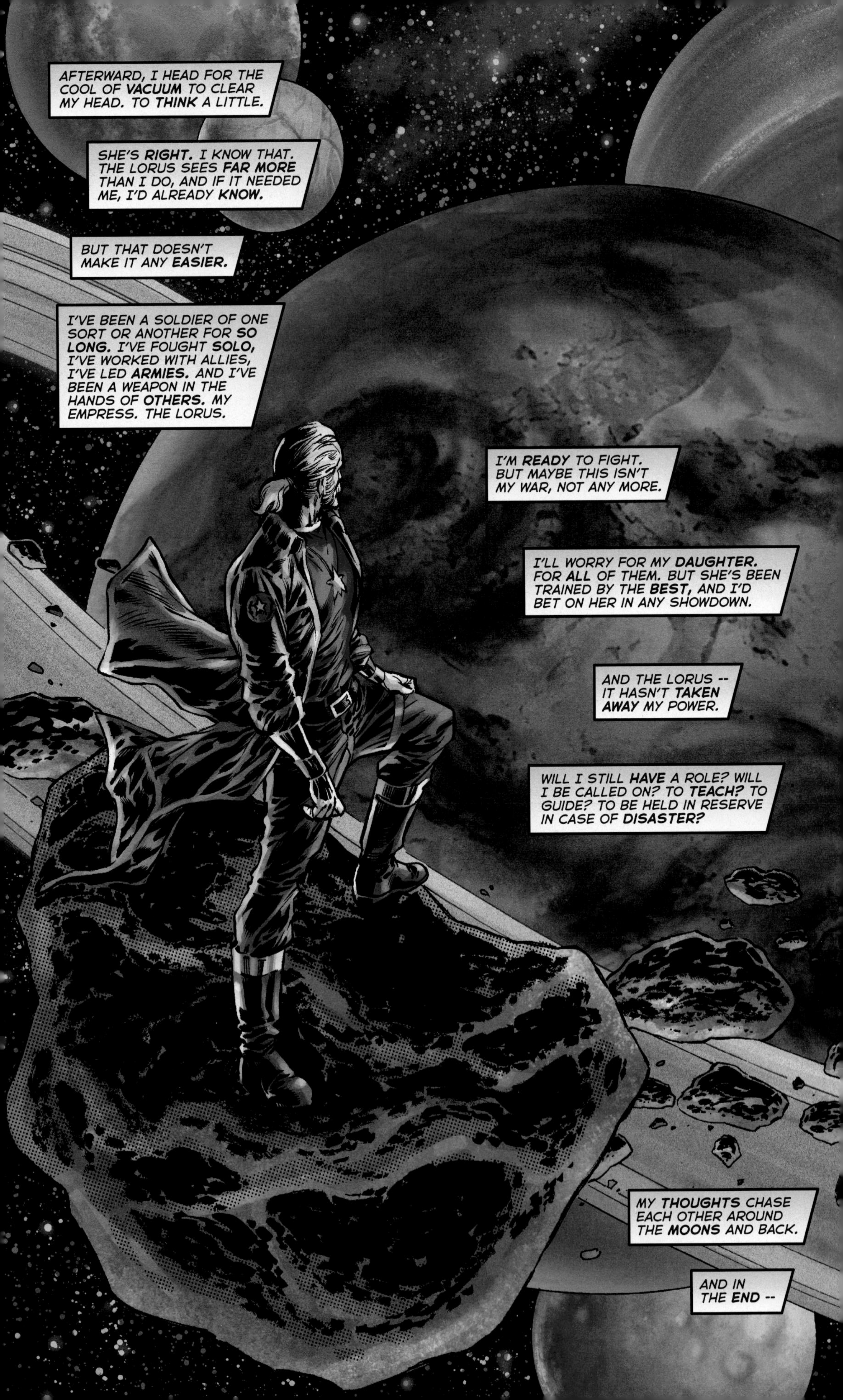
AFTERWARD, I HEAD FOR THE COOL OF **VACUUM** TO CLEAR MY HEAD. TO **THINK** A LITTLE.
SHE'S **RIGHT.** I KNOW THAT. THE LORUS SEES **FAR MORE** THAN I DO, AND IF IT NEEDED ME, I'D ALREADY **KNOW.**
BUT THAT DOESN'T MAKE IT ANY **EASIER.**
I'VE BEEN A SOLDIER OF ONE SORT OR ANOTHER FOR **SO LONG.** I'VE FOUGHT **SOLO,** I'VE WORKED WITH ALLIES, I'VE LED **ARMIES.** AND I'VE BEEN A WEAPON IN THE HANDS OF **OTHERS.** MY EMPRESS. THE LORUS.
I'M **READY** TO FIGHT. BUT MAYBE THIS ISN'T MY WAR, NOT ANY MORE.
I'LL WORRY FOR MY **DAUGHTER.** FOR **ALL** OF THEM. BUT SHE'S BEEN TRAINED BY THE **BEST,** AND I'D BET ON HER IN ANY SHOWDOWN.
AND THE LORUS -- IT HASN'T **TAKEN AWAY** MY POWER.
WILL I STILL **HAVE** A ROLE? WILL I BE CALLED ON? TO **TEACH?** TO GUIDE? TO BE HELD IN RESERVE IN CASE OF **DISASTER?**
MY **THOUGHTS** CHASE EACH OTHER AROUND THE **MOONS** AND BACK.
AND IN THE **END** --

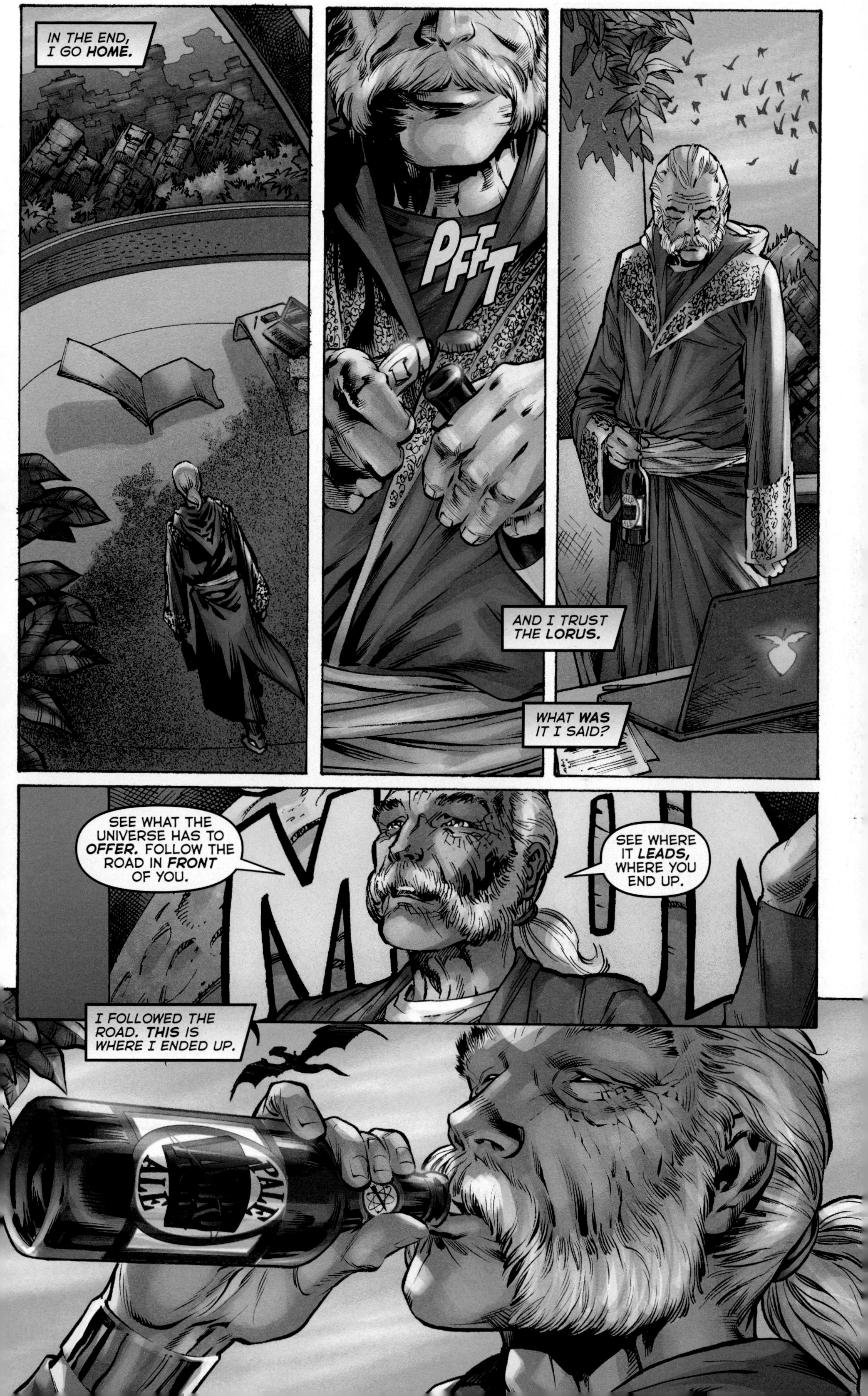
IN THE END, I GO HOME.
PFFT
AND I TRUST THE LORUS.
WHAT WAS IT I SAID?
SEE WHAT THE UNIVERSE HAS TO OFFER. FOLLOW THE ROAD IN FRONT OF YOU.
SEE WHERE IT LEADS, WHERE YOU END UP.
I FOLLOWED THE ROAD. THIS IS WHERE I ENDED UP.
PALE ALE

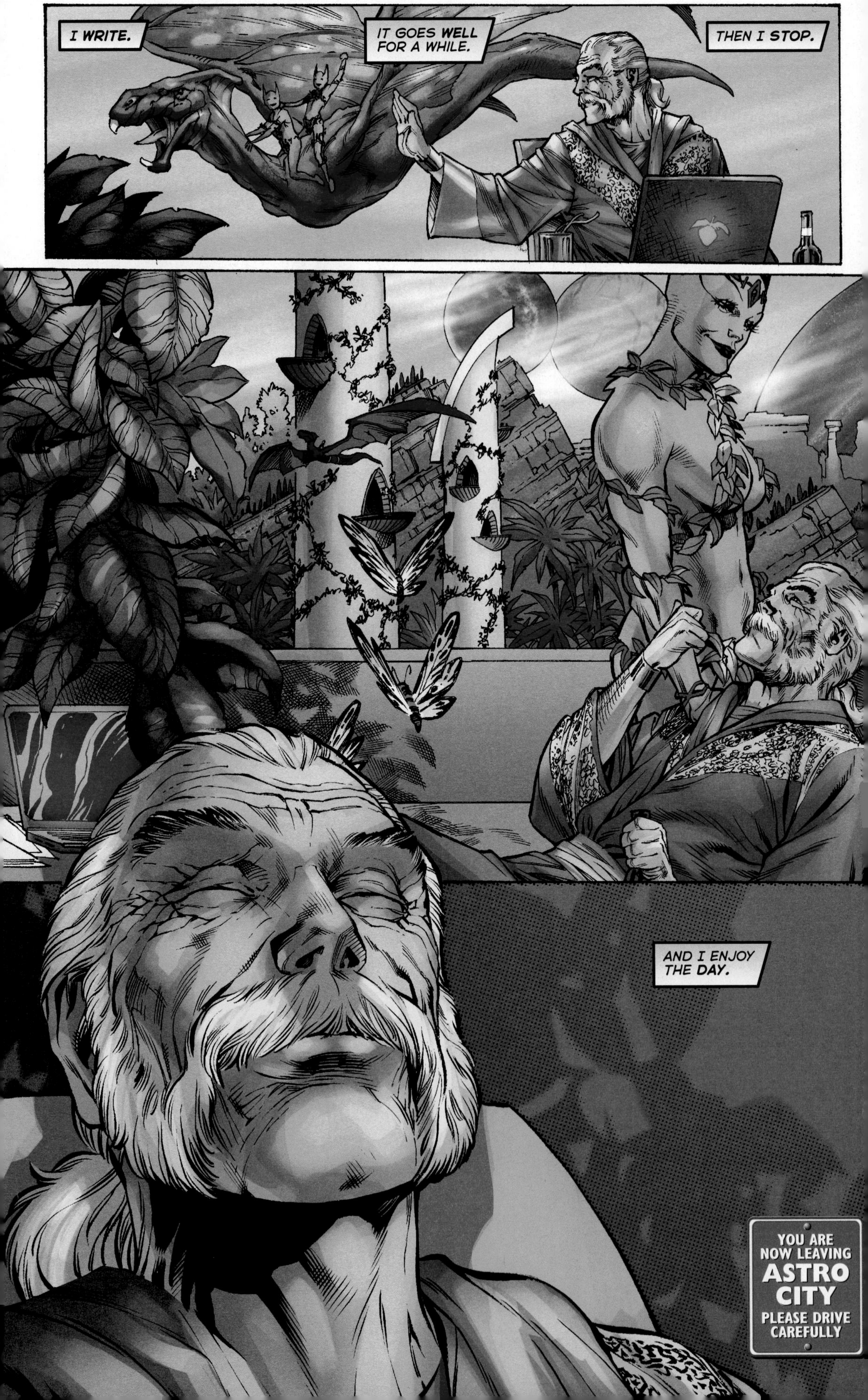
I WRITE.
IT GOES WELL FOR A WHILE.
THEN I STOP.
AND I ENJOY THE DAY.
YOU ARE NOW LEAVING ASTRO CITY PLEASE DRIVE CAREFULLY

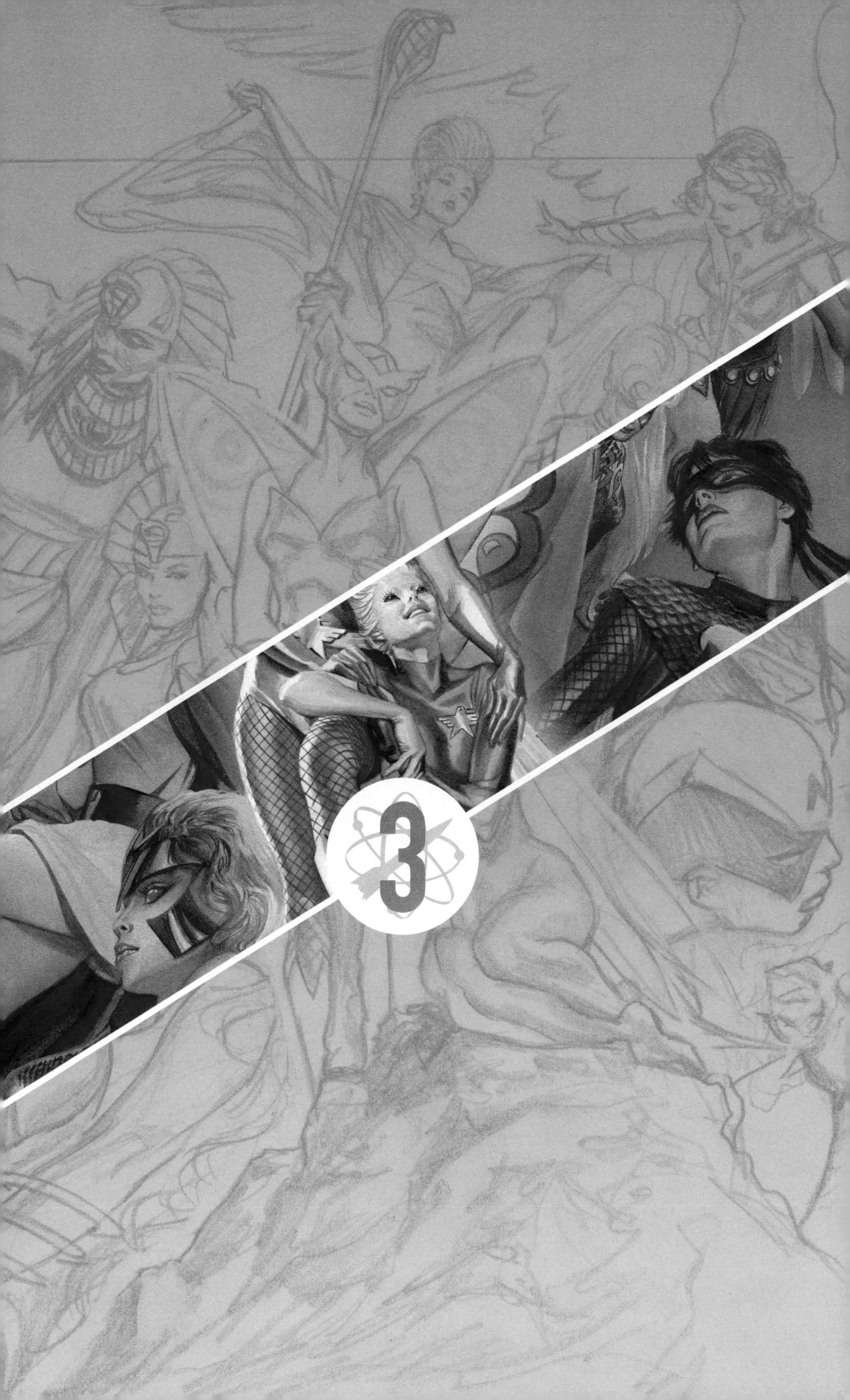
3

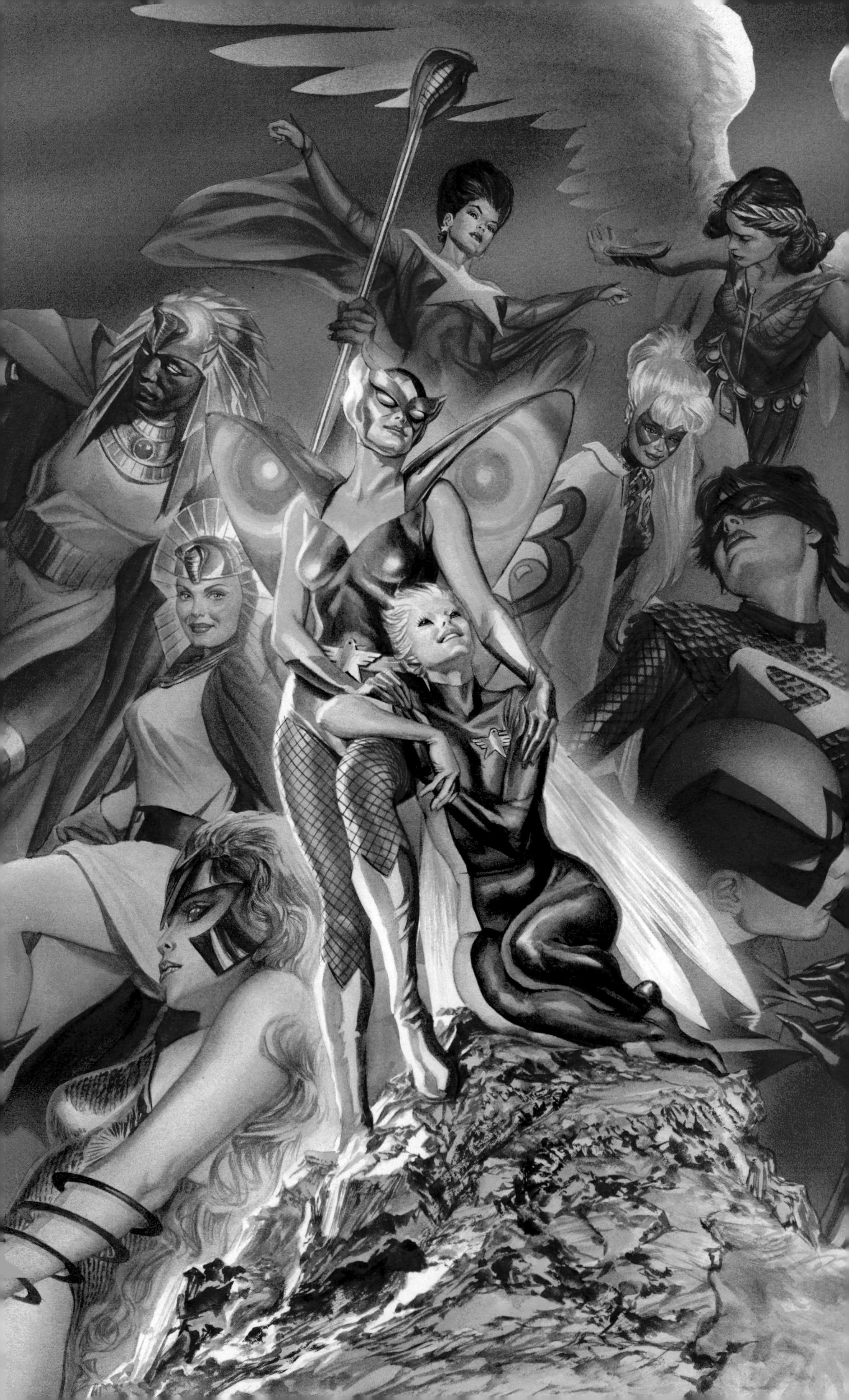

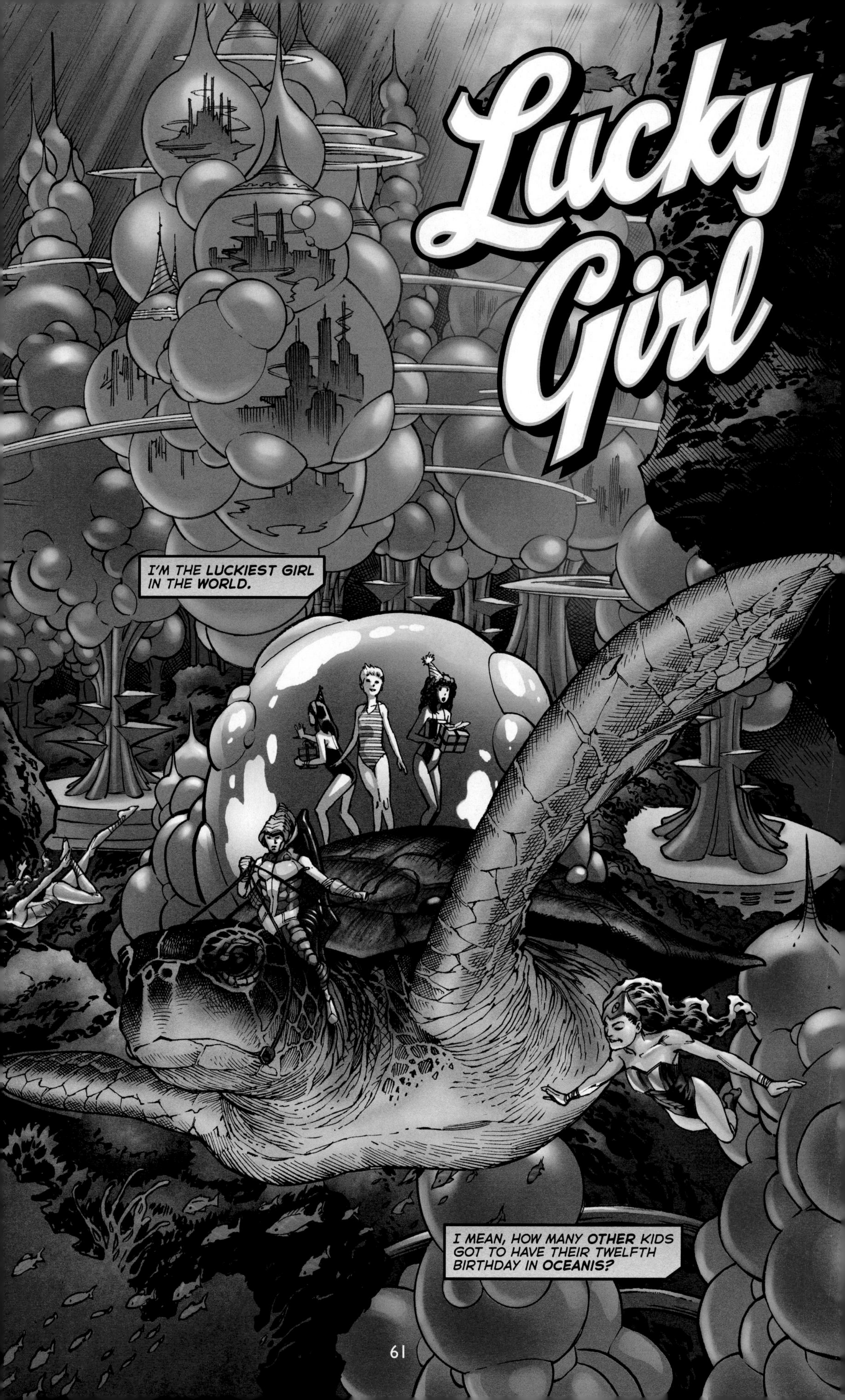
Lucky Girl
I'M THE LUCKIEST GIRL IN THE WORLD.
I MEAN, HOW MANY OTHER KIDS GOT TO HAVE THEIR TWELFTH BIRTHDAY IN OCEANIS?

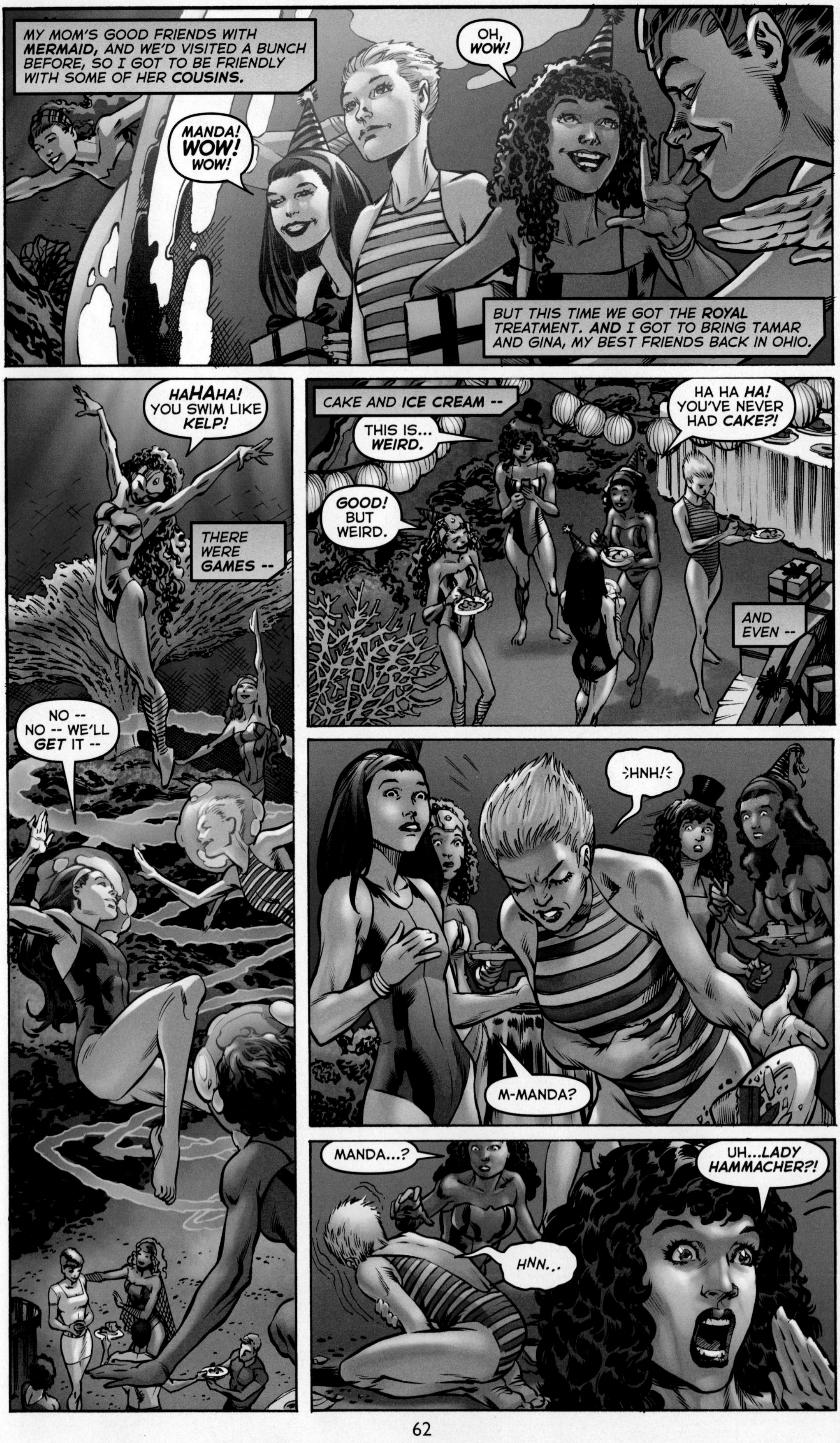
MY MOM'S GOOD FRIENDS WITH MERMAID, AND WE'D VISITED A BUNCH BEFORE, SO I GOT TO BE FRIENDLY WITH SOME OF HER COUSINS.
MANDA! WOW! WOW!
OH, WOW!
BUT THIS TIME WE GOT THE ROYAL TREATMENT. AND I GOT TO BRING TAMAR AND GINA, MY BEST FRIENDS BACK IN OHIO.
HAHAHA! YOU SWIM LIKE KELP!
THERE WERE GAMES --
NO -- NO -- WE'LL GET IT --
CAKE AND ICE CREAM --
THIS IS... WEIRD.
GOOD! BUT WEIRD.
HA HA HA! YOU'VE NEVER HAD CAKE?!
AND EVEN --
HNH!
M-MANDA?
MANDA...?
UH...LADY HAMMACHER?!
HNN...

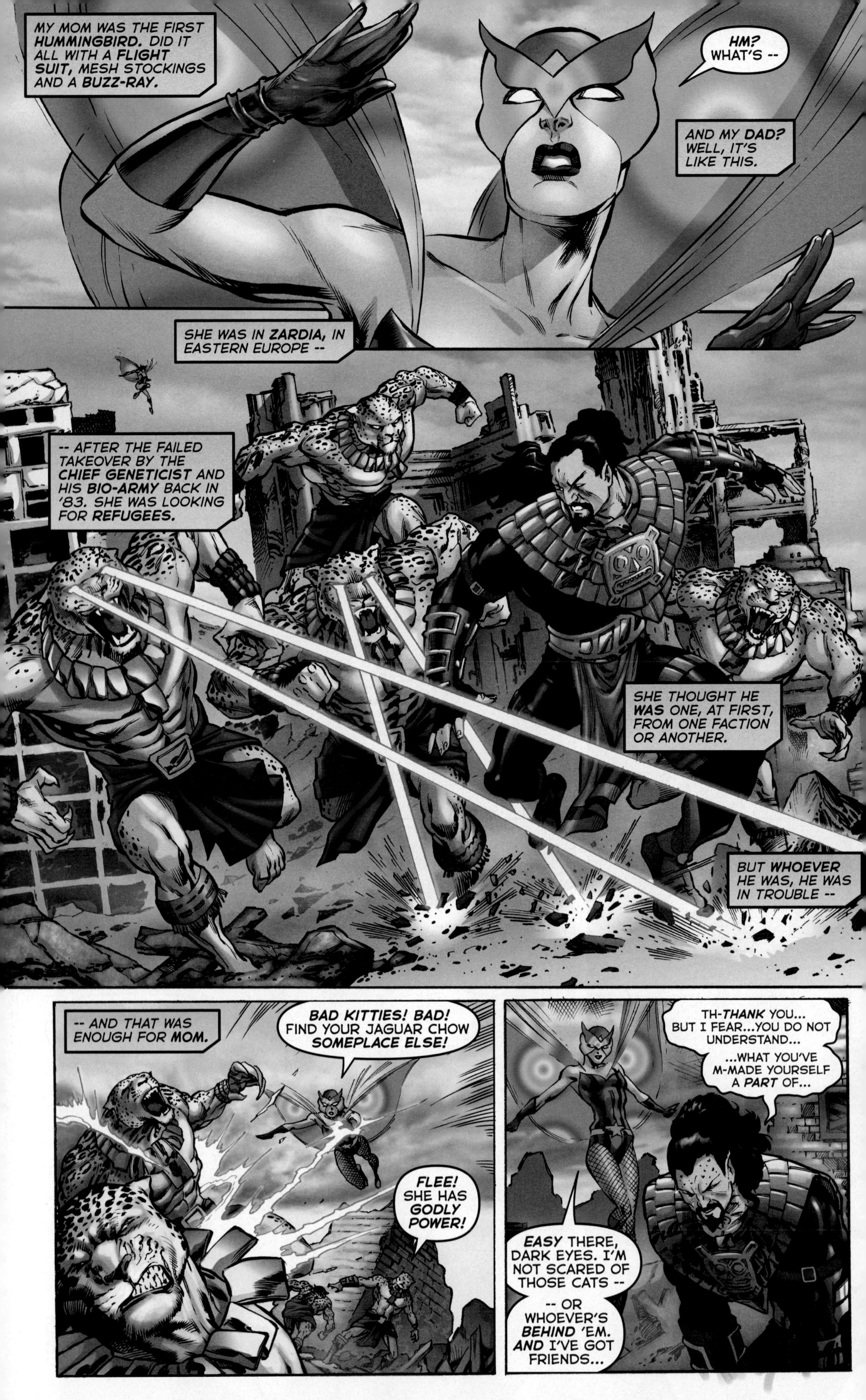
MY MOM WAS THE FIRST HUMMINGBIRD. DID IT ALL WITH A FLIGHT SUIT, MESH STOCKINGS AND A BUZZ-RAY.
HM? WHAT'S --
AND MY DAD? WELL, IT'S LIKE THIS.
SHE WAS IN ZARDIA, IN EASTERN EUROPE --
-- AFTER THE FAILED TAKEOVER BY THE CHIEF GENETICIST AND HIS BIO-ARMY BACK IN '83. SHE WAS LOOKING FOR REFUGEES.
SHE THOUGHT HE WAS ONE, AT FIRST, FROM ONE FACTION OR ANOTHER.
BUT WHOEVER HE WAS, HE WAS IN TROUBLE --
-- AND THAT WAS ENOUGH FOR MOM.
BAD KITTIES! BAD! FIND YOUR JAGUAR CHOW SOMEPLACE ELSE!
FLEE! SHE HAS GODLY POWER!
TH-THANK YOU... BUT I FEAR...YOU DO NOT UNDERSTAND...
...WHAT YOU'VE M-MADE YOURSELF A PART OF...
EASY THERE, DARK EYES. I'M NOT SCARED OF THOSE CATS --
-- OR WHOEVER'S BEHIND 'EM. AND I'VE GOT FRIENDS...

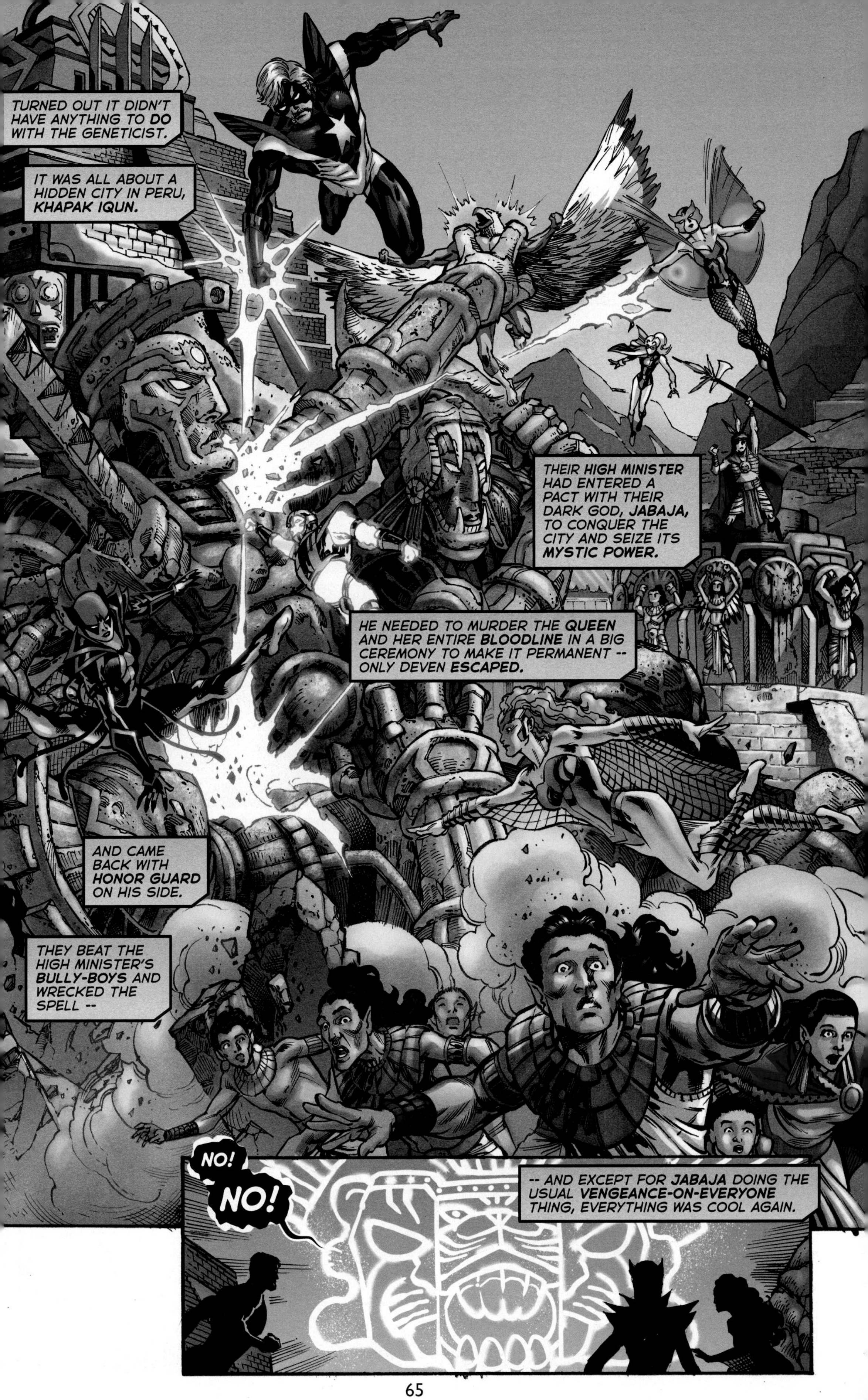

TURNED OUT IT DIDN'T HAVE ANYTHING TO DO WITH THE GENETICIST.
IT WAS ALL ABOUT A HIDDEN CITY IN PERU, KHAPAK IQUN.
THEIR HIGH MINISTER HAD ENTERED A PACT WITH THEIR DARK GOD, JABAJA, TO CONQUER THE CITY AND SEIZE ITS MYSTIC POWER.
HE NEEDED TO MURDER THE QUEEN AND HER ENTIRE BLOODLINE IN A BIG CEREMONY TO MAKE IT PERMANENT -- ONLY DEVEN ESCAPED.
AND CAME BACK WITH HONOR GUARD ON HIS SIDE.
THEY BEAT THE HIGH MINISTER'S BULLY-BOYS AND WRECKED THE SPELL --
NO!
NO!
-- AND EXCEPT FOR JABAJA DOING THE USUAL VENGEANCE-ON-EVERYONE THING, EVERYTHING WAS COOL AGAIN.

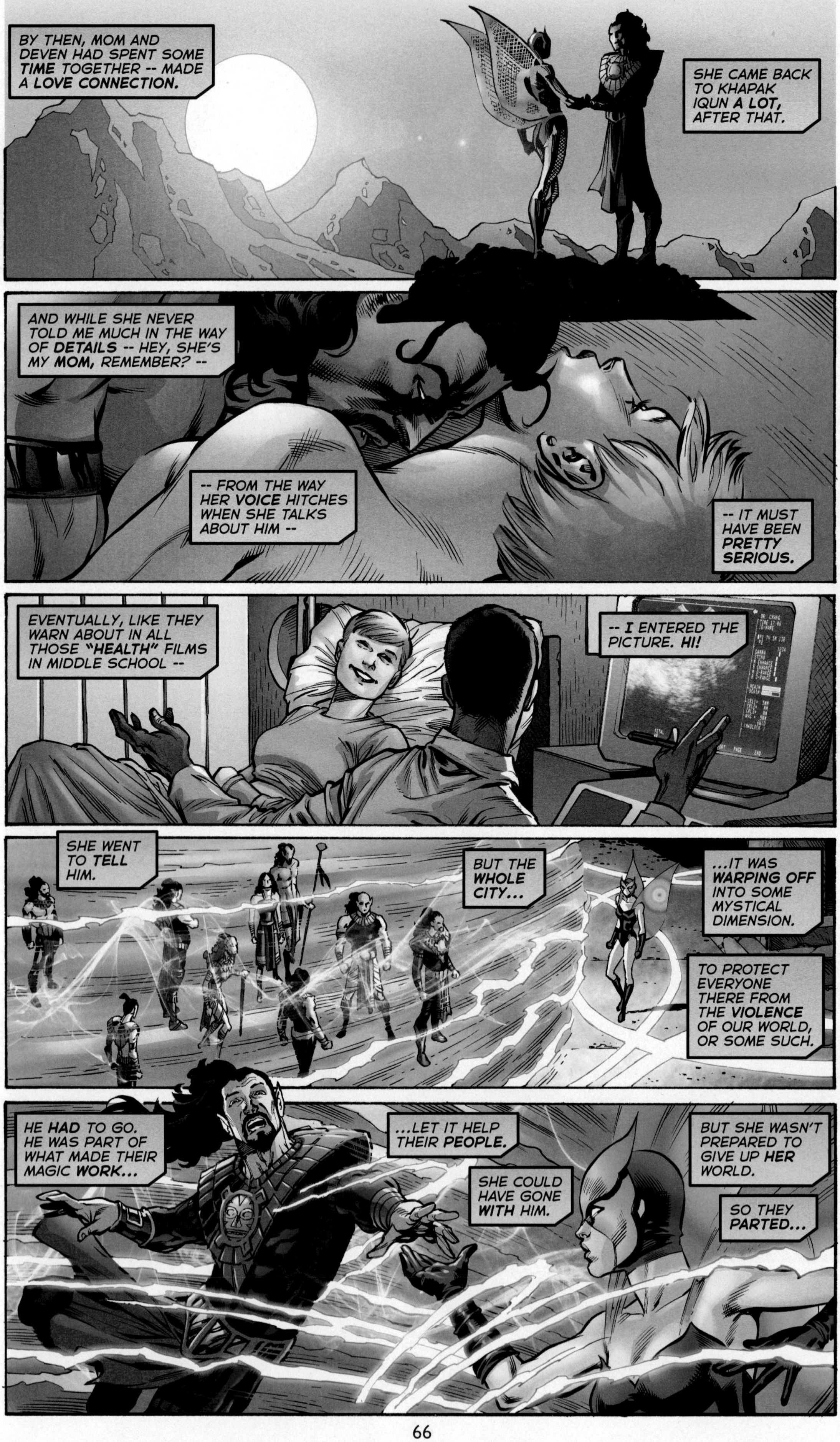

BY THEN, MOM AND DEVEN HAD SPENT SOME TIME TOGETHER -- MADE A LOVE CONNECTION.
SHE CAME BACK TO KHAPAK IQUN A LOT, AFTER THAT.
AND WHILE SHE NEVER TOLD ME MUCH IN THE WAY OF DETAILS -- HEY, SHE'S MY MOM, REMEMBER? --
-- FROM THE WAY HER VOICE HITCHES WHEN SHE TALKS ABOUT HIM --
-- IT MUST HAVE BEEN PRETTY SERIOUS.
EVENTUALLY, LIKE THEY WARN ABOUT IN ALL THOSE "HEALTH" FILMS IN MIDDLE SCHOOL --
-- I ENTERED THE PICTURE. HI!
SHE WENT TO TELL HIM.
BUT THE WHOLE CITY...
...IT WAS WARPING OFF INTO SOME MYSTICAL DIMENSION.
TO PROTECT EVERYONE THERE FROM THE VIOLENCE OF OUR WORLD, OR SOME SUCH.
HE HAD TO GO. HE WAS PART OF WHAT MADE THEIR MAGIC WORK...
...LET IT HELP THEIR PEOPLE.
SHE COULD HAVE GONE WITH HIM.
BUT SHE WASN'T PREPARED TO GIVE UP HER WORLD.
SO THEY PARTED...

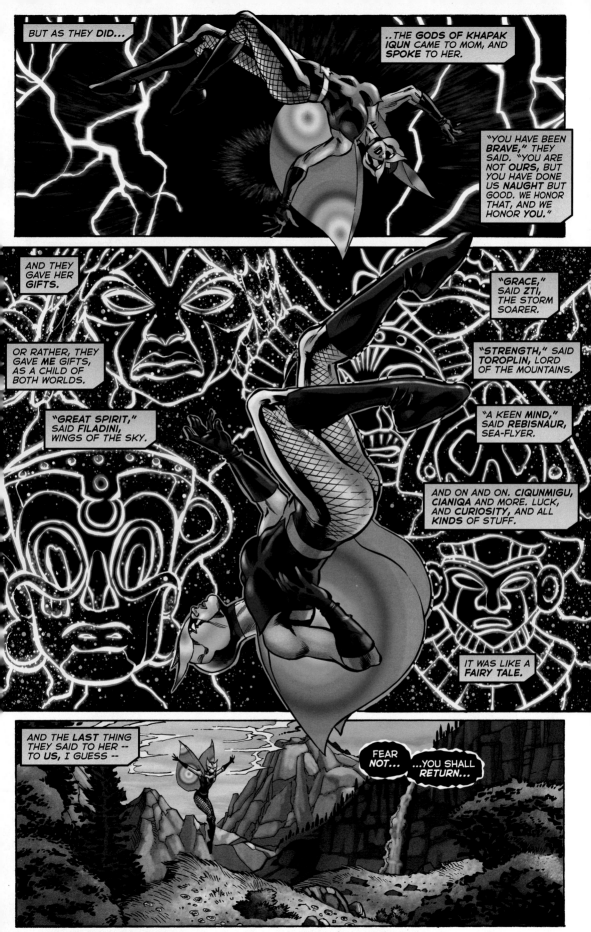

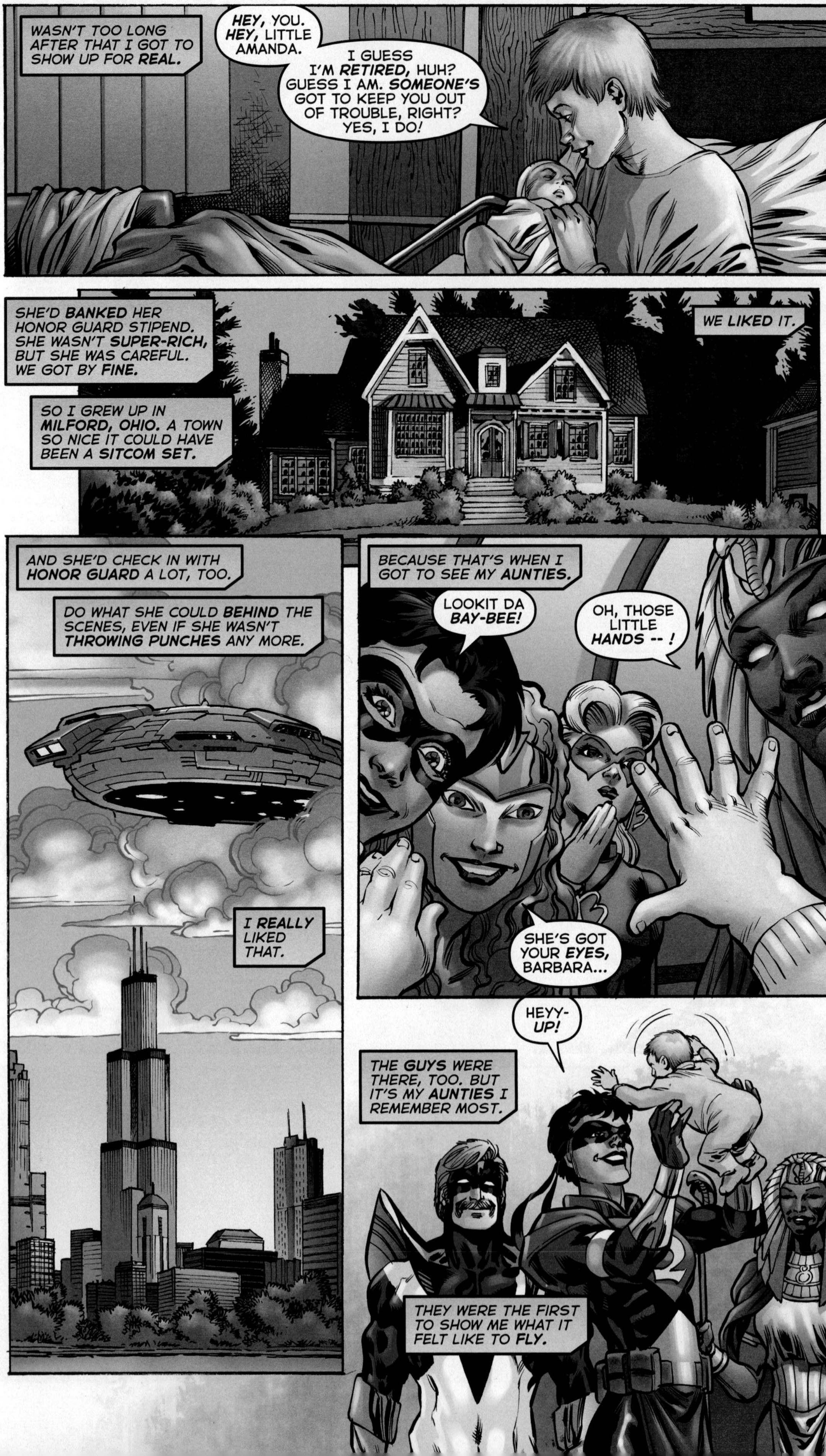
WASN'T TOO LONG AFTER THAT I GOT TO SHOW UP FOR REAL.
HEY, YOU. HEY, LITTLE AMANDA.
I GUESS I'M RETIRED, HUH? GUESS I AM. SOMEONE'S GOT TO KEEP YOU OUT OF TROUBLE, RIGHT? YES, I DO!
SHE'D BANKED HER HONOR GUARD STIPEND. SHE WASN'T SUPER-RICH, BUT SHE WAS CAREFUL. WE GOT BY FINE.
SO I GREW UP IN MILFORD, OHIO. A TOWN SO NICE IT COULD HAVE BEEN A SITCOM SET.
WE LIKED IT.
AND SHE'D CHECK IN WITH HONOR GUARD A LOT, TOO.
DO WHAT SHE COULD BEHIND THE SCENES, EVEN IF SHE WASN'T THROWING PUNCHES ANY MORE.
I REALLY LIKED THAT.
BECAUSE THAT'S WHEN I GOT TO SEE MY AUNTIES.
LOOKIT DA BAY-BEE!
OH, THOSE LITTLE HANDS -- !
SHE'S GOT YOUR EYES, BARBARA...
HEYY-UP!
THE GUYS WERE THERE, TOO. BUT IT'S MY AUNTIES I REMEMBER MOST.
THEY WERE THE FIRST TO SHOW ME WHAT IT FELT LIKE TO FLY.

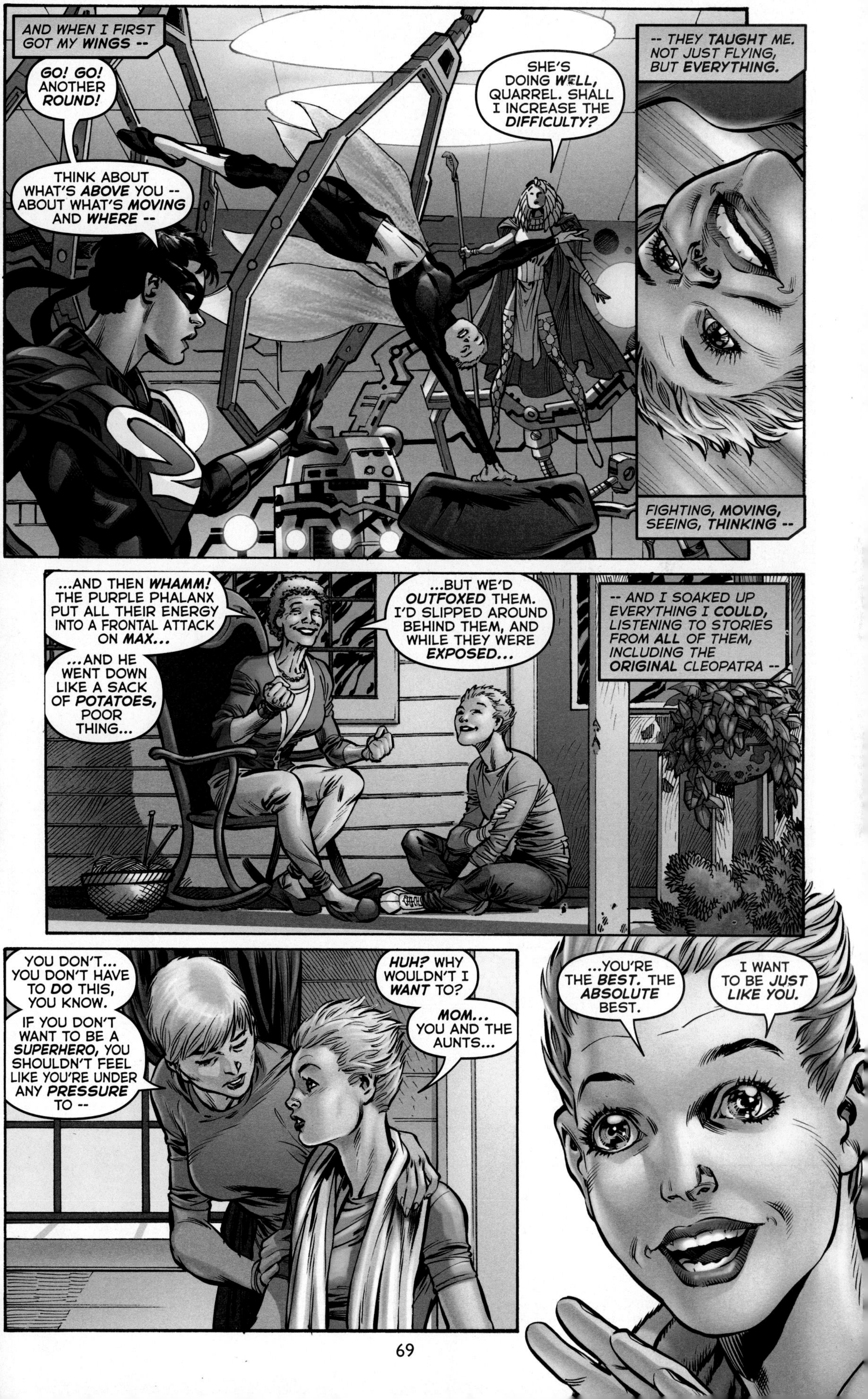
AND WHEN I FIRST GOT MY WINGS --
GO! GO! ANOTHER ROUND!
THINK ABOUT WHAT'S ABOVE YOU -- ABOUT WHAT'S MOVING AND WHERE --
SHE'S DOING WELL, QUARREL. SHALL I INCREASE THE DIFFICULTY?
-- THEY TAUGHT ME. NOT JUST FLYING, BUT EVERYTHING.
FIGHTING, MOVING, SEEING, THINKING --
...AND THEN WHAMM! THE PURPLE PHALANX PUT ALL THEIR ENERGY INTO A FRONTAL ATTACK ON MAX...
...AND HE WENT DOWN LIKE A SACK OF POTATOES, POOR THING...
...BUT WE'D OUTFOXED THEM. I'D SLIPPED AROUND BEHIND THEM, AND WHILE THEY WERE EXPOSED...
-- AND I SOAKED UP EVERYTHING I COULD, LISTENING TO STORIES FROM ALL OF THEM, INCLUDING THE ORIGINAL CLEOPATRA --
YOU DON'T... YOU DON'T HAVE TO DO THIS, YOU KNOW.
IF YOU DON'T WANT TO BE A SUPERHERO, YOU SHOULDN'T FEEL LIKE YOU'RE UNDER ANY PRESSURE TO --
HUH? WHY WOULDN'T I WANT TO?
MOM... YOU AND THE AUNTS...
...YOU'RE THE BEST. THE ABSOLUTE BEST.
I WANT TO BE JUST LIKE YOU.

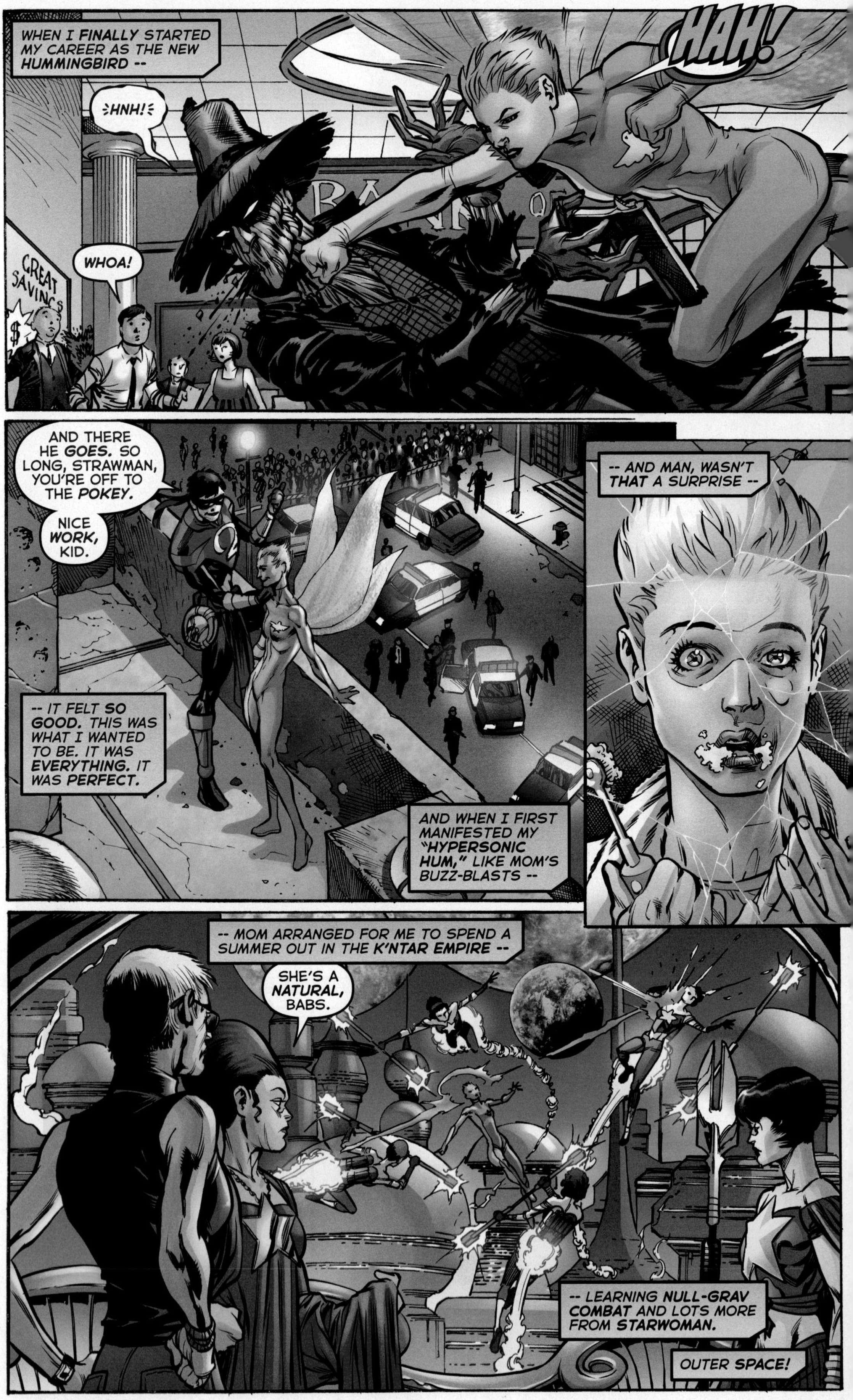

WHEN I FINALLY STARTED MY CAREER AS THE NEW HUMMINGBIRD --
HAH!
HNH!
WHOA!
GREAT SAVINGS
AND THERE HE GOES. SO LONG, STRAWMAN, YOU'RE OFF TO THE POKEY.
NICE WORK, KID.
-- IT FELT SO GOOD. THIS WAS WHAT I WANTED TO BE. IT WAS EVERYTHING. IT WAS PERFECT.
AND WHEN I FIRST MANIFESTED MY "HYPERSONIC HUM," LIKE MOM'S BUZZ-BLASTS --
-- AND MAN, WASN'T THAT A SURPRISE --
-- MOM ARRANGED FOR ME TO SPEND A SUMMER OUT IN THE K'NTAR EMPIRE --
SHE'S A NATURAL, BABS.
-- LEARNING NULL-GRAV COMBAT AND LOTS MORE FROM STARWOMAN.
OUTER SPACE!

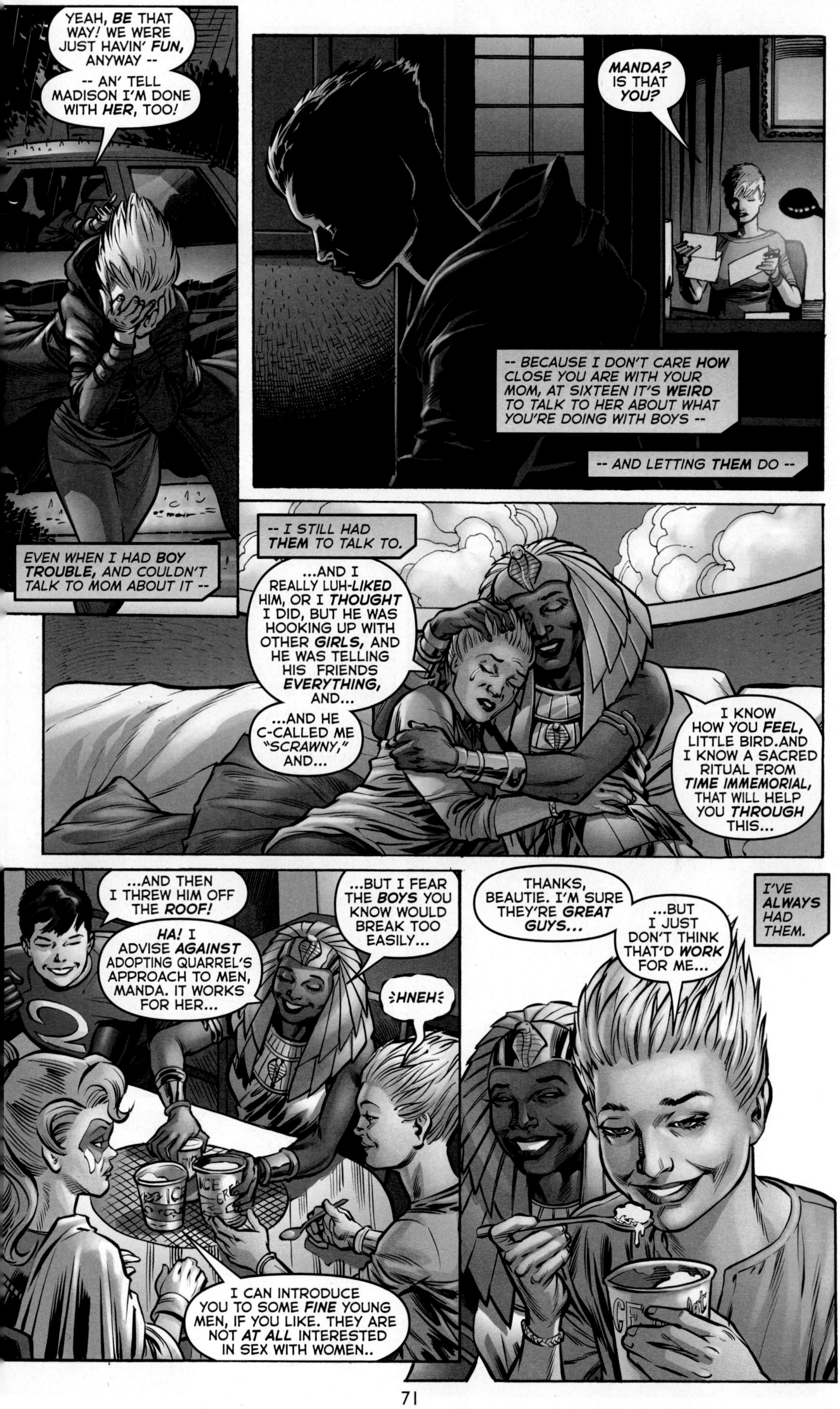
YEAH, BE THAT WAY! WE WERE JUST HAVIN' FUN, ANYWAY --
-- AN' TELL MADISON I'M DONE WITH HER, TOO!
MANDA? IS THAT YOU?
-- BECAUSE I DON'T CARE HOW CLOSE YOU ARE WITH YOUR MOM, AT SIXTEEN IT'S WEIRD TO TALK TO HER ABOUT WHAT YOU'RE DOING WITH BOYS --
-- AND LETTING THEM DO --
EVEN WHEN I HAD BOY TROUBLE, AND COULDN'T TALK TO MOM ABOUT IT --
-- I STILL HAD THEM TO TALK TO.
...AND I REALLY LUH-LIKED HIM, OR I THOUGHT I DID, BUT HE WAS HOOKING UP WITH OTHER GIRLS, AND HE WAS TELLING HIS FRIENDS EVERYTHING, AND...
...AND HE C-CALLED ME "SCRAWNY," AND...
I KNOW HOW YOU FEEL, LITTLE BIRD.AND I KNOW A SACRED RITUAL FROM TIME IMMEMORIAL, THAT WILL HELP YOU THROUGH THIS...
...AND THEN I THREW HIM OFF THE ROOF!
HA! I ADVISE AGAINST ADOPTING QUARREL'S APPROACH TO MEN, MANDA. IT WORKS FOR HER...
...BUT I FEAR THE BOYS YOU KNOW WOULD BREAK TOO EASILY...
HNEH
I CAN INTRODUCE YOU TO SOME FINE YOUNG MEN, IF YOU LIKE. THEY ARE NOT AT ALL INTERESTED IN SEX WITH WOMEN..
THANKS, BEAUTIE. I'M SURE THEY'RE GREAT GUYS...
...BUT I JUST DON'T THINK THAT'D WORK FOR ME...
I'VE ALWAYS HAD THEM.

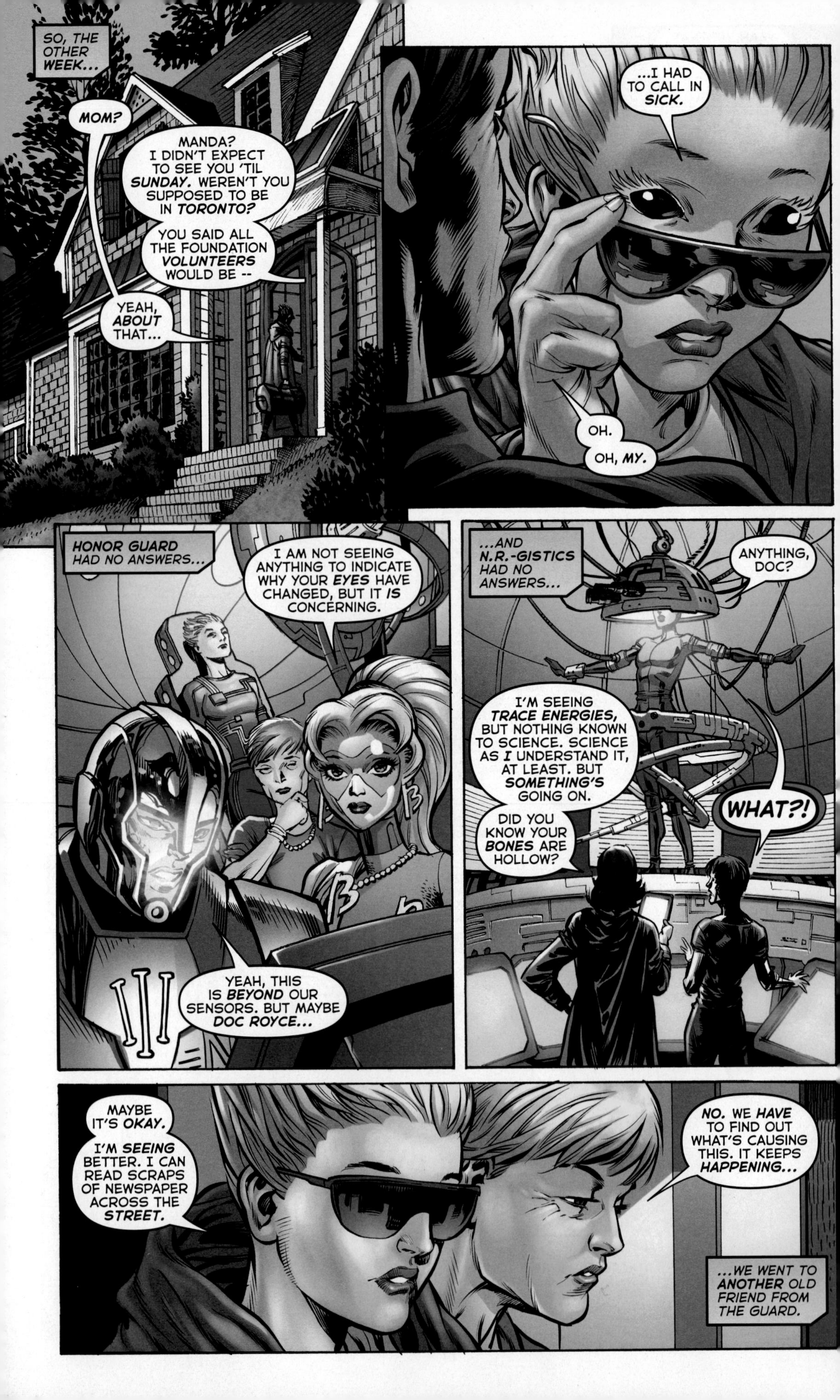
SO, THE OTHER WEEK...
MOM?
MANDA? I DIDN'T EXPECT TO SEE YOU 'TIL SUNDAY. WEREN'T YOU SUPPOSED TO BE IN TORONTO?
YOU SAID ALL THE FOUNDATION VOLUNTEERS WOULD BE --
YEAH, ABOUT THAT...
...I HAD TO CALL IN SICK.
OH.
OH, MY.
HONOR GUARD HAD NO ANSWERS...
I AM NOT SEEING ANYTHING TO INDICATE WHY YOUR EYES HAVE CHANGED, BUT IT IS CONCERNING.
YEAH, THIS IS BEYOND OUR SENSORS. BUT MAYBE DOC ROYCE...
...AND N.R.-GISTICS HAD NO ANSWERS...
ANYTHING, DOC?
I'M SEEING TRACE ENERGIES, BUT NOTHING KNOWN TO SCIENCE. SCIENCE AS I UNDERSTAND IT, AT LEAST. BUT SOMETHING'S GOING ON.
DID YOU KNOW YOUR BONES ARE HOLLOW?
WHAT?!
MAYBE IT'S OKAY.
I'M SEEING BETTER. I CAN READ SCRAPS OF NEWSPAPER ACROSS THE STREET.
NO. WE HAVE TO FIND OUT WHAT'S CAUSING THIS. IT KEEPS HAPPENING...
...WE WENT TO ANOTHER OLD FRIEND FROM THE GUARD.

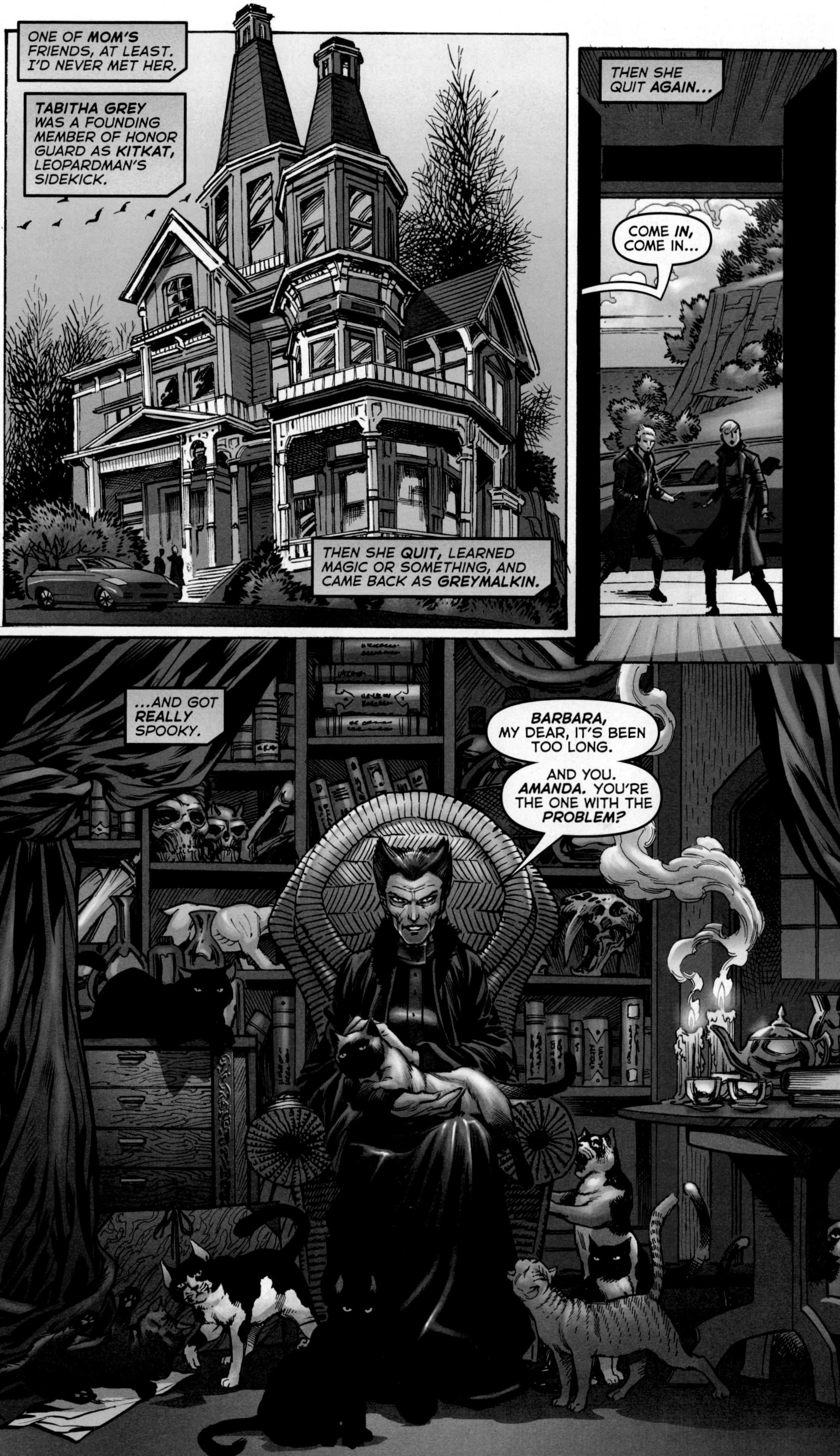
ONE OF MOM'S FRIENDS, AT LEAST. I'D NEVER MET HER.
TABITHA GREY WAS A FOUNDING MEMBER OF HONOR GUARD AS KITKAT, LEOPARDMAN'S SIDEKICK.
THEN SHE QUIT, LEARNED MAGIC OR SOMETHING, AND CAME BACK AS GREYMALKIN.
THEN SHE QUIT AGAIN...
COME IN, COME IN...
...AND GOT REALLY SPOOKY.
BARBARA, MY DEAR, IT'S BEEN TOO LONG.
AND YOU. AMANDA. YOU'RE THE ONE WITH THE PROBLEM?

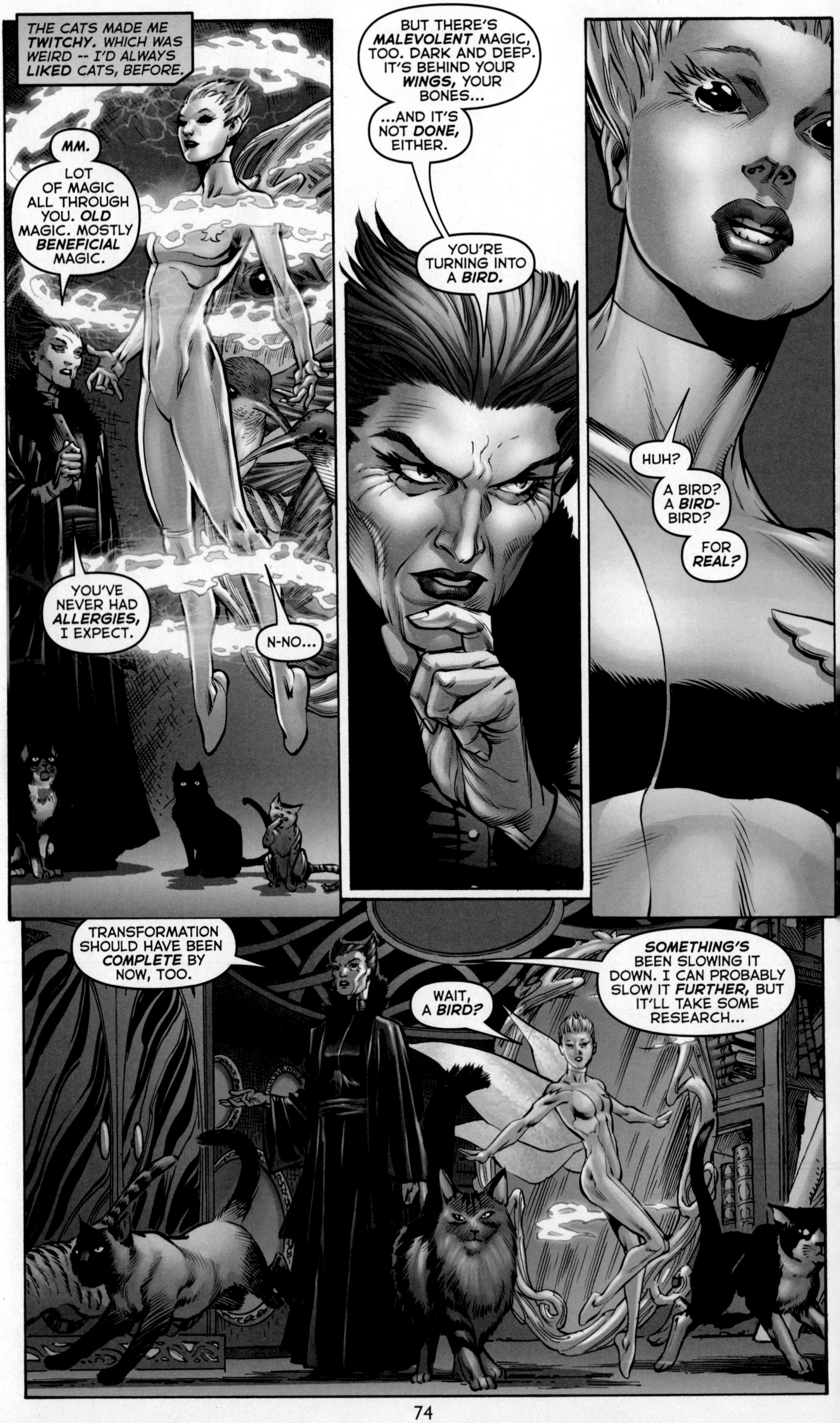
THE CATS MADE ME TWITCHY. WHICH WAS WEIRD -- I'D ALWAYS LIKED CATS, BEFORE.
MM.
LOT OF MAGIC ALL THROUGH YOU. OLD MAGIC. MOSTLY BENEFICIAL MAGIC.
YOU'VE NEVER HAD ALLERGIES, I EXPECT.
N-NO...
BUT THERE'S MALEVOLENT MAGIC, TOO. DARK AND DEEP. IT'S BEHIND YOUR WINGS, YOUR BONES...
...AND IT'S NOT DONE, EITHER.
YOU'RE TURNING INTO A BIRD.
HUH?
A BIRD? A BIRD-BIRD?
FOR REAL?
TRANSFORMATION SHOULD HAVE BEEN COMPLETE BY NOW, TOO.
WAIT, A BIRD?
SOMETHING'S BEEN SLOWING IT DOWN. I CAN PROBABLY SLOW IT FURTHER, BUT IT'LL TAKE SOME RESEARCH...

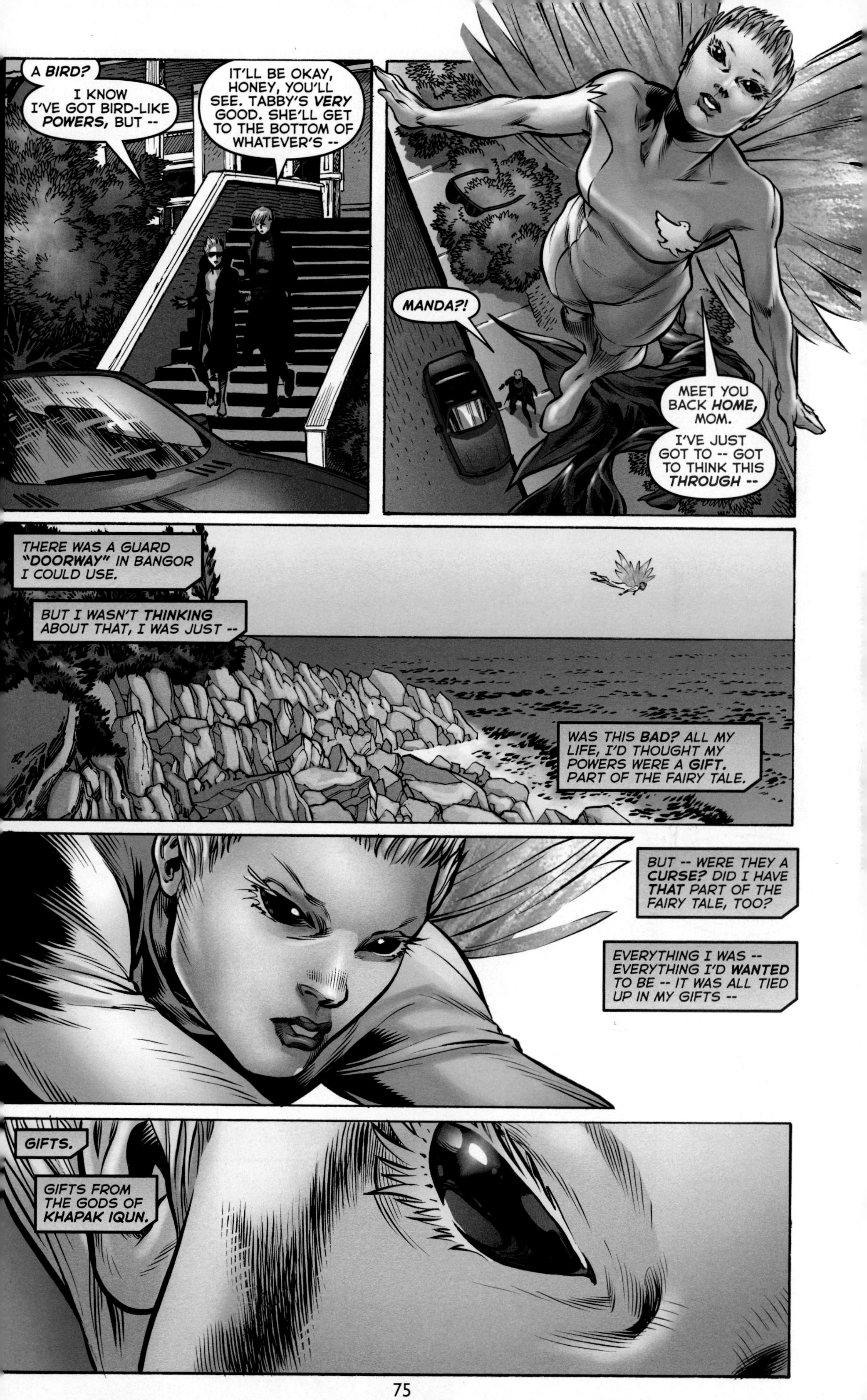
A BIRD?
I KNOW I'VE GOT BIRD-LIKE POWERS, BUT --
IT'LL BE OKAY, HONEY, YOU'LL SEE. TABBY'S VERY GOOD. SHE'LL GET TO THE BOTTOM OF WHATEVER'S --
MANDA?!
MEET YOU BACK HOME, MOM.
I'VE JUST GOT TO -- GOT TO THINK THIS THROUGH --
THERE WAS A GUARD "DOORWAY" IN BANGOR I COULD USE.
BUT I WASN'T THINKING ABOUT THAT, I WAS JUST --
WAS THIS BAD? ALL MY LIFE, I'D THOUGHT MY POWERS WERE A GIFT. PART OF THE FAIRY TALE.
BUT -- WERE THEY A CURSE? DID I HAVE THAT PART OF THE FAIRY TALE, TOO?
EVERYTHING I WAS -- EVERYTHING I'D WANTED TO BE -- IT WAS ALL TIED UP IN MY GIFTS --
GIFTS.
GIFTS FROM THE GODS OF KHAPAK IQUN.

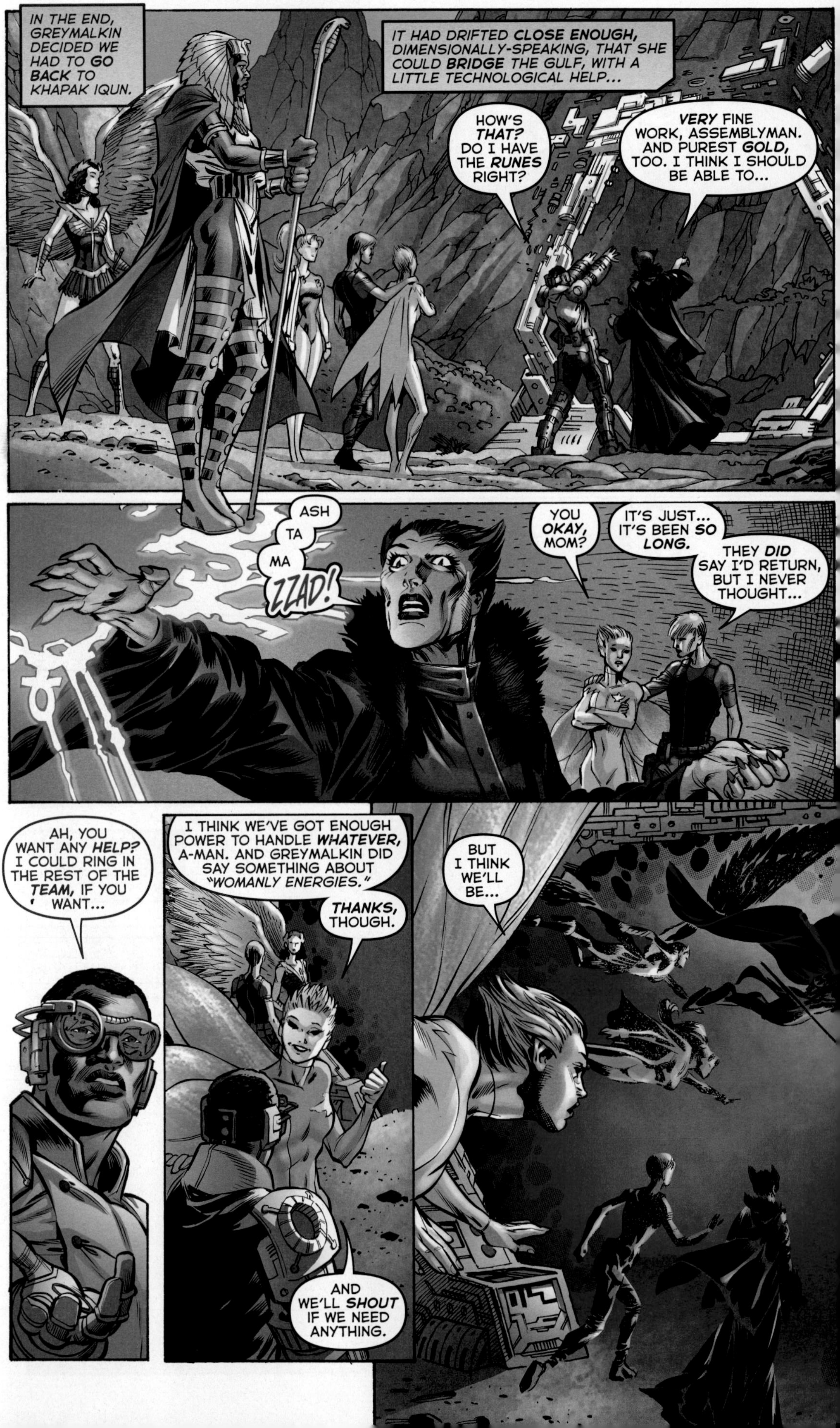
IN THE END, GREYMALKIN DECIDED WE HAD TO GO BACK TO KHAPAK IQUN.
IT HAD DRIFTED CLOSE ENOUGH, DIMENSIONALLY-SPEAKING, THAT SHE COULD BRIDGE THE GULF, WITH A LITTLE TECHNOLOGICAL HELP...
HOW'S THAT? DO I HAVE THE RUNES RIGHT?
VERY FINE WORK, ASSEMBLYMAN. AND PUREST GOLD, TOO. I THINK I SHOULD BE ABLE TO...
ASH
TA
MA
ZZAD!
YOU OKAY, MOM?
IT'S JUST... IT'S BEEN SO LONG.
THEY DID SAY I'D RETURN, BUT I NEVER THOUGHT...
AH, YOU WANT ANY HELP? I COULD RING IN THE REST OF THE TEAM, IF YOU WANT...
I THINK WE'VE GOT ENOUGH POWER TO HANDLE WHATEVER, A-MAN. AND GREYMALKIN DID SAY SOMETHING ABOUT "WOMANLY ENERGIES."
THANKS, THOUGH.
AND WE'LL SHOUT IF WE NEED ANYTHING.
BUT I THINK WE'LL BE...

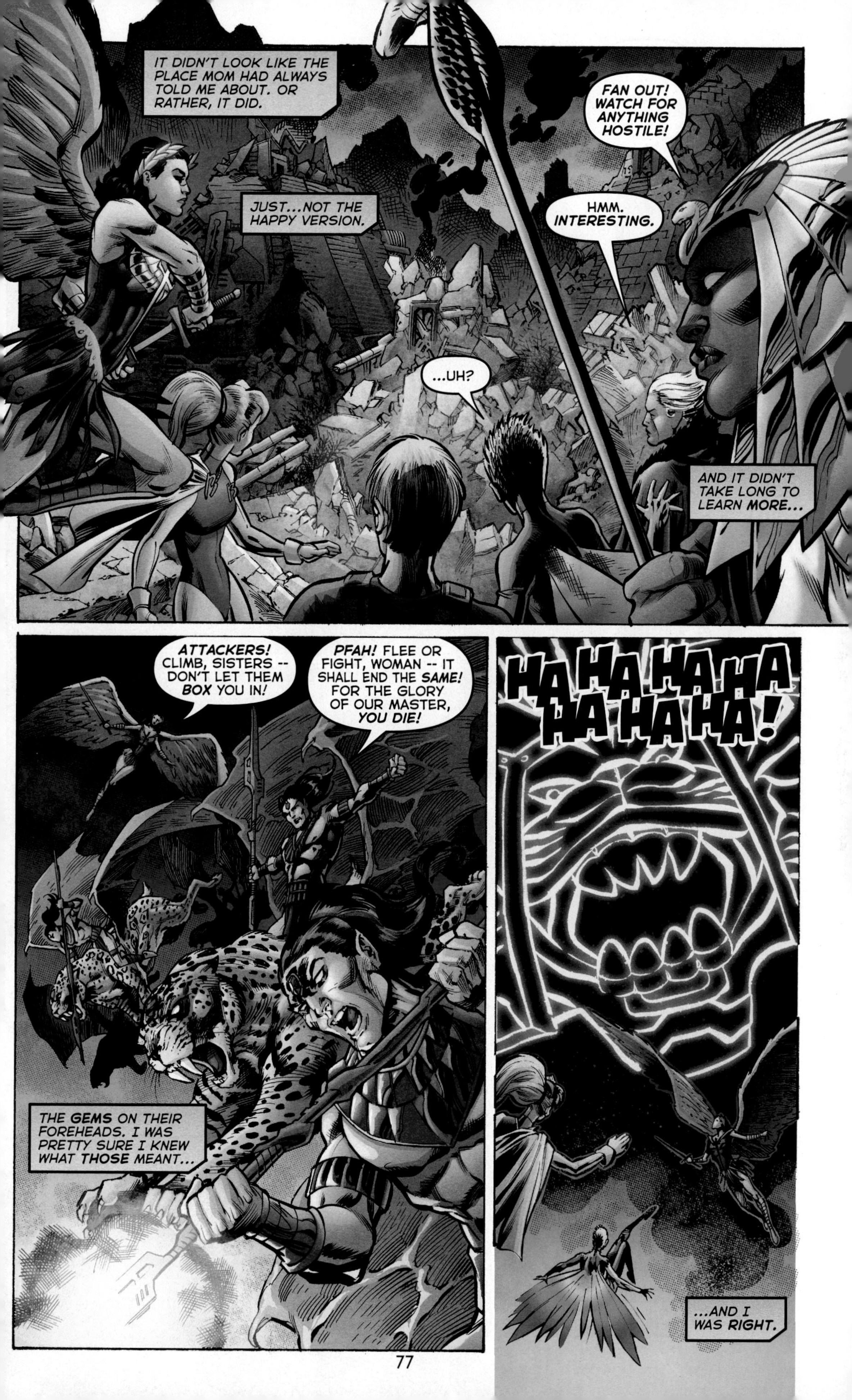
IT DIDN'T LOOK LIKE THE PLACE MOM HAD ALWAYS TOLD ME ABOUT. OR RATHER, IT DID.
JUST...NOT THE HAPPY VERSION.
FAN OUT! WATCH FOR ANYTHING HOSTILE!
HMM. INTERESTING.
...UH?
AND IT DIDN'T TAKE LONG TO LEARN MORE...
ATTACKERS! CLIMB, SISTERS -- DON'T LET THEM BOX YOU IN!
PFAH! FLEE OR FIGHT, WOMAN -- IT SHALL END THE SAME! FOR THE GLORY OF OUR MASTER, YOU DIE!
THE GEMS ON THEIR FOREHEADS. I WAS PRETTY SURE I KNEW WHAT THOSE MEANT...
HA HA HA HA HA HA HA HA HA!
...AND I WAS RIGHT.

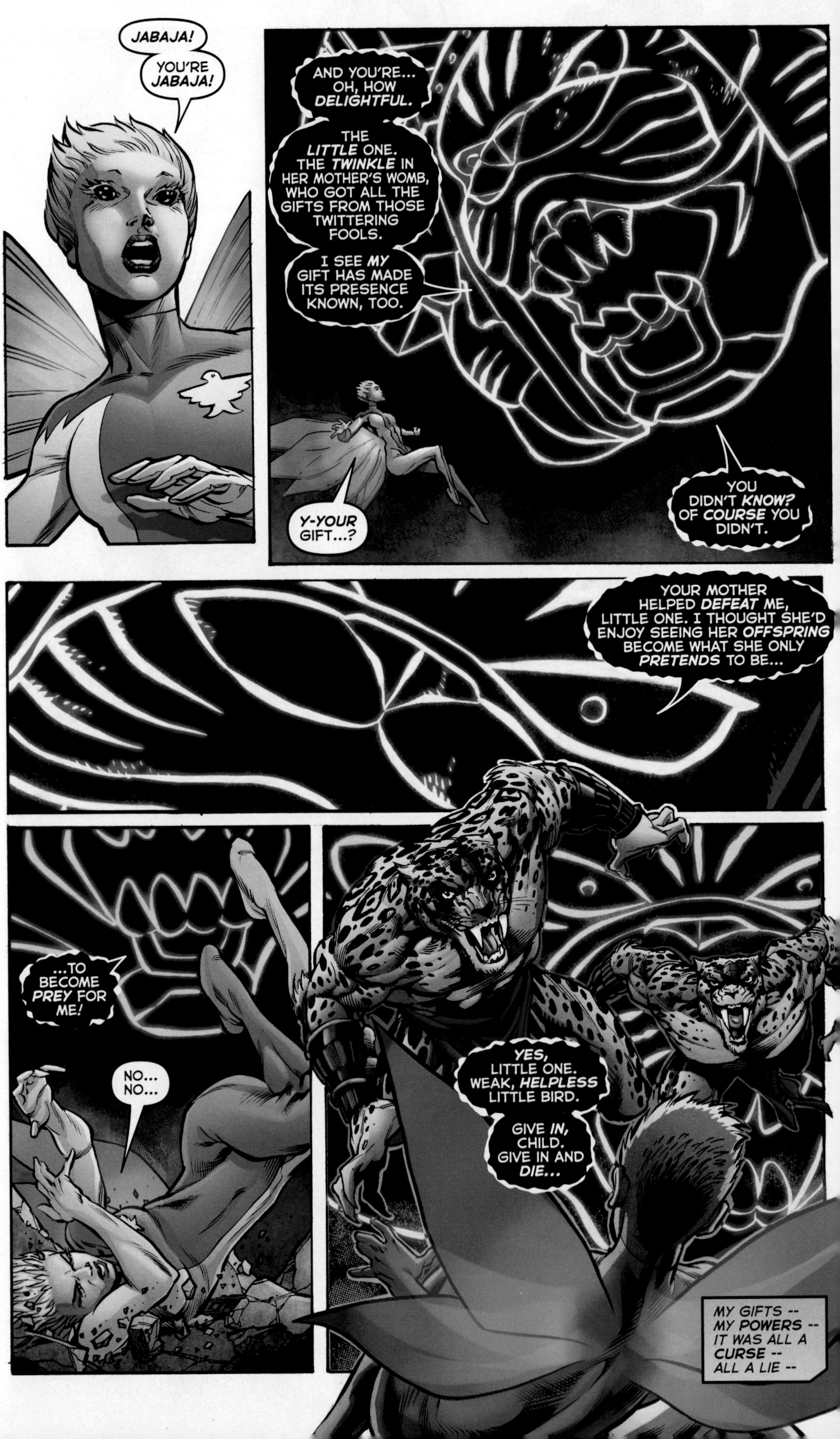
JABAJA!
YOU'RE JABAJA!
AND YOU'RE... OH, HOW DELIGHTFUL.
THE LITTLE ONE. THE TWINKLE IN HER MOTHER'S WOMB, WHO GOT ALL THE GIFTS FROM THOSE TWITTERING FOOLS.
I SEE MY GIFT HAS MADE ITS PRESENCE KNOWN, TOO.
Y-YOUR GIFT...?
YOU DIDN'T KNOW? OF COURSE YOU DIDN'T.
YOUR MOTHER HELPED DEFEAT ME, LITTLE ONE. I THOUGHT SHE'D ENJOY SEEING HER OFFSPRING BECOME WHAT SHE ONLY PRETENDS TO BE...
...TO BECOME PREY FOR ME!
NO... NO...
YES, LITTLE ONE. WEAK, HELPLESS LITTLE BIRD.
GIVE IN, CHILD. GIVE IN AND DIE...
MY GIFTS -- MY POWERS -- IT WAS ALL A CURSE -- ALL A LIE --

NO!

OH, *PLEASE,* BIRDLING.

YOU ARE *OUTNUMBERED.* OUT-*TALONED.* WHY, YOU DON'T EVEN HAVE YOUR *CLAWS* YET --

CLAWS? NOT SURE I LIKE THE *SOUND* OF THAT...

HE WAS *RIGHT.* THEY *HAD* ME ON POWER AND POINTY BITS.

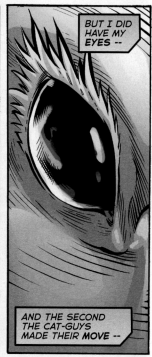

BUT I DID HAVE MY *EYES* --

AND THE SECOND THE CAT-GUYS MADE THEIR *MOVE* --

RRRAHH!!

AH-AH! SORRY, JABAJA -- MAYBE YOU *MEANT* TO CURSE ME, BUT I DO *OKAY* WITH WHAT I'VE GOT. MAYBE NO CLAWS, BUT I'VE STILL GOT SPEED, *REFLEXES* --

-- AND --

AND I *SAW* IT, DEEP IN THE SHADOWS. A SINGLE *GLINT* -- WITHOUT MY NEW EYES, I'D NEVER HAVE *SPOTTED* IT, BUT --

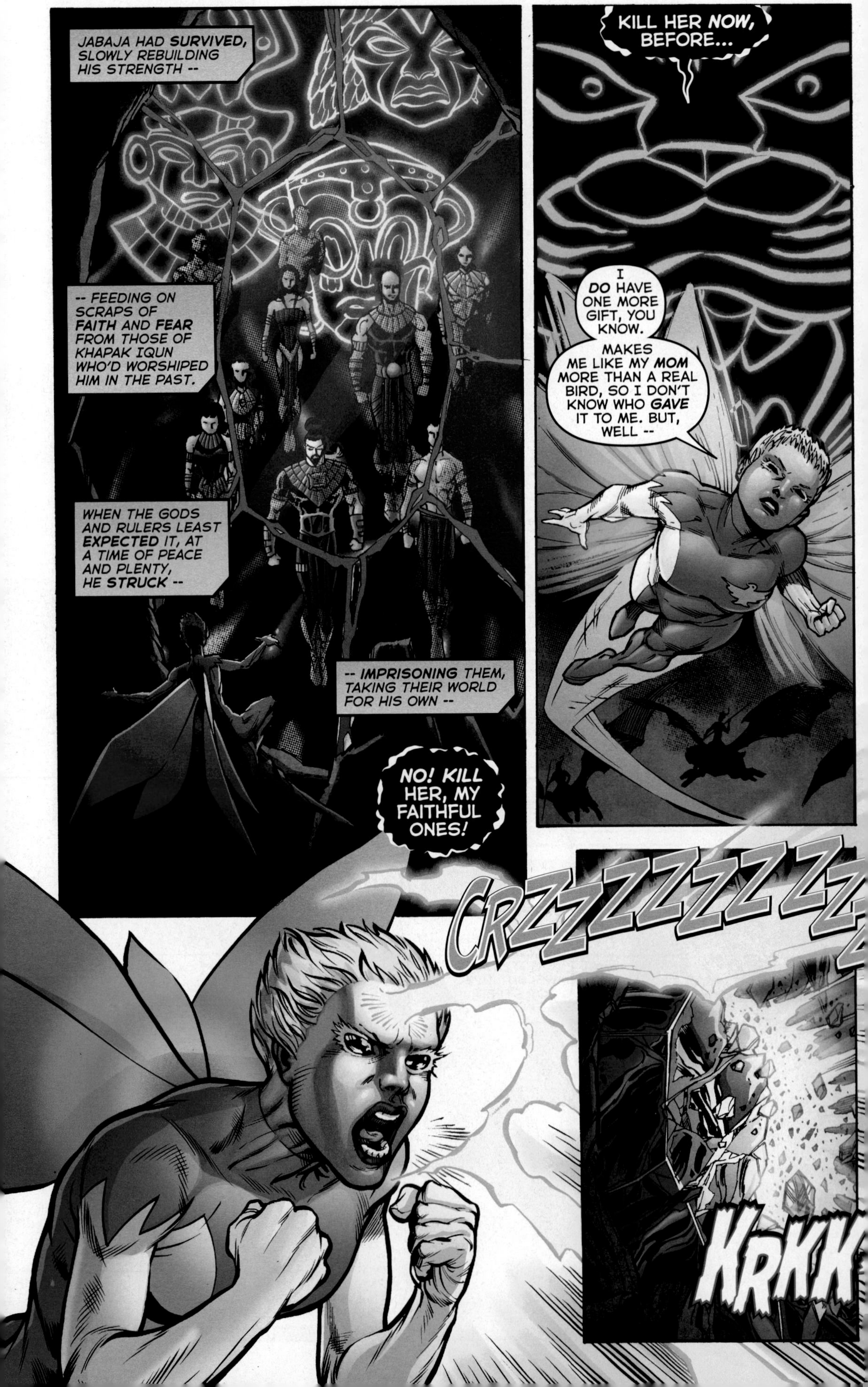
JABAJA HAD SURVIVED, SLOWLY REBUILDING HIS STRENGTH --
-- FEEDING ON SCRAPS OF FAITH AND FEAR FROM THOSE OF KHAPAK IQUN WHO'D WORSHIPED HIM IN THE PAST.
WHEN THE GODS AND RULERS LEAST EXPECTED IT, AT A TIME OF PEACE AND PLENTY, HE STRUCK --
-- IMPRISONING THEM, TAKING THEIR WORLD FOR HIS OWN --
NO! KILL HER, MY FAITHFUL ONES!
KILL HER NOW, BEFORE...
I DO HAVE ONE MORE GIFT, YOU KNOW.
MAKES ME LIKE MY MOM MORE THAN A REAL BIRD, SO I DON'T KNOW WHO GAVE IT TO ME. BUT, WELL --
CRZZZZZZZZ
KRKK

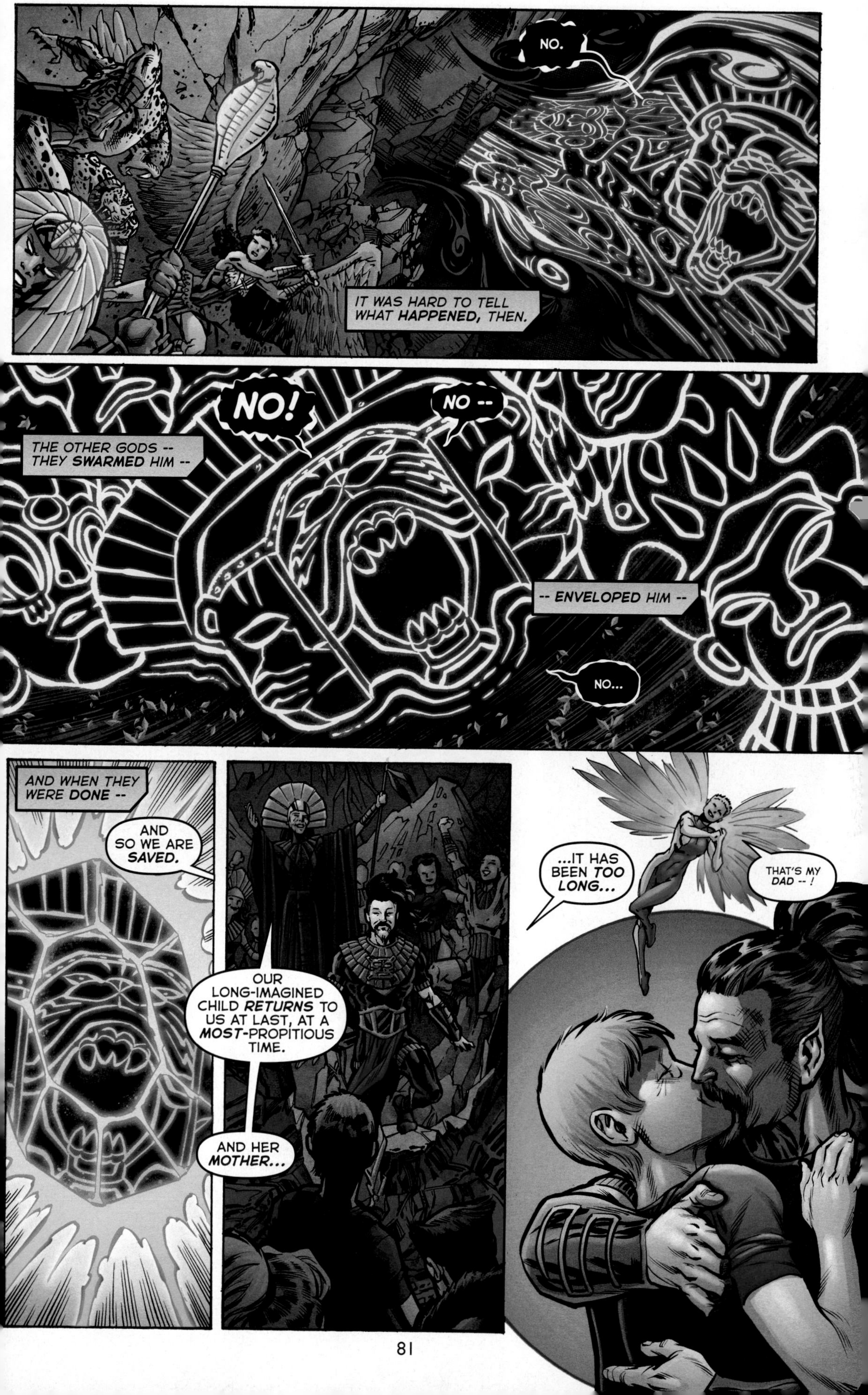
NO.
IT WAS HARD TO TELL WHAT HAPPENED, THEN.
NO!
NO --
THE OTHER GODS -- THEY SWARMED HIM --
-- ENVELOPED HIM --
NO...
AND WHEN THEY WERE DONE --
AND SO WE ARE SAVED.
OUR LONG-IMAGINED CHILD RETURNS TO US AT LAST, AT A MOST-PROPITIOUS TIME.
AND HER MOTHER...
...IT HAS BEEN TOO LONG...
THAT'S MY DAD -- !

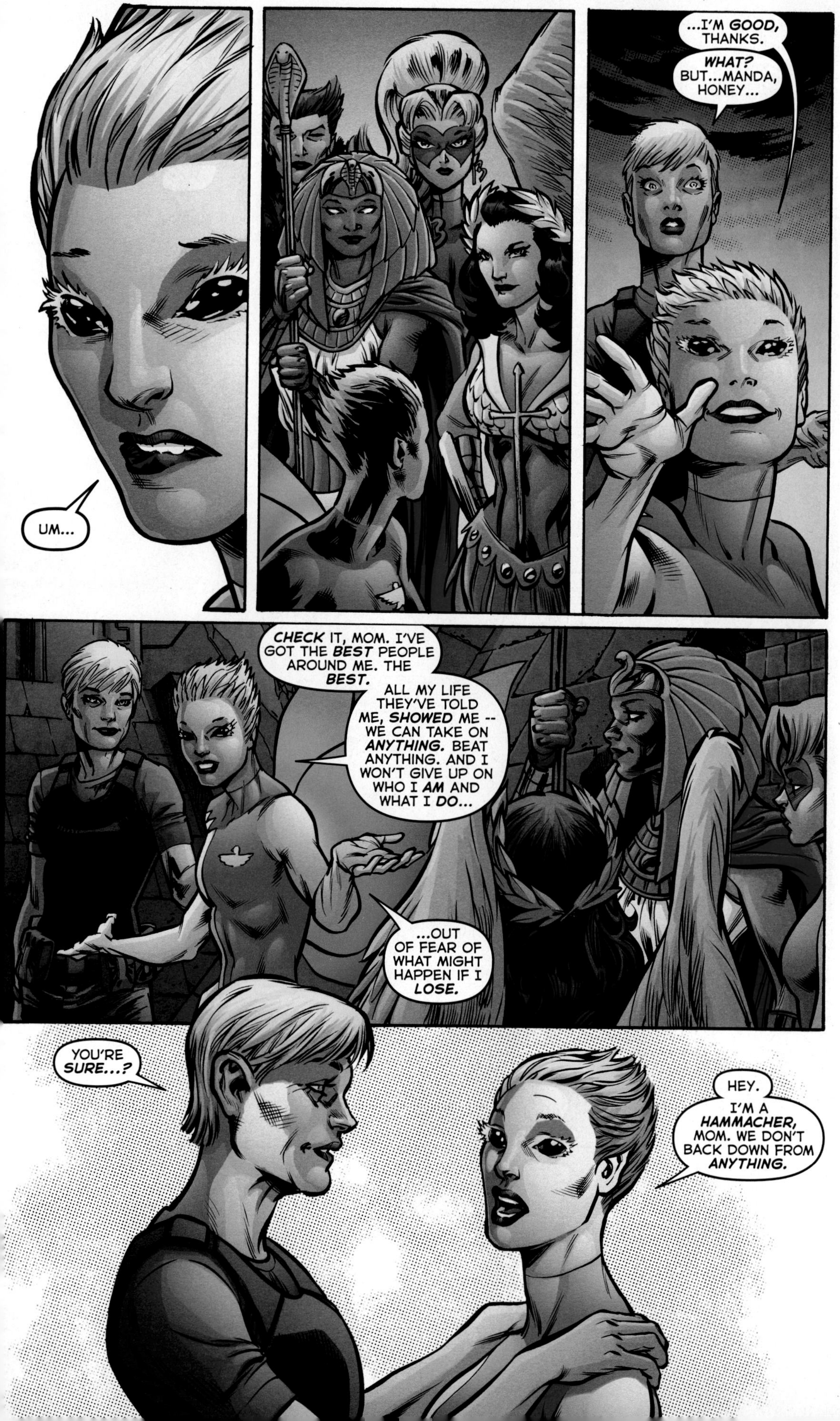
UM...
...I'M GOOD, THANKS.
WHAT? BUT...MANDA, HONEY...
CHECK IT, MOM. I'VE GOT THE BEST PEOPLE AROUND ME. THE BEST.
ALL MY LIFE THEY'VE TOLD ME, SHOWED ME -- WE CAN TAKE ON ANYTHING. BEAT ANYTHING. AND I WON'T GIVE UP ON WHO I AM AND WHAT I DO...
...OUT OF FEAR OF WHAT MIGHT HAPPEN IF I LOSE.
YOU'RE SURE...?
HEY.
I'M A HAMMACHER, MOM. WE DON'T BACK DOWN FROM ANYTHING.

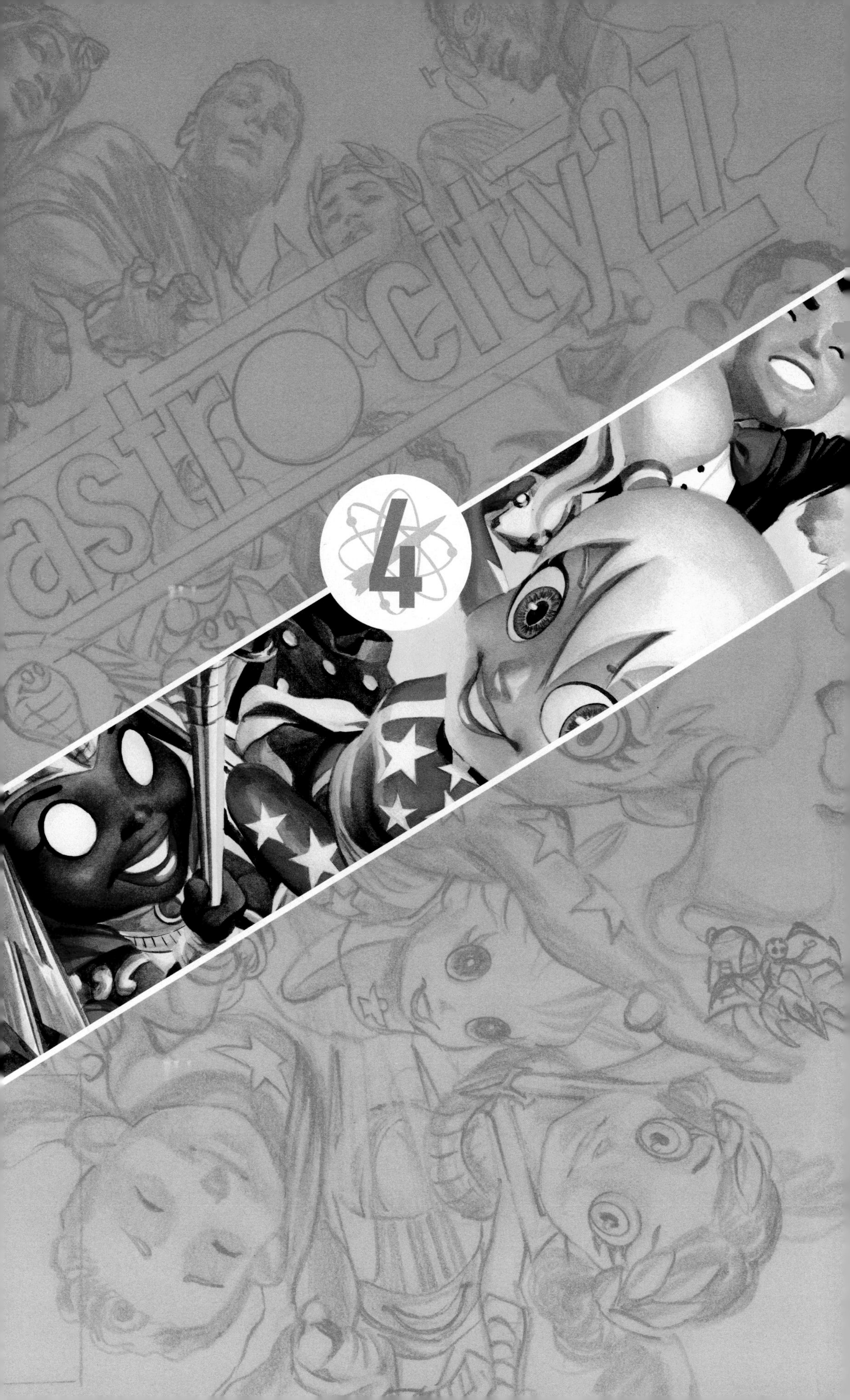
astro city 27
4

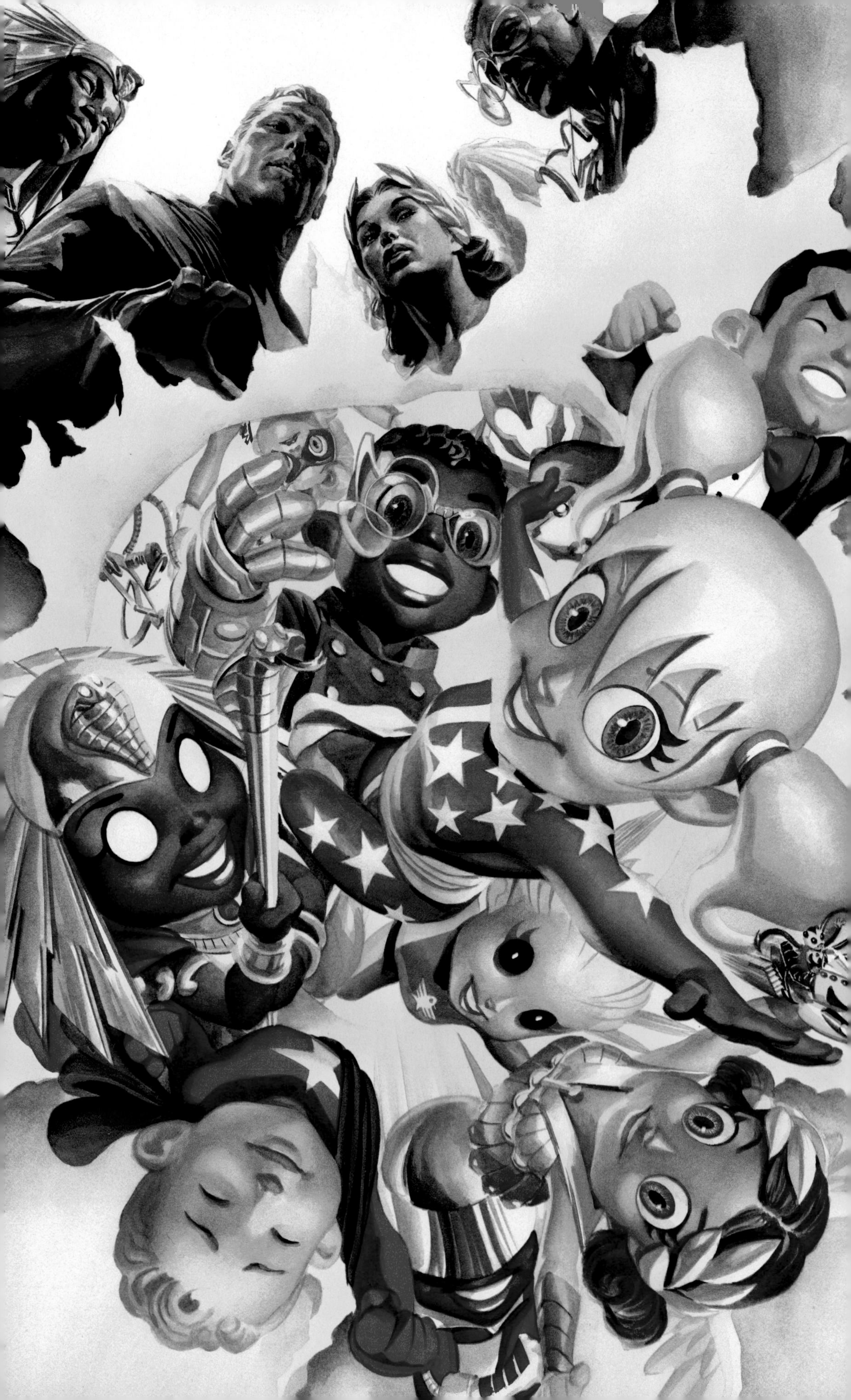

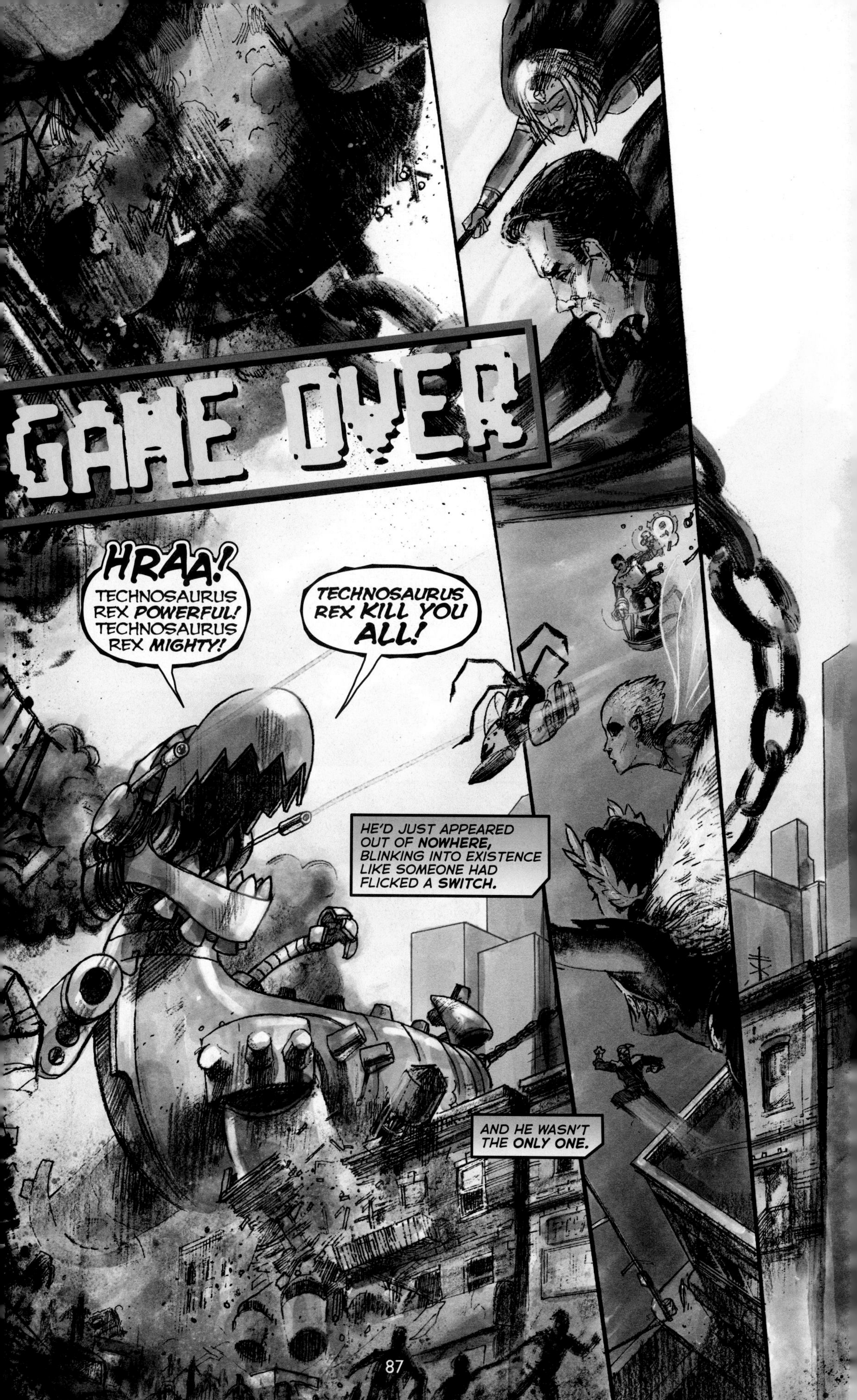
GAME OVER
HRAA! TECHNOSAURUS REX POWERFUL! TECHNOSAURUS REX MIGHTY!
TECHNOSAURUS REX KILL YOU ALL!
HE'D JUST APPEARED OUT OF NOWHERE, BLINKING INTO EXISTENCE LIKE SOMEONE HAD FLICKED A SWITCH.
AND HE WASN'T THE ONLY ONE.

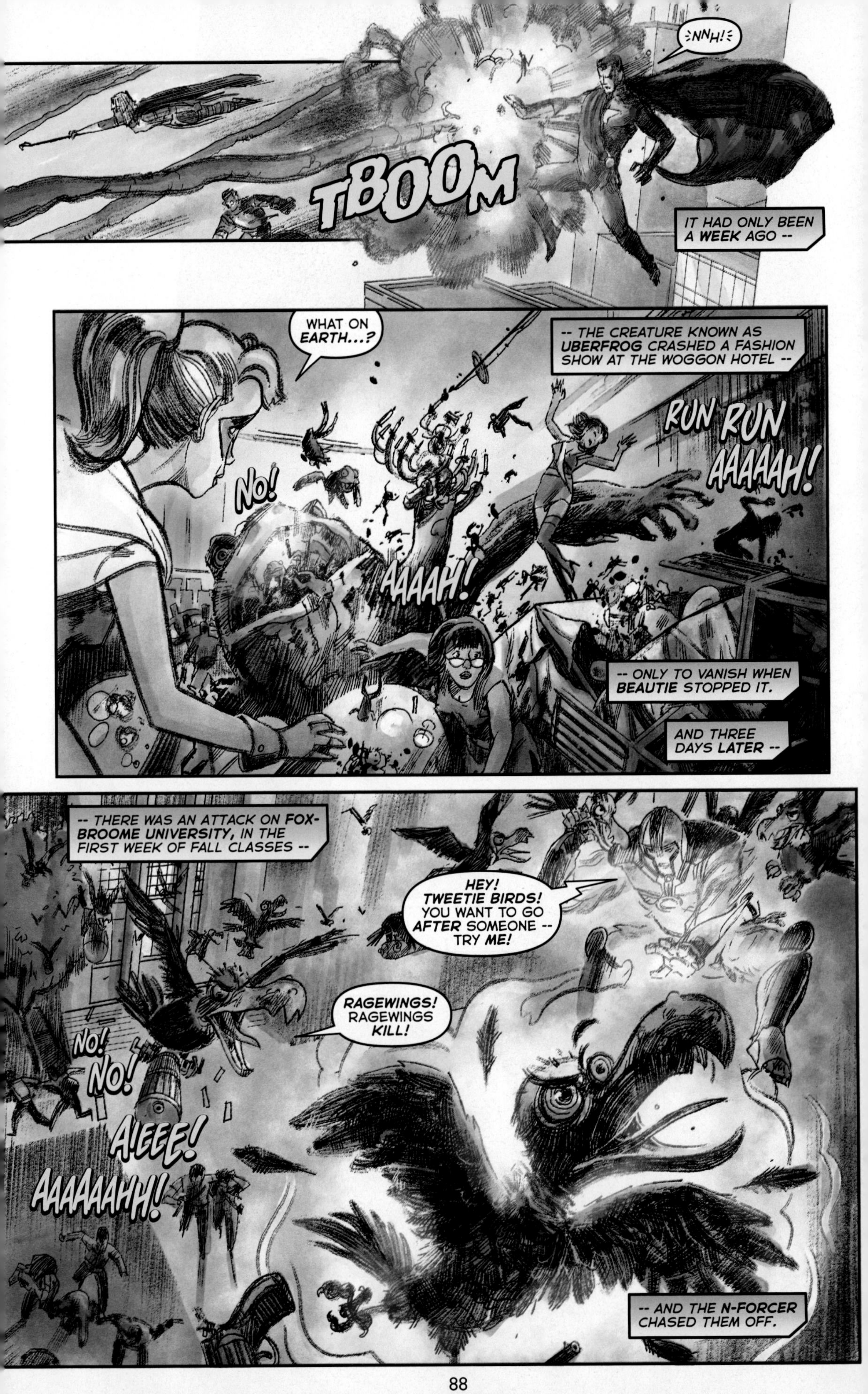
NNH!
TBOOM
IT HAD ONLY BEEN A WEEK AGO --
WHAT ON EARTH...?
-- THE CREATURE KNOWN AS UBERFROG CRASHED A FASHION SHOW AT THE WOGGON HOTEL --
RUN RUN
AAAAAH!
NO!
AAAAH!
-- ONLY TO VANISH WHEN BEAUTIE STOPPED IT.
AND THREE DAYS LATER --
-- THERE WAS AN ATTACK ON FOX-BROOME UNIVERSITY, IN THE FIRST WEEK OF FALL CLASSES --
HEY! TWEETIE BIRDS! YOU WANT TO GO AFTER SOMEONE -- TRY ME!
RAGEWINGS! RAGEWINGS KILL!
NO! NO!
AIEEE!
AAAAAAHH!
-- AND THE N-FORCER CHASED THEM OFF.

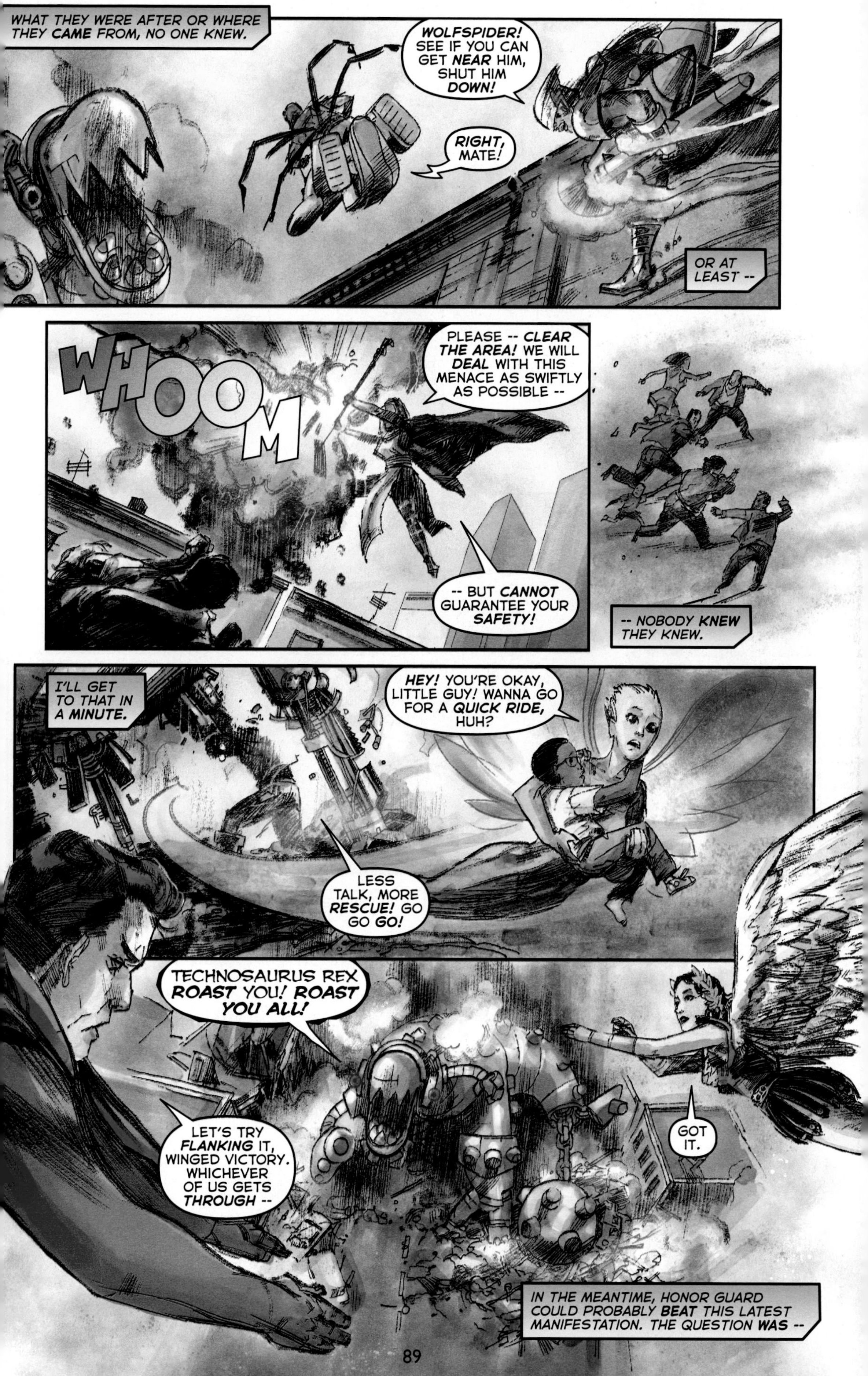

WHAT THEY WERE AFTER OR WHERE THEY CAME FROM, NO ONE KNEW.
WOLFSPIDER! SEE IF YOU CAN GET NEAR HIM, SHUT HIM DOWN!
RIGHT, MATE!
OR AT LEAST --
WHOOOM
PLEASE -- CLEAR THE AREA! WE WILL DEAL WITH THIS MENACE AS SWIFTLY AS POSSIBLE --
-- BUT CANNOT GUARANTEE YOUR SAFETY!
-- NOBODY KNEW THEY KNEW.
I'LL GET TO THAT IN A MINUTE.
HEY! YOU'RE OKAY, LITTLE GUY! WANNA GO FOR A QUICK RIDE, HUH?
LESS TALK, MORE RESCUE! GO GO GO!
TECHNOSAURUS REX ROAST YOU! ROAST YOU ALL!
LET'S TRY FLANKING IT, WINGED VICTORY. WHICHEVER OF US GETS THROUGH --
GOT IT.
IN THE MEANTIME, HONOR GUARD COULD PROBABLY BEAT THIS LATEST MANIFESTATION. THE QUESTION WAS --

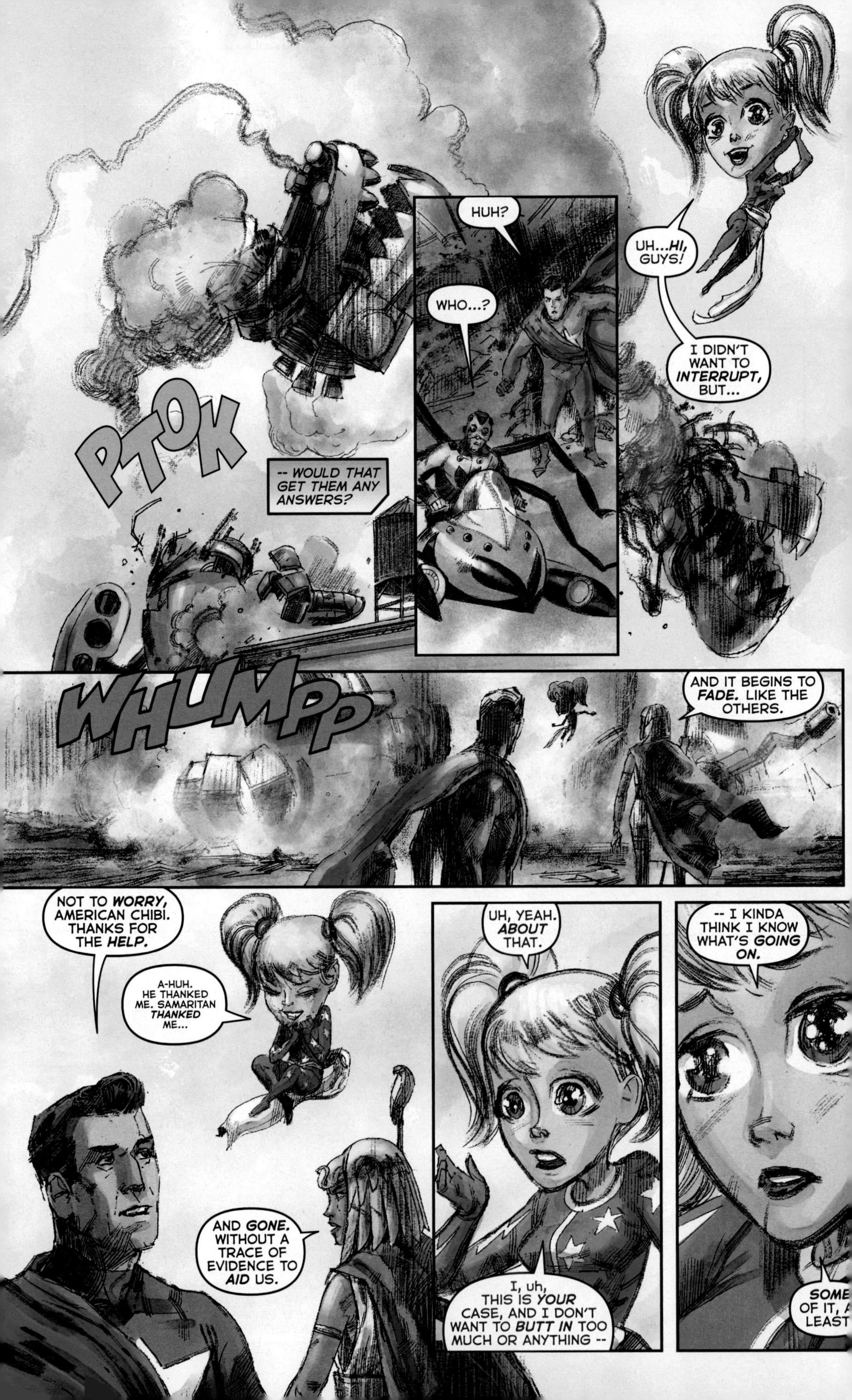
PTOK
-- WOULD THAT GET THEM ANY ANSWERS?
HUH?
WHO...?
UH...HI, GUYS!
I DIDN'T WANT TO INTERRUPT, BUT...
WHUMPP
AND IT BEGINS TO FADE. LIKE THE OTHERS.
NOT TO WORRY, AMERICAN CHIBI. THANKS FOR THE HELP.
A-HUH. HE THANKED ME. SAMARITAN THANKED ME...
AND GONE. WITHOUT A TRACE OF EVIDENCE TO AID US.
UH, YEAH. ABOUT THAT.
I, uh, THIS IS YOUR CASE, AND I DON'T WANT TO BUTT IN TOO MUCH OR ANYTHING --
-- I KINDA THINK I KNOW WHAT'S GOING ON.

91

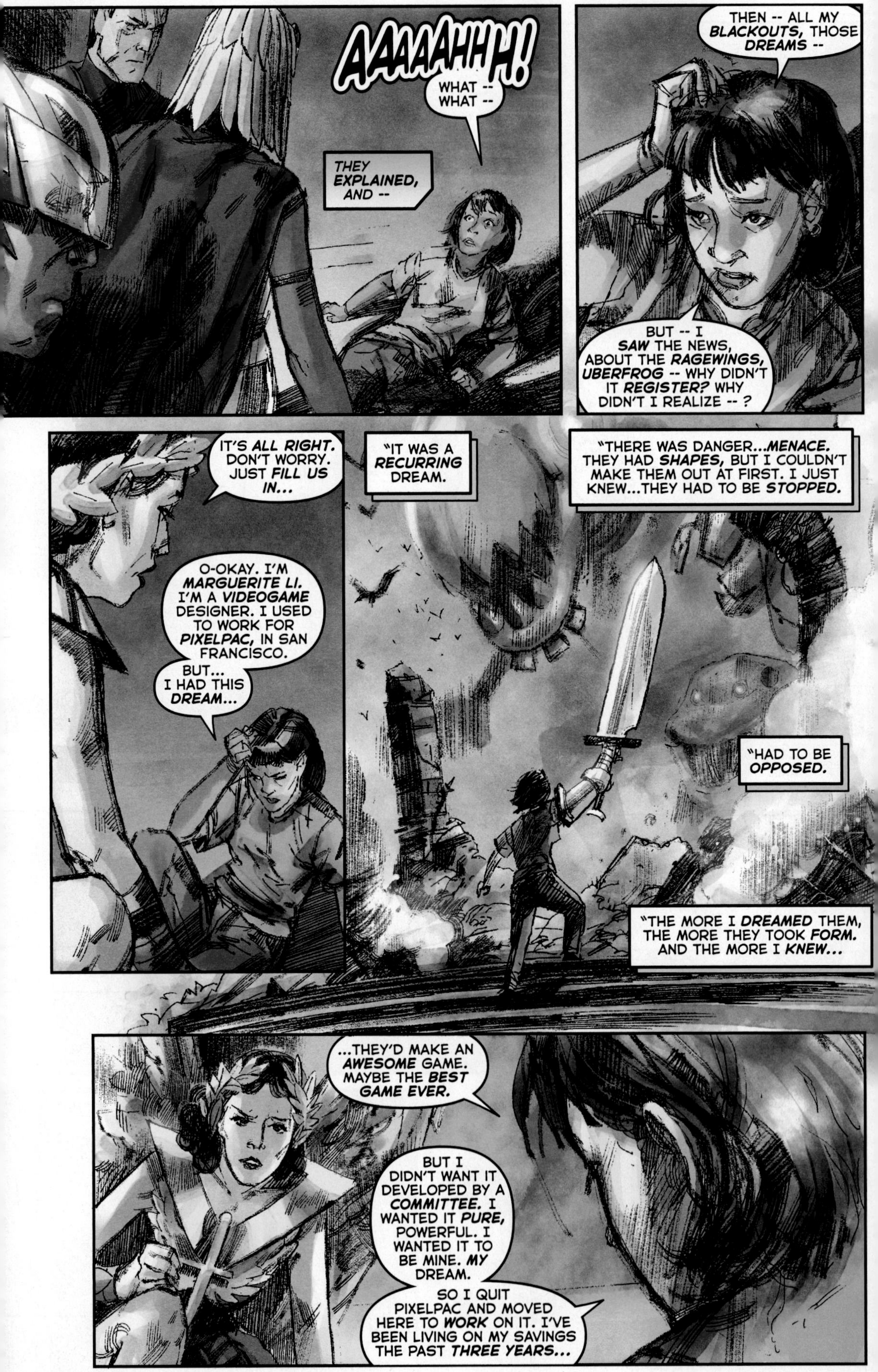
AAAAAHHH!
WHAT -- WHAT --
THEY EXPLAINED, AND --
THEN -- ALL MY BLACKOUTS, THOSE DREAMS --
BUT -- I SAW THE NEWS, ABOUT THE RAGEWINGS, UBERFROG -- WHY DIDN'T IT REGISTER? WHY DIDN'T I REALIZE -- ?
IT'S ALL RIGHT. DON'T WORRY. JUST FILL US IN...
O-OKAY. I'M MARGUERITE LI. I'M A VIDEOGAME DESIGNER. I USED TO WORK FOR PIXELPAC, IN SAN FRANCISCO.
BUT... I HAD THIS DREAM...
"IT WAS A RECURRING DREAM.
"THERE WAS DANGER...MENACE. THEY HAD SHAPES, BUT I COULDN'T MAKE THEM OUT AT FIRST. I JUST KNEW...THEY HAD TO BE STOPPED.
"HAD TO BE OPPOSED.
"THE MORE I DREAMED THEM, THE MORE THEY TOOK FORM. AND THE MORE I KNEW...
...THEY'D MAKE AN AWESOME GAME. MAYBE THE BEST GAME EVER.
BUT I DIDN'T WANT IT DEVELOPED BY A COMMITTEE. I WANTED IT PURE, POWERFUL. I WANTED IT TO BE MINE. MY DREAM.
SO I QUIT PIXELPAC AND MOVED HERE TO WORK ON IT. I'VE BEEN LIVING ON MY SAVINGS THE PAST THREE YEARS...

I DESIGNED A **HEROINE.** I WANTED SOMEONE **FUN,** BRIGHT, **LIFE-AFFIRMING.**

MYSTIC SCRUNCHIES?

THREE YEARS. RIGHT WHEN AMERICAN CHIBI...

WHEN SHE **DEBUTED.** YES.

AND I...I **REMEMBER** IT, NOW, BUT I DON'T KNOW WHY IT DIDN'T REGISTER. I'D **CREATED** HER, BUT IT NEVER STRUCK ME AS ODD.

A **CHIBI-TYPE HERO.** STRONG, FAST, POWERED BY HER MYSTIC **HAIR** SCRUNCHIES...

I'M BETTING THAT WAS WHEN YOUR **BLACKOUTS** STARTED, TOO.

LET ME **GUESS.** THESE **CREATURES** THAT HAVE BEEN APPEARING. THEY'RE ALL FROM THE **GAME,** RIGHT?

YES, BUT **HOW --**

THE **UNBODIED.**

"**SOME** OF THEM, ANYWAY. MYTHS WHOSE **BELIEVERS** HAVE DIED OUT.

"THEY **LINGER,** SEEKING NEW FORMS, NEW WAYS **BACK INTO** THE WORLD.

"**YOU** REMEMBER, HUMMINGBIRD. WE FOUGHT THAT **CULT** IN NEW ORLEANS? DEDICATED TO MAKING THE **LOVECRAFT MYTHOS** A REALITY?"

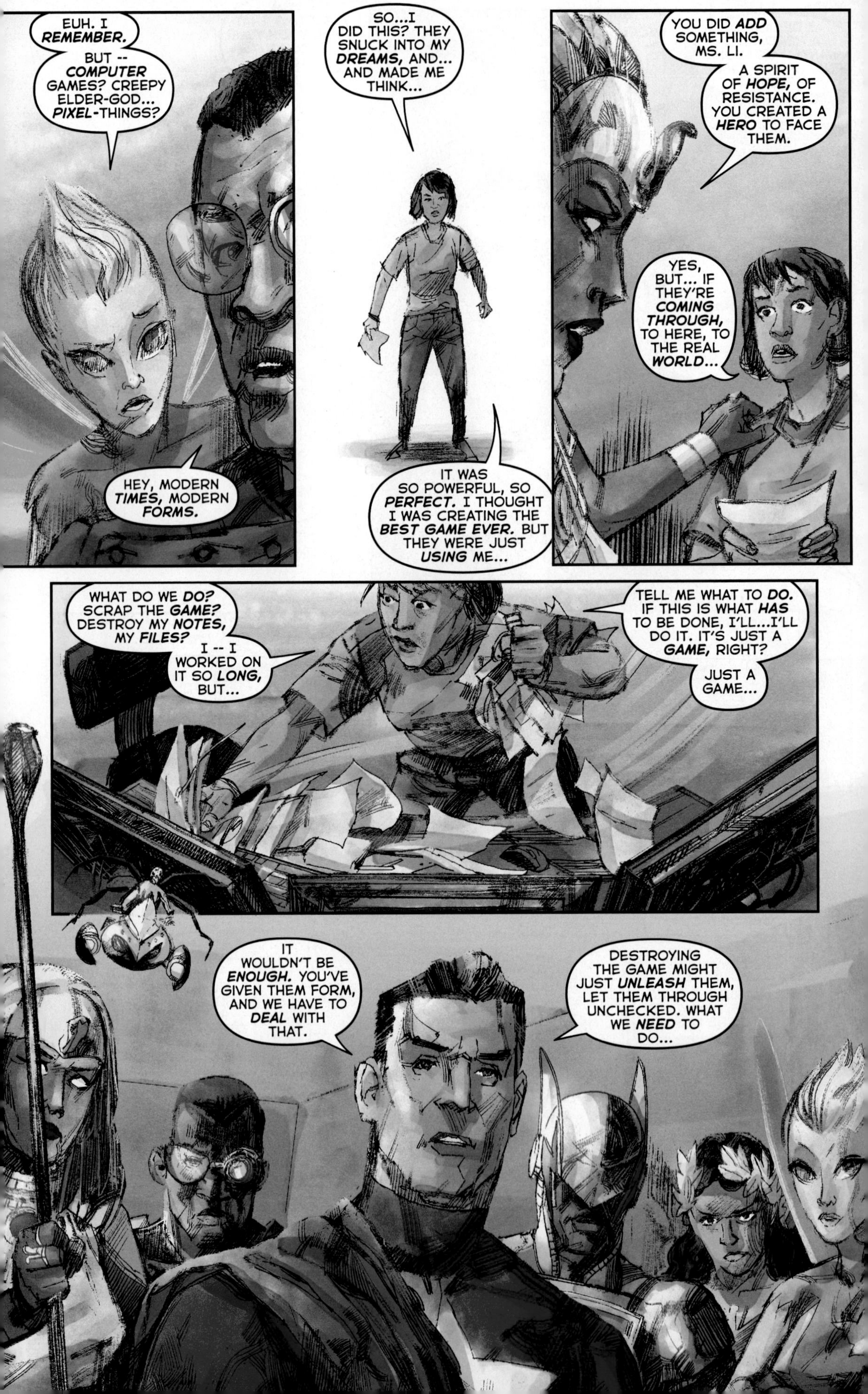

EUH. I REMEMBER.
BUT -- COMPUTER GAMES? CREEPY ELDER-GOD... PIXEL-THINGS?
HEY, MODERN TIMES, MODERN FORMS.
SO...I DID THIS? THEY SNUCK INTO MY DREAMS, AND... AND MADE ME THINK...
IT WAS SO POWERFUL, SO PERFECT. I THOUGHT I WAS CREATING THE BEST GAME EVER. BUT THEY WERE JUST USING ME...
YOU DID ADD SOMETHING, MS. LI.
A SPIRIT OF HOPE, OF RESISTANCE. YOU CREATED A HERO TO FACE THEM.
YES, BUT... IF THEY'RE COMING THROUGH, TO HERE, TO THE REAL WORLD...
WHAT DO WE DO? SCRAP THE GAME? DESTROY MY NOTES, MY FILES?
I -- I WORKED ON IT SO LONG, BUT...
TELL ME WHAT TO DO. IF THIS IS WHAT HAS TO BE DONE, I'LL...I'LL DO IT. IT'S JUST A GAME, RIGHT?
JUST A GAME...
IT WOULDN'T BE ENOUGH. YOU'VE GIVEN THEM FORM, AND WE HAVE TO DEAL WITH THAT.
DESTROYING THE GAME MIGHT JUST UNLEASH THEM, LET THEM THROUGH UNCHECKED. WHAT WE NEED TO DO...

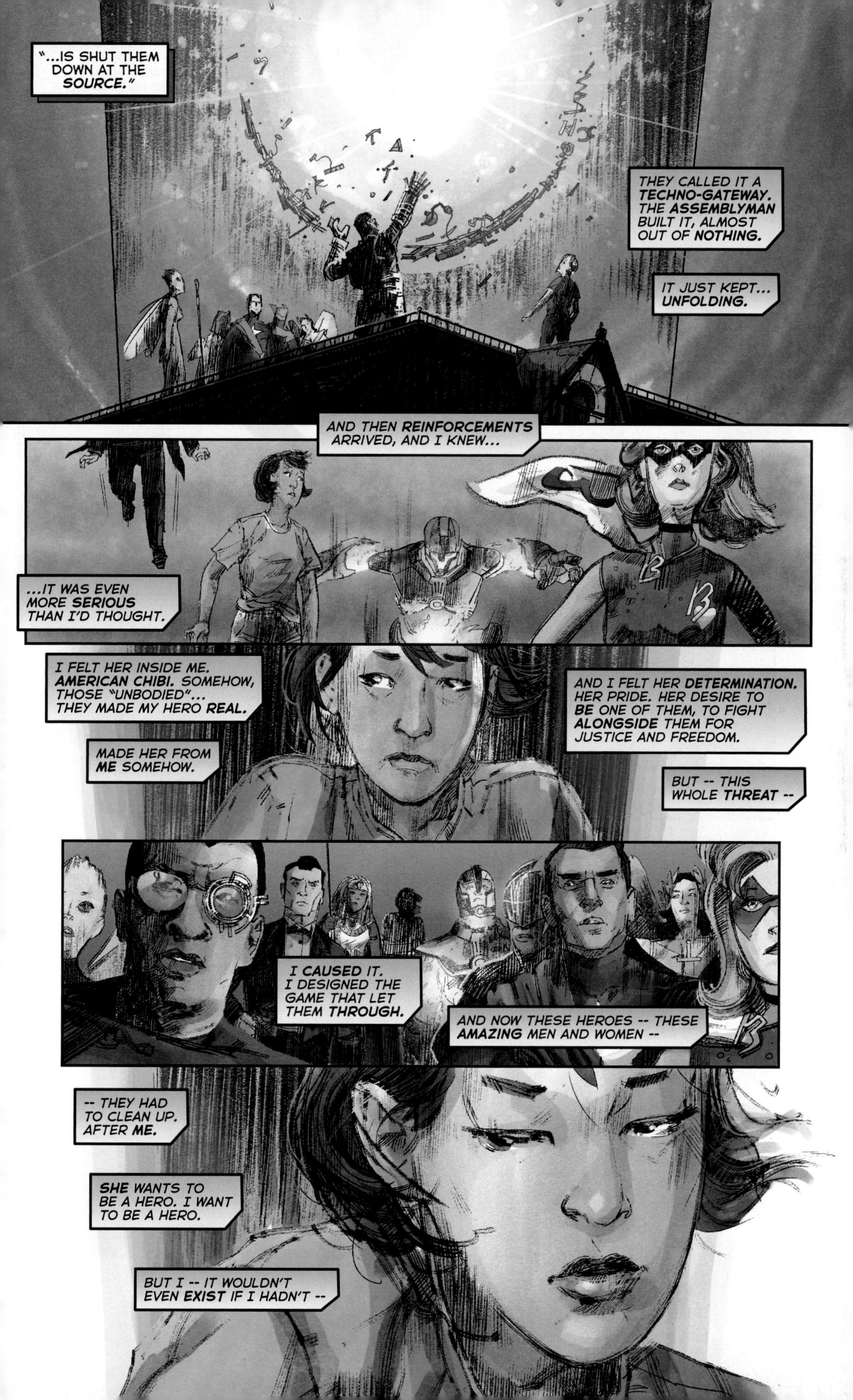
"...IS SHUT THEM DOWN AT THE SOURCE."
THEY CALLED IT A TECHNO-GATEWAY. THE ASSEMBLYMAN BUILT IT, ALMOST OUT OF NOTHING.
IT JUST KEPT... UNFOLDING.
AND THEN REINFORCEMENTS ARRIVED, AND I KNEW...
...IT WAS EVEN MORE SERIOUS THAN I'D THOUGHT.
I FELT HER INSIDE ME. AMERICAN CHIBI. SOMEHOW, THOSE "UNBODIED"... THEY MADE MY HERO REAL.
MADE HER FROM ME SOMEHOW.
AND I FELT HER DETERMINATION. HER PRIDE. HER DESIRE TO BE ONE OF THEM, TO FIGHT ALONGSIDE THEM FOR JUSTICE AND FREEDOM.
BUT -- THIS WHOLE THREAT --
I CAUSED IT. I DESIGNED THE GAME THAT LET THEM THROUGH.
AND NOW THESE HEROES -- THESE AMAZING MEN AND WOMEN --
-- THEY HAD TO CLEAN UP AFTER ME.
SHE WANTS TO BE A HERO. I WANT TO BE A HERO.
BUT I -- IT WOULDN'T EVEN EXIST IF I HADN'T --

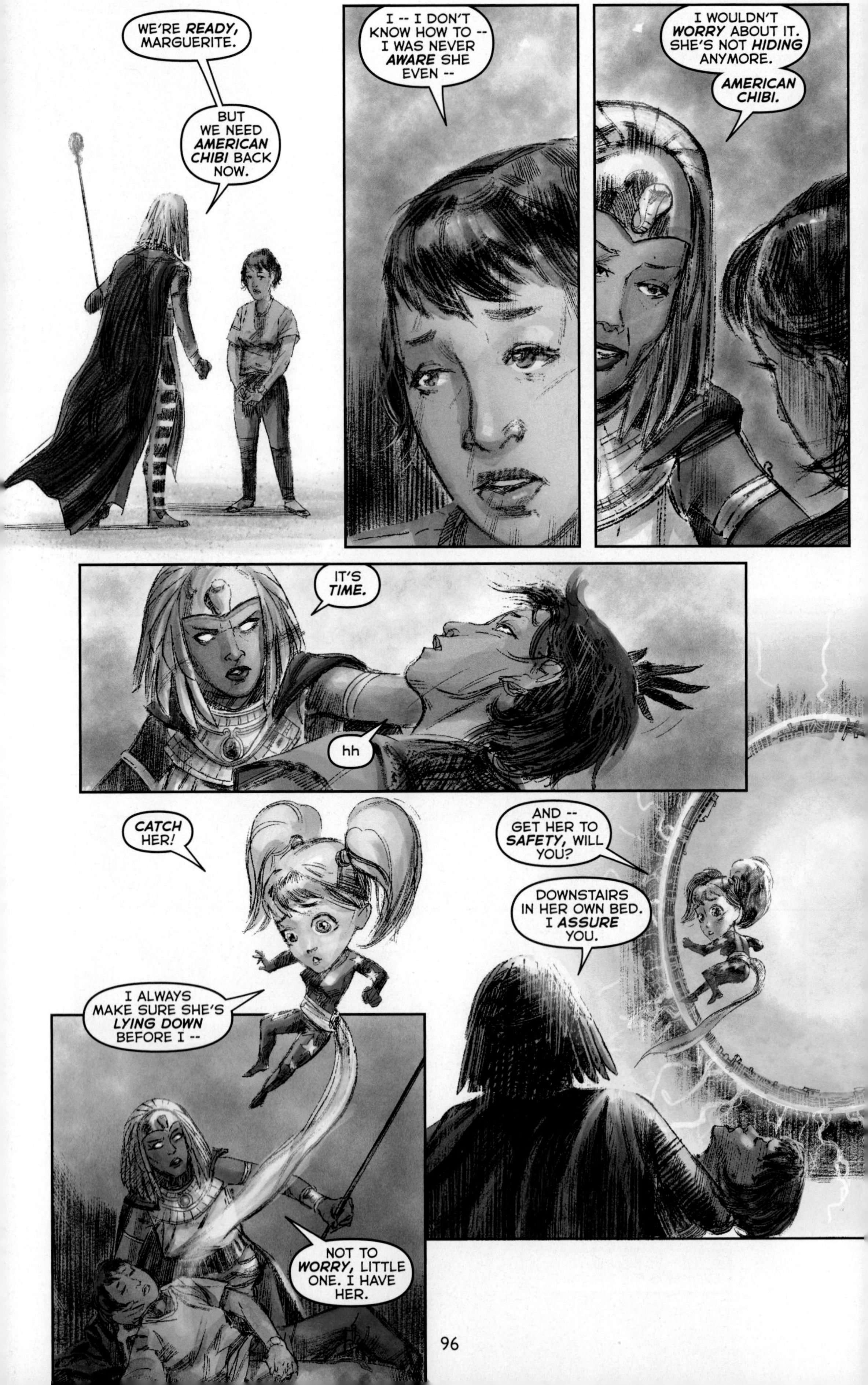
WE'RE READY, MARGUERITE.
BUT WE NEED AMERICAN CHIBI BACK NOW.
I -- I DON'T KNOW HOW TO -- I WAS NEVER AWARE SHE EVEN --
I WOULDN'T WORRY ABOUT IT. SHE'S NOT HIDING ANYMORE.
AMERICAN CHIBI.
IT'S TIME.
hh
CATCH HER!
AND -- GET HER TO SAFETY, WILL YOU?
DOWNSTAIRS IN HER OWN BED. I ASSURE YOU.
I ALWAYS MAKE SURE SHE'S LYING DOWN BEFORE I --
NOT TO WORRY, LITTLE ONE. I HAVE HER.

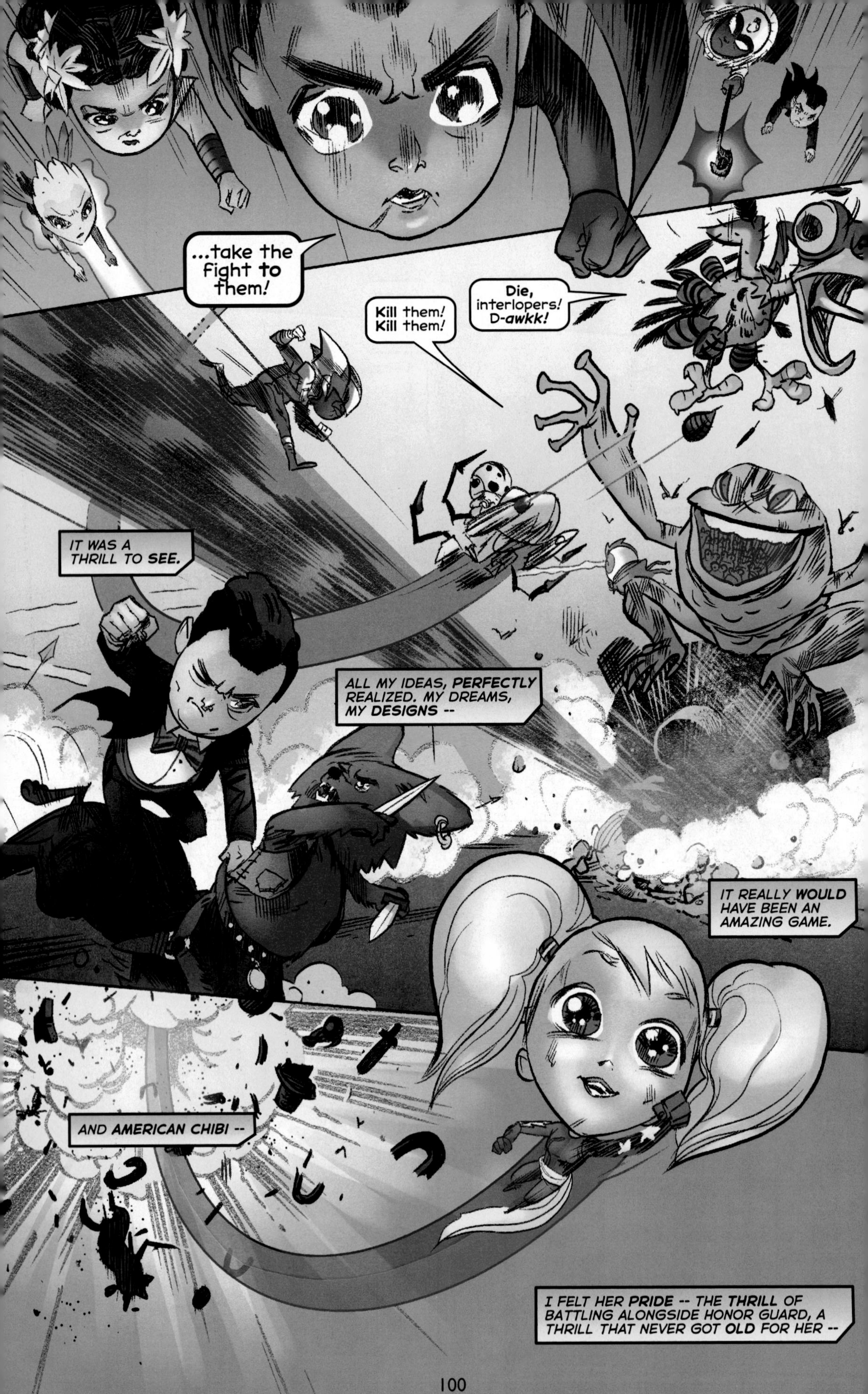

...take the fight to them!
Kill them! Kill them!
Die, interlopers! D-awkk!
IT WAS A THRILL TO SEE.
ALL MY IDEAS, PERFECTLY REALIZED. MY DREAMS, MY DESIGNS --
IT REALLY WOULD HAVE BEEN AN AMAZING GAME.
AND AMERICAN CHIBI --
I FELT HER PRIDE -- THE THRILL OF BATTLING ALONGSIDE HONOR GUARD, A THRILL THAT NEVER GOT OLD FOR HER --

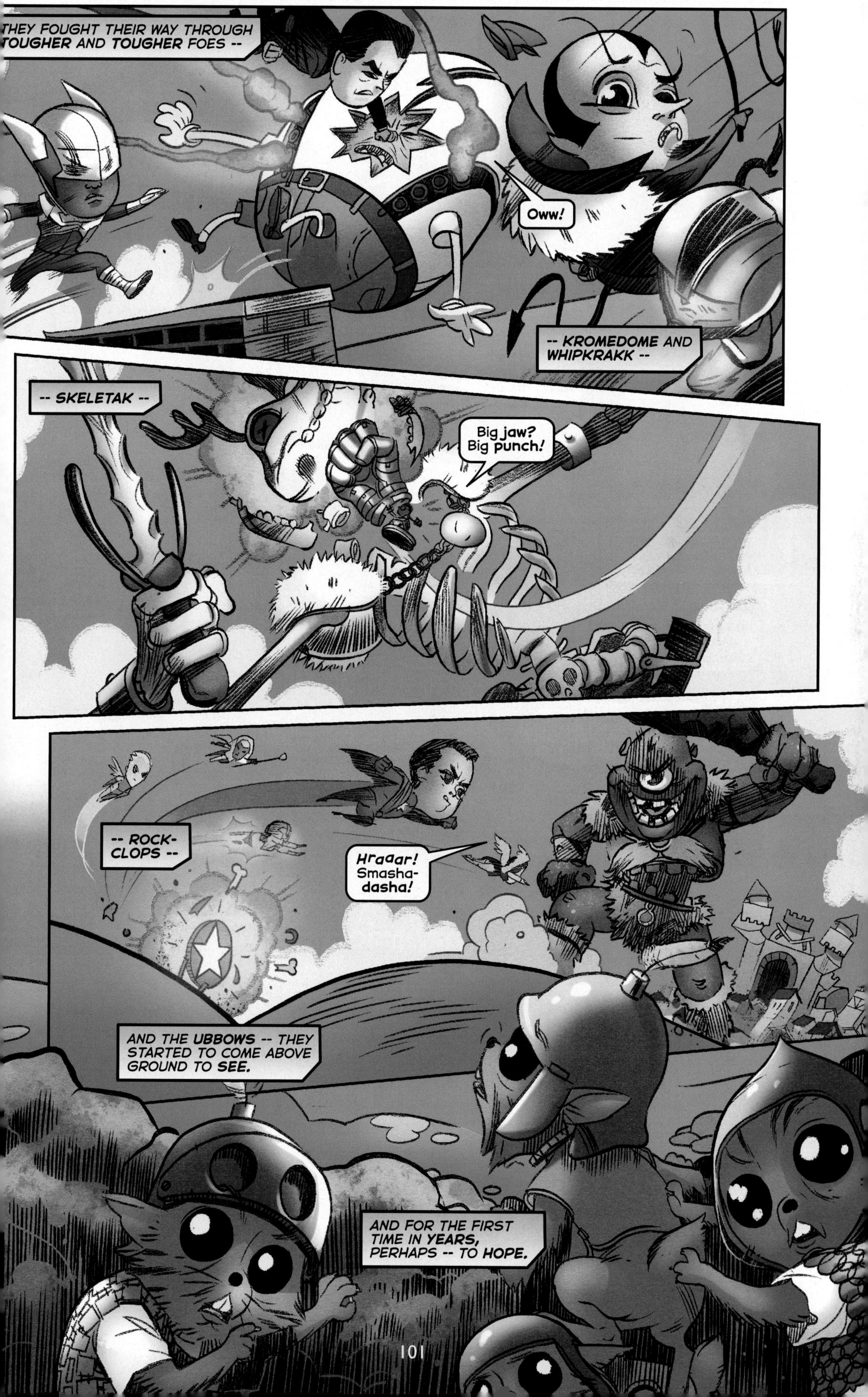

THEY FOUGHT THEIR WAY THROUGH TOUGHER AND TOUGHER FOES --
Oww!
-- KROMEDOME AND WHIPKRAKK --
-- SKELETAK --
Big jaw? Big punch!
-- ROCK-CLOPS --
Hraaar! Smasha-dasha!
AND THE UBBOWS -- THEY STARTED TO COME ABOVE GROUND TO SEE.
AND FOR THE FIRST TIME IN YEARS, PERHAPS -- TO HOPE.

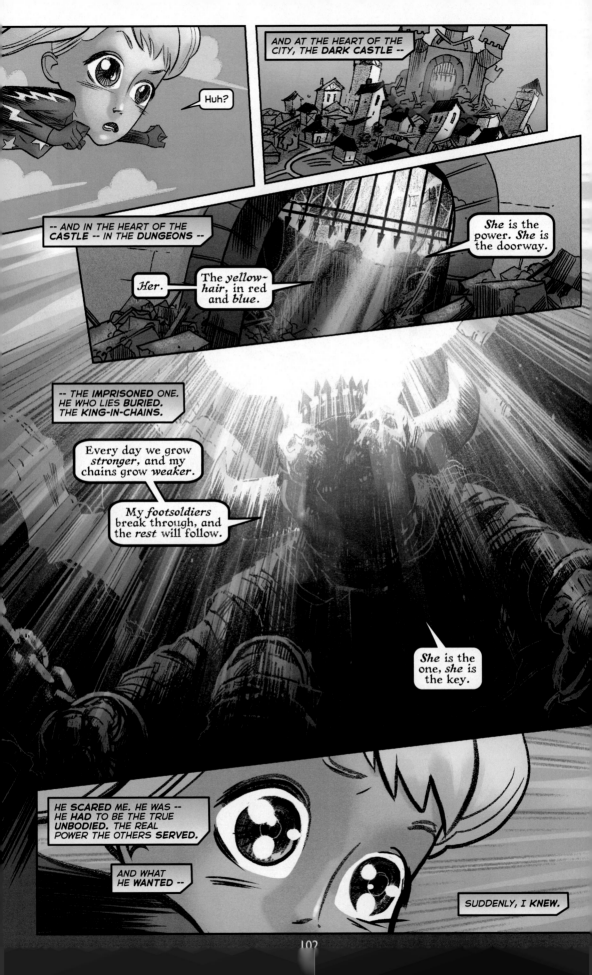

Huh?

AND AT THE HEART OF THE CITY, THE DARK CASTLE --

-- AND IN THE HEART OF THE CASTLE -- IN THE DUNGEONS --

She is the power. *She* is the doorway.

Her.

The *yellow-hair,* in red and *blue.*

-- THE IMPRISONED ONE. HE WHO LIES BURIED. THE KING-IN-CHAINS.

Every day we grow *stronger,* and my chains grow *weaker.*

My *footsoldiers* break through, and the *rest* will follow.

She is the one, *she* is the key.

HE SCARED ME. HE WAS -- HE HAD TO BE THE TRUE UNBODIED. THE REAL POWER THE OTHERS SERVED.

AND WHAT HE WANTED --

SUDDENLY, I KNEW.

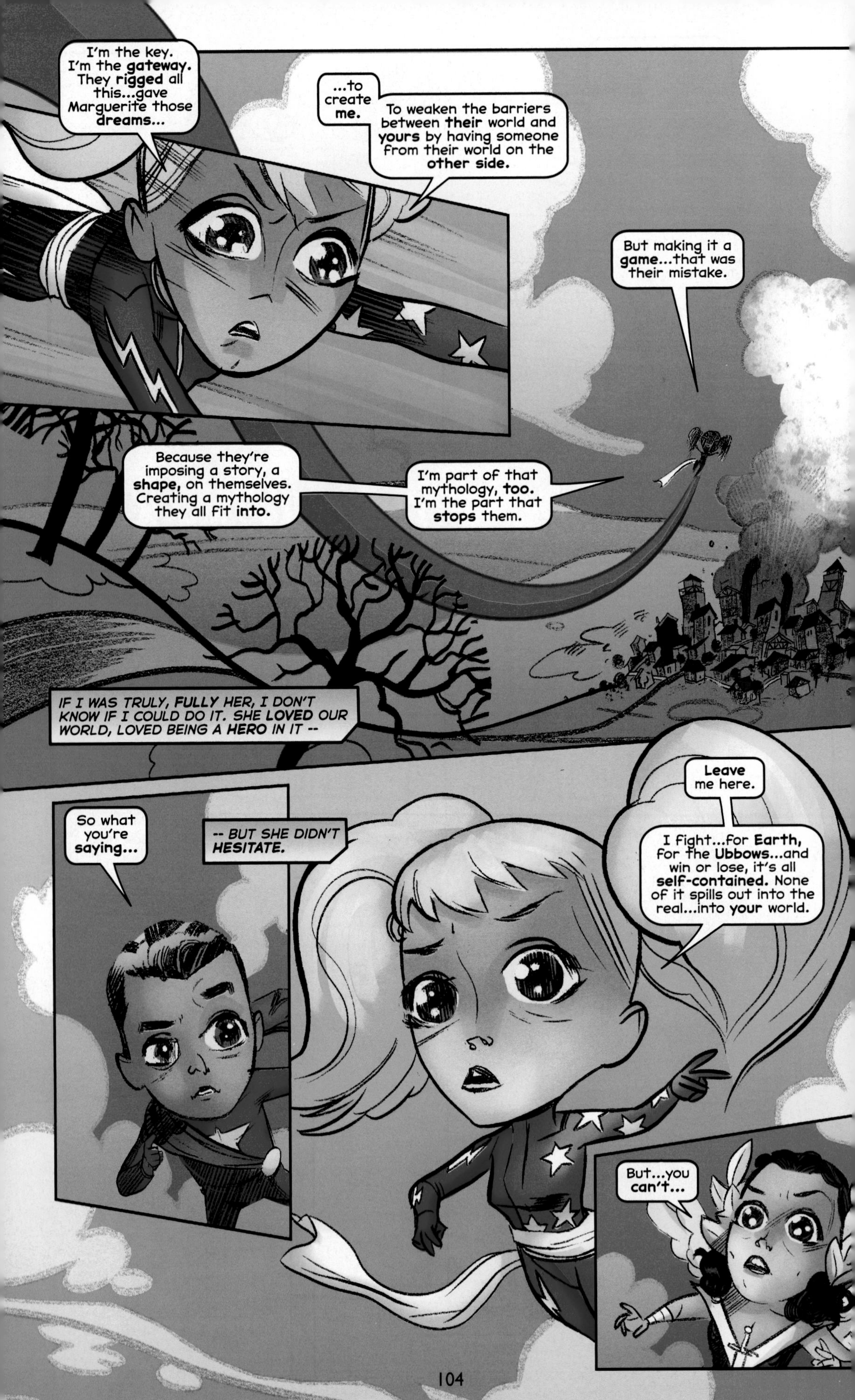

I'm the key. I'm the gateway. They rigged all this...gave Marguerite those dreams...
...to create me.
To weaken the barriers between their world and yours by having someone from their world on the other side.
But making it a game...that was their mistake.
Because they're imposing a story, a shape, on themselves. Creating a mythology they all fit into.
I'm part of that mythology, too. I'm the part that stops them.
IF I WAS TRULY, FULLY HER, I DON'T KNOW IF I COULD DO IT. SHE LOVED OUR WORLD, LOVED BEING A HERO IN IT --
So what you're saying...
-- BUT SHE DIDN'T HESITATE.
Leave me here.
I fight...for Earth, for the Ubbows...and win or lose, it's all self-contained. None of it spills out into the real...into your world.
But...you can't...

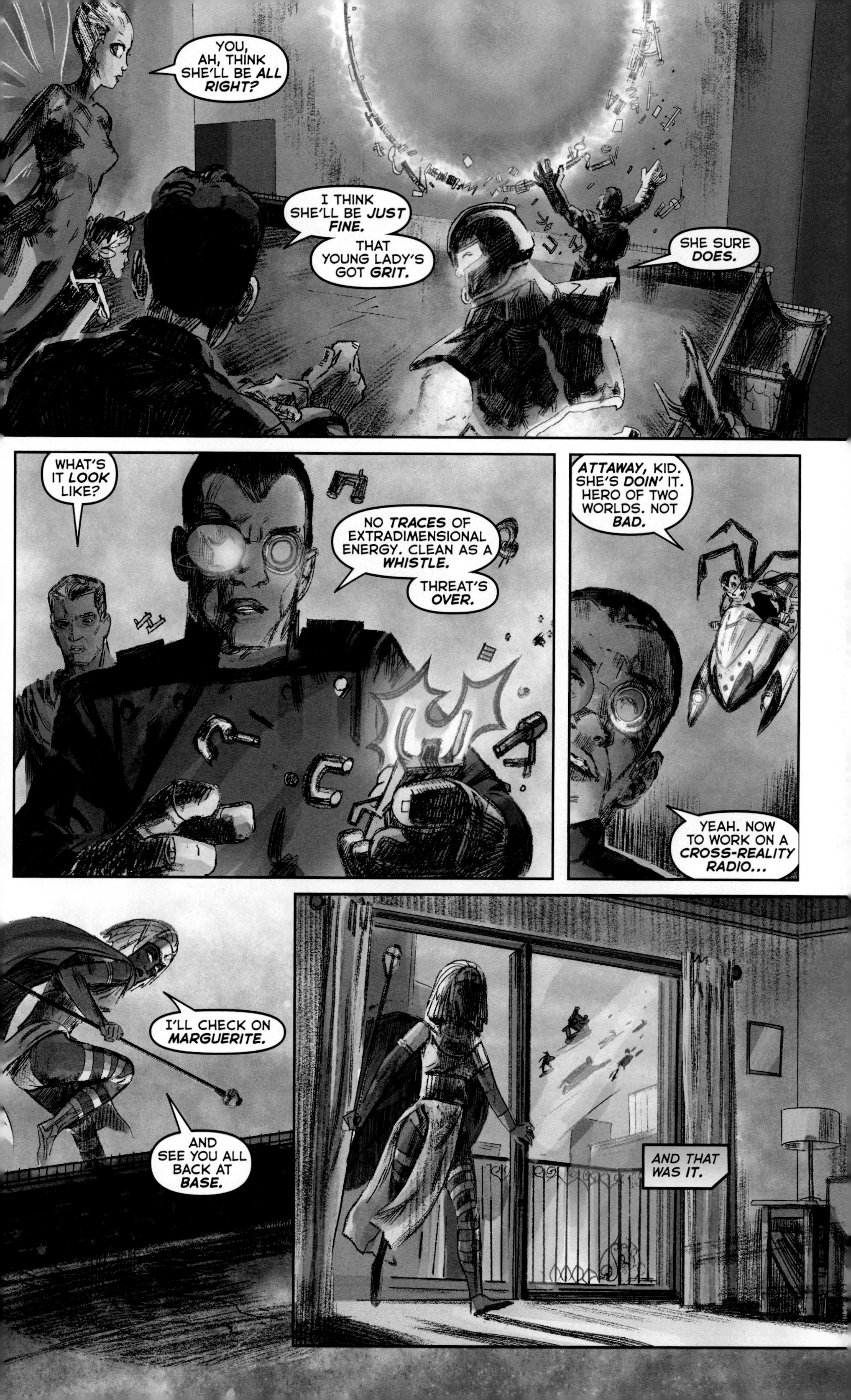
YOU, AH, THINK SHE'LL BE ALL RIGHT?
I THINK SHE'LL BE JUST FINE.
THAT YOUNG LADY'S GOT GRIT.
SHE SURE DOES.
WHAT'S IT LOOK LIKE?
NO TRACES OF EXTRADIMENSIONAL ENERGY. CLEAN AS A WHISTLE.
THREAT'S OVER.
ATTAWAY, KID. SHE'S DOIN' IT. HERO OF TWO WORLDS. NOT BAD.
YEAH. NOW TO WORK ON A CROSS-REALITY RADIO...
I'LL CHECK ON MARGUERITE.
AND SEE YOU ALL BACK AT BASE.
AND THAT WAS IT.

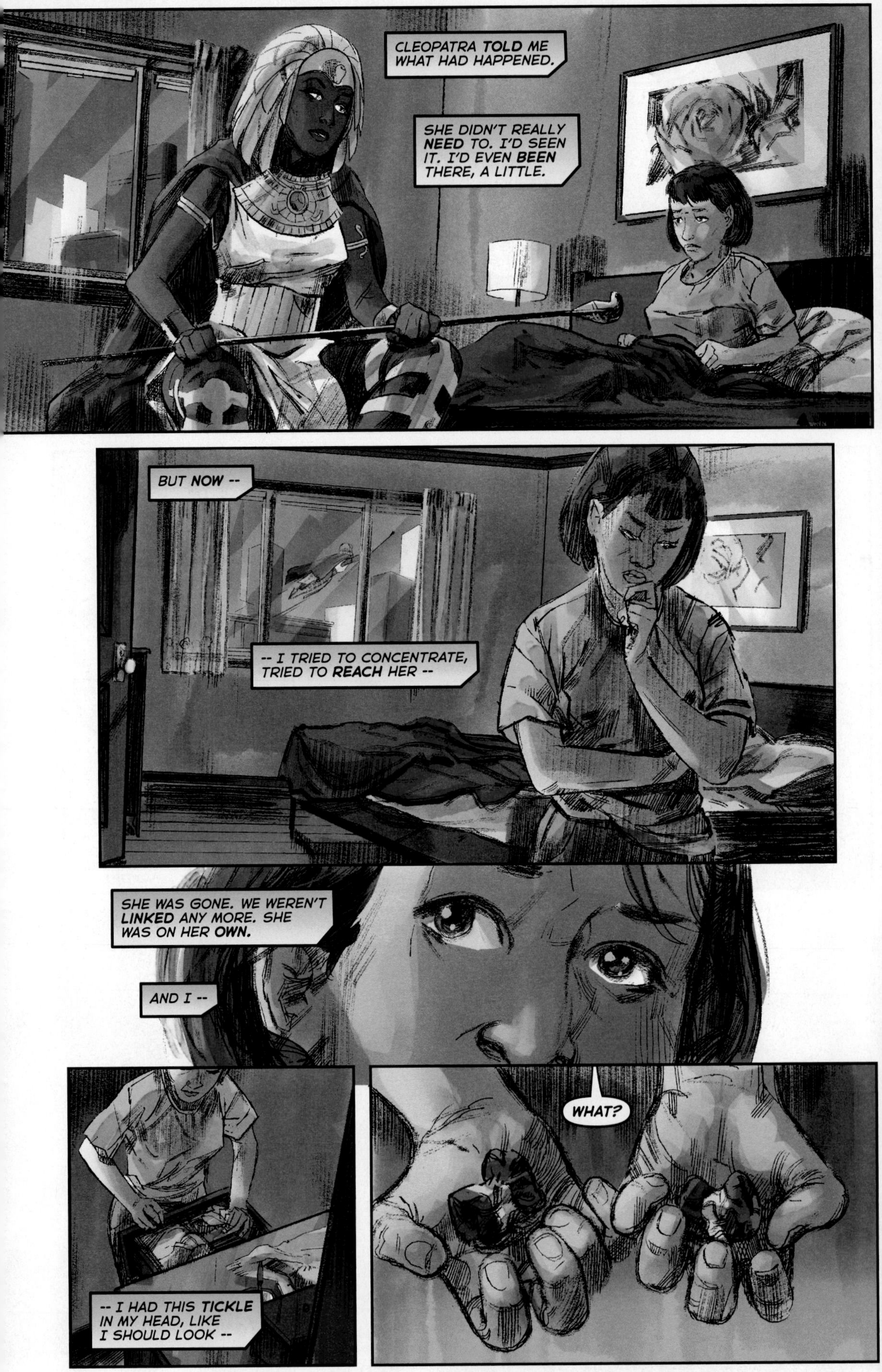
CLEOPATRA TOLD ME WHAT HAD HAPPENED.
SHE DIDN'T REALLY NEED TO. I'D SEEN IT. I'D EVEN BEEN THERE, A LITTLE.
BUT NOW --
-- I TRIED TO CONCENTRATE, TRIED TO REACH HER --
SHE WAS GONE. WE WEREN'T LINKED ANY MORE. SHE WAS ON HER OWN.
AND I --
-- I HAD THIS TICKLE IN MY HEAD, LIKE I SHOULD LOOK --
WHAT?

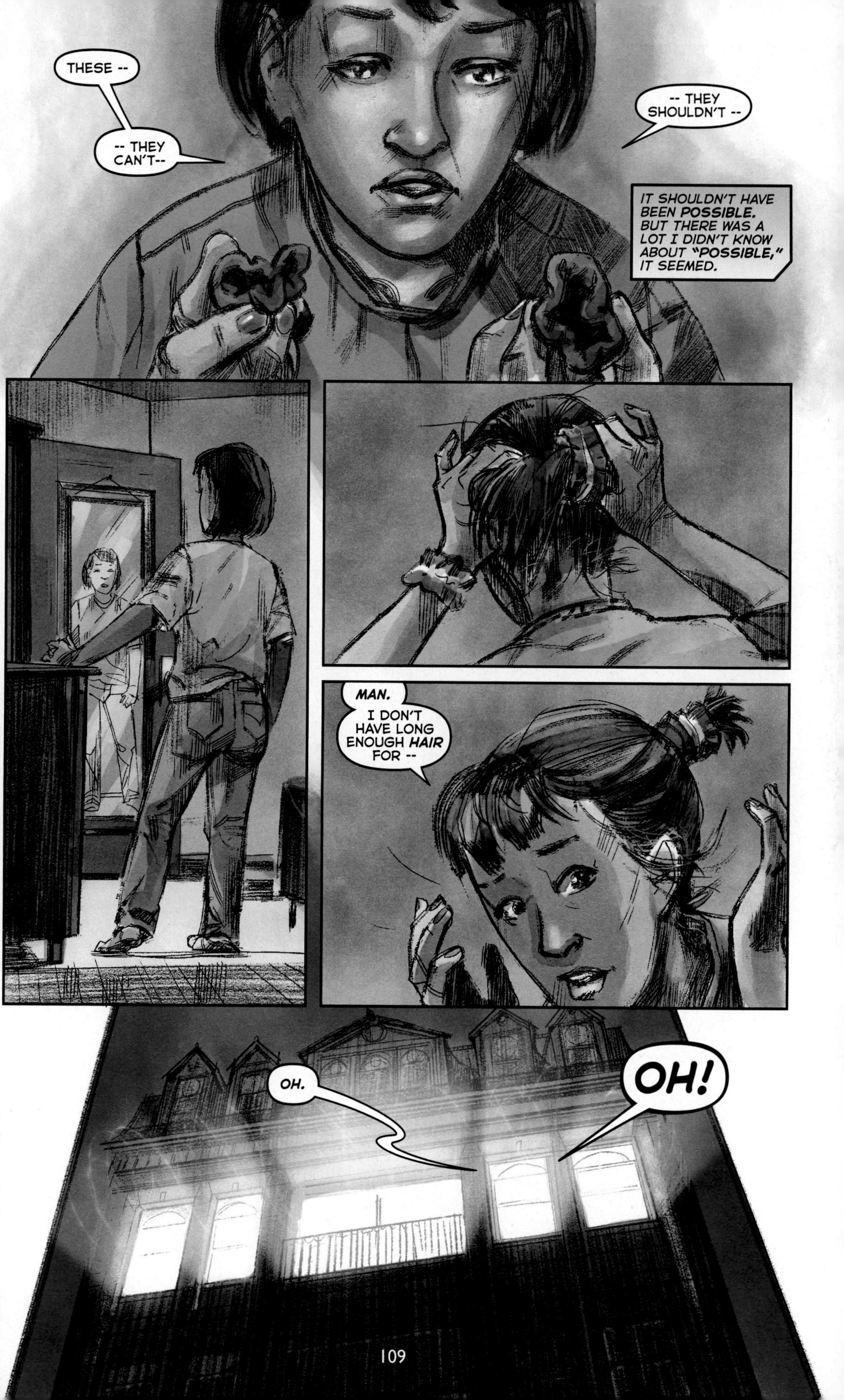
THESE --
-- THEY CAN'T--
-- THEY SHOULDN'T --
IT SHOULDN'T HAVE BEEN POSSIBLE. BUT THERE WAS A LOT I DIDN'T KNOW ABOUT "POSSIBLE," IT SEEMED.
MAN.
I DON'T HAVE LONG ENOUGH HAIR FOR --
OH.
OH!

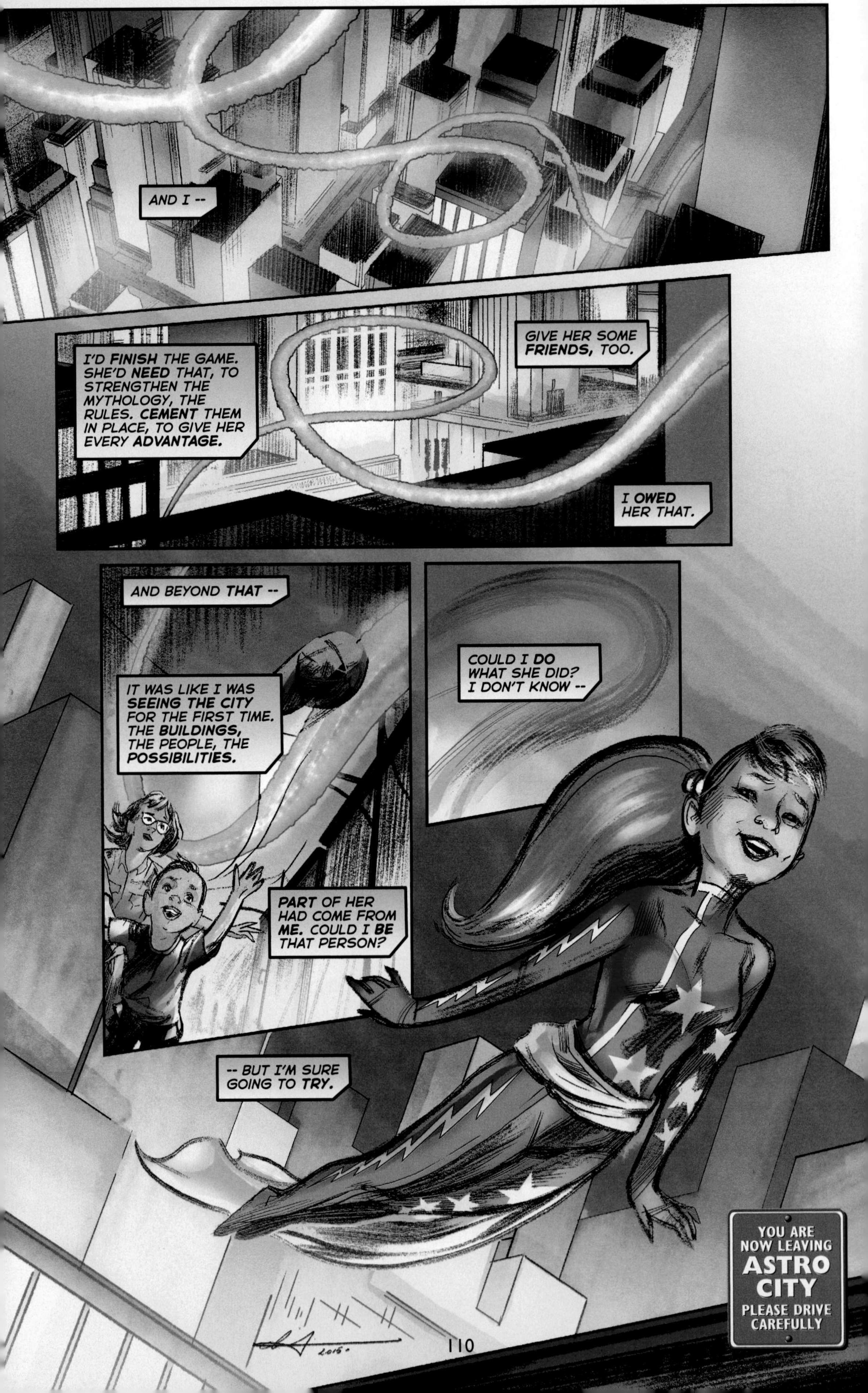
AND I --
I'D FINISH THE GAME. SHE'D NEED THAT, TO STRENGTHEN THE MYTHOLOGY, THE RULES. CEMENT THEM IN PLACE, TO GIVE HER EVERY ADVANTAGE.
GIVE HER SOME FRIENDS, TOO.
I OWED HER THAT.
AND BEYOND THAT --
IT WAS LIKE I WAS SEEING THE CITY FOR THE FIRST TIME. THE BUILDINGS, THE PEOPLE, THE POSSIBILITIES.
PART OF HER HAD COME FROM ME. COULD I BE THAT PERSON?
COULD I DO WHAT SHE DID? I DON'T KNOW --
-- BUT I'M SURE GOING TO TRY.
YOU ARE NOW LEAVING ASTRO CITY PLEASE DRIVE CAREFULLY
2015

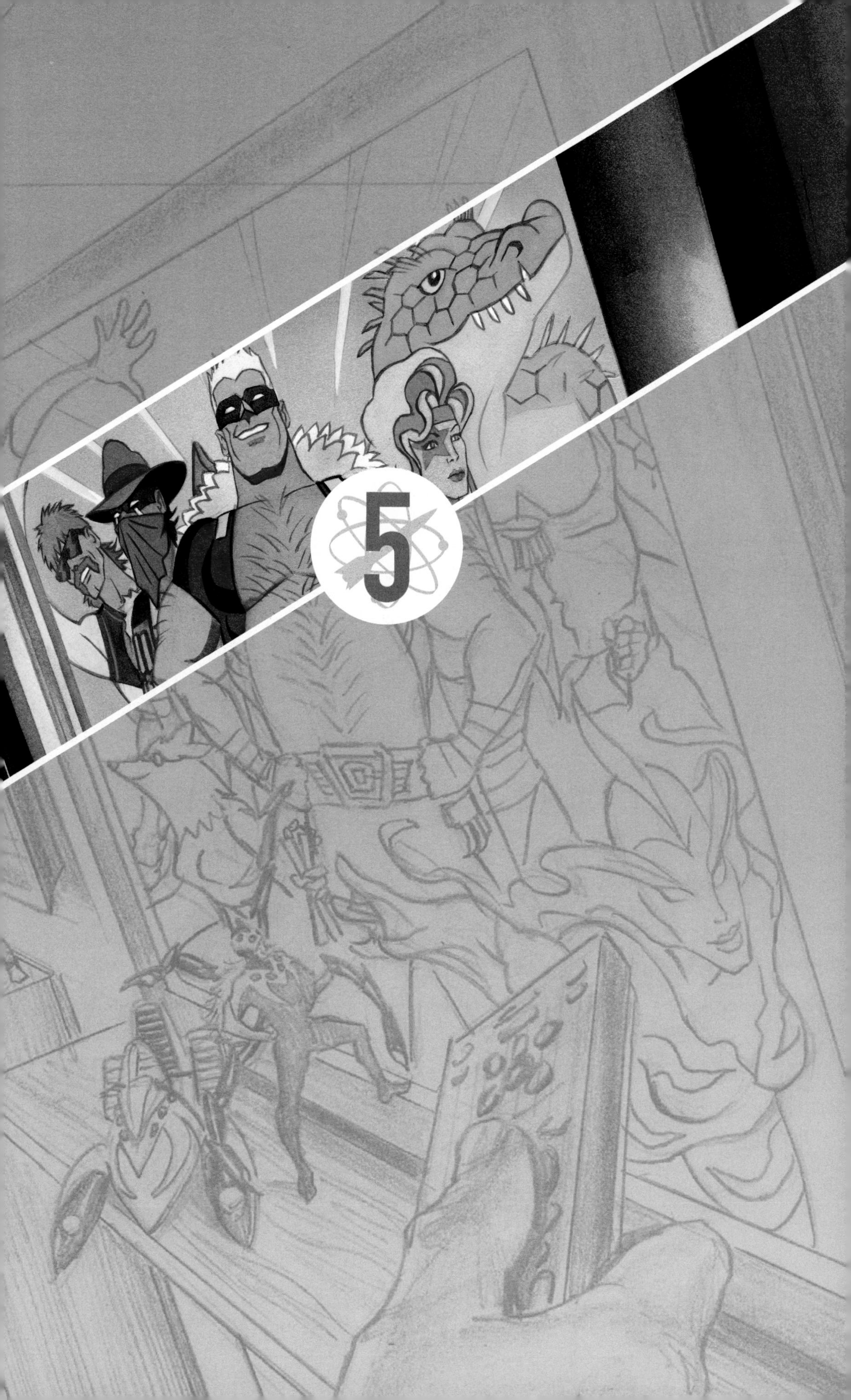
5

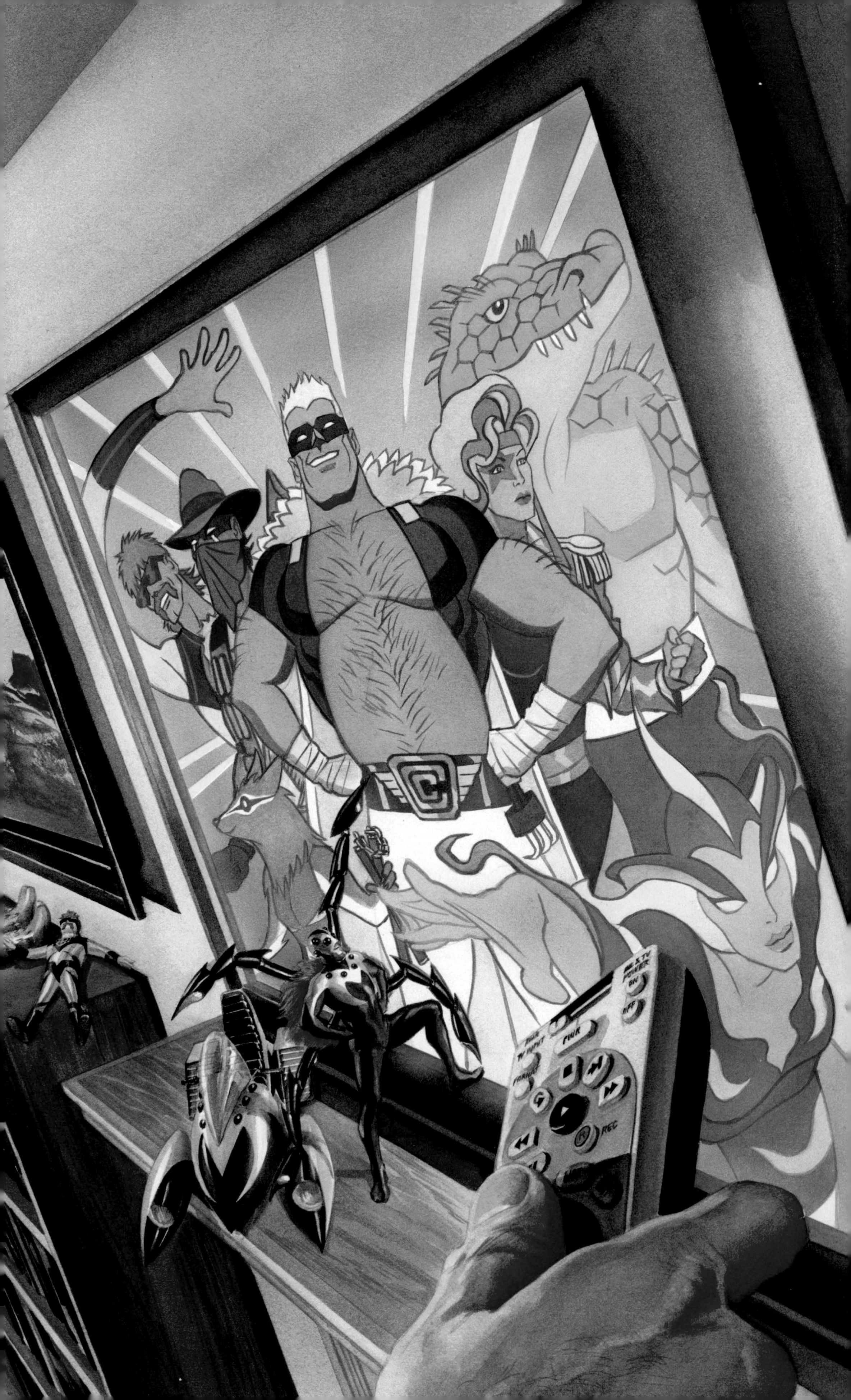
POWER
ON
OFF
TV INPUT
PWR
FORMAT
REC

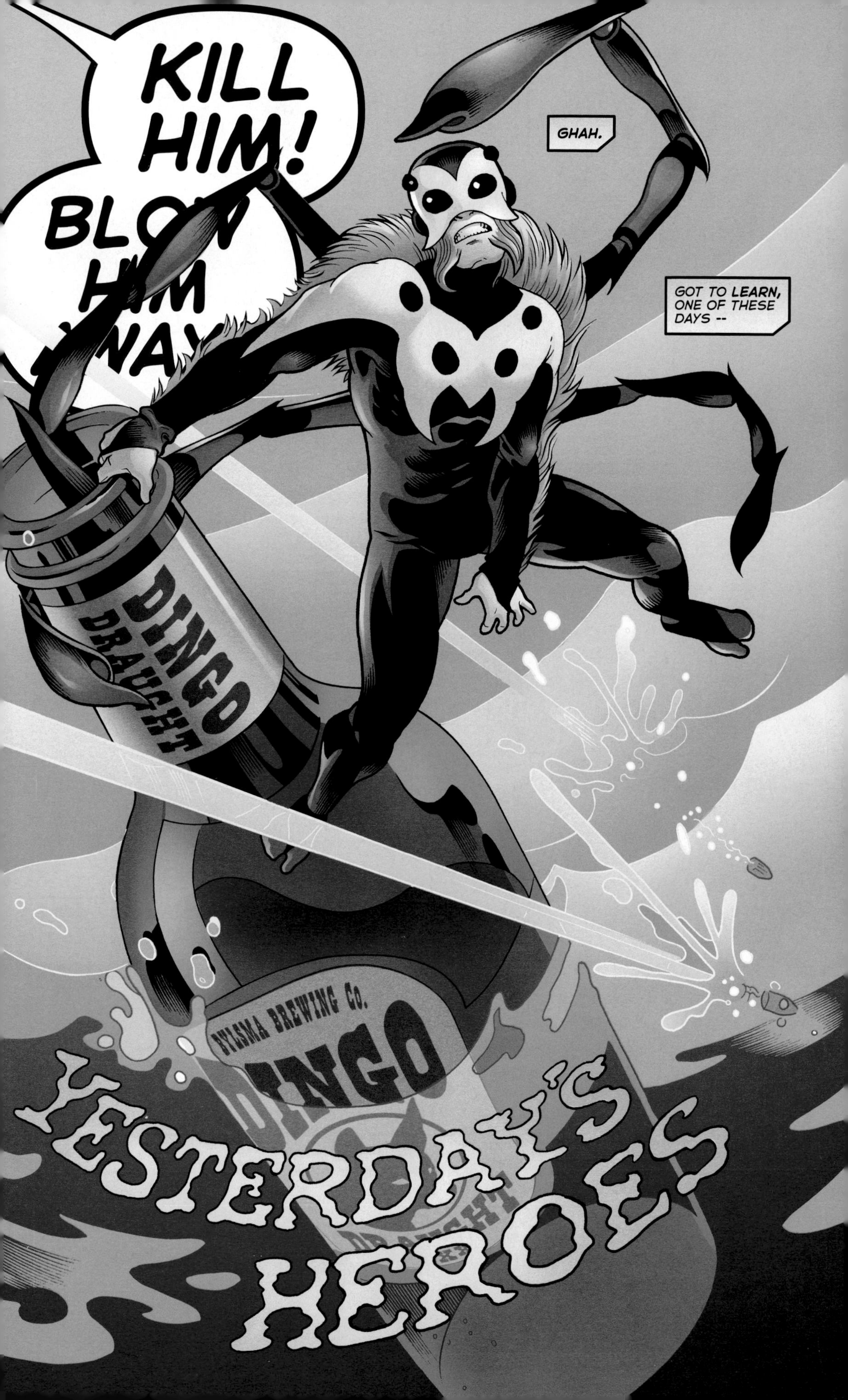
KILL HIM!
GHAH.
GOT TO LEARN, ONE OF THESE DAYS --
DINGO DRAUGHT
BYLSMA BREWING CO.
DINGO
YESTERDAY'S HEROES

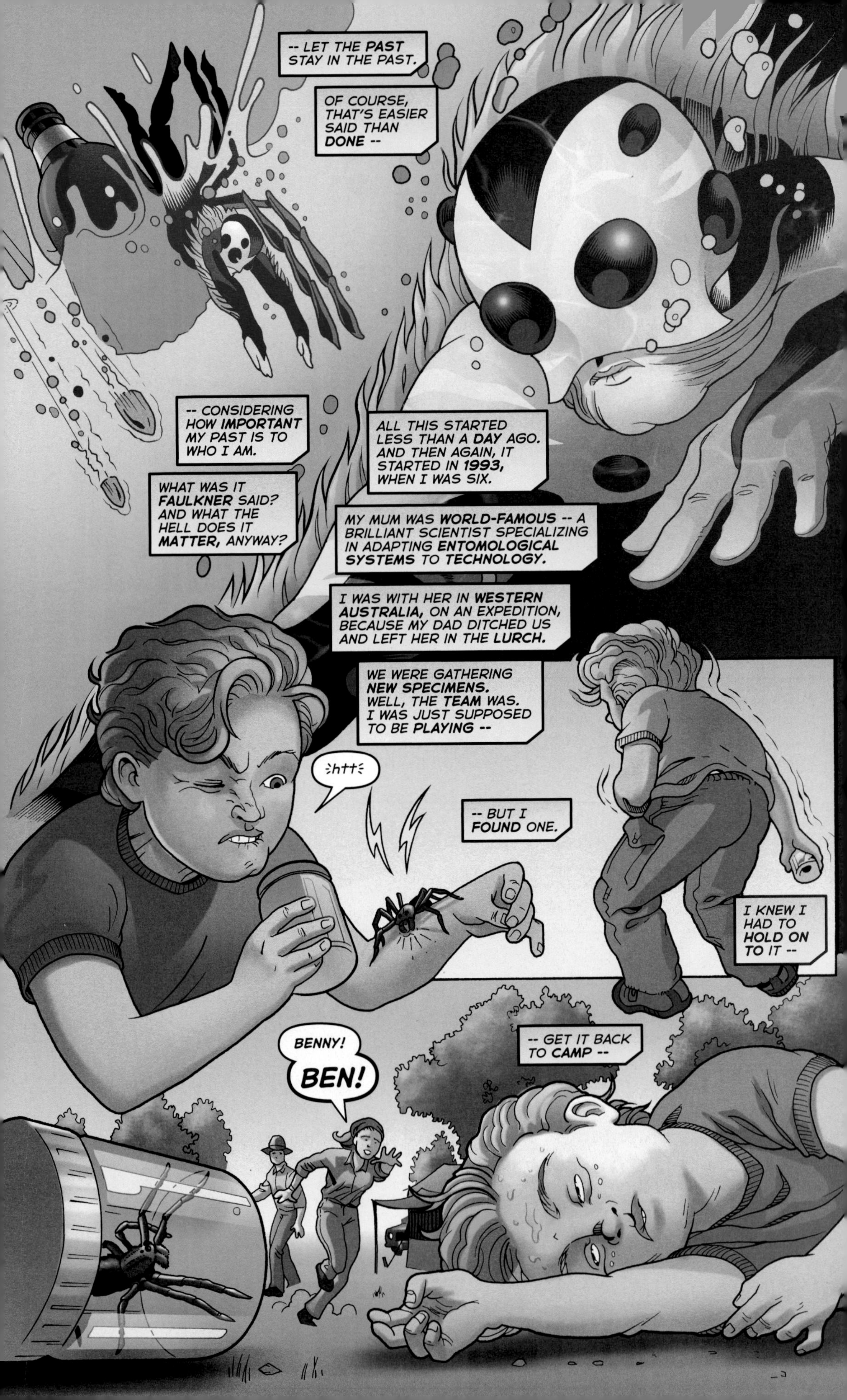
-- LET THE **PAST** STAY IN THE PAST.
OF COURSE, THAT'S EASIER SAID THAN **DONE** --
-- CONSIDERING HOW **IMPORTANT** MY PAST IS TO WHO I AM.
WHAT WAS IT **FAULKNER** SAID? AND WHAT THE HELL DOES IT **MATTER,** ANYWAY?
ALL THIS STARTED LESS THAN A **DAY** AGO. AND THEN AGAIN, IT STARTED IN **1993,** WHEN I WAS SIX.
MY MUM WAS **WORLD-FAMOUS** -- A BRILLIANT SCIENTIST SPECIALIZING IN ADAPTING **ENTOMOLOGICAL SYSTEMS** TO **TECHNOLOGY.**
I WAS WITH HER IN **WESTERN AUSTRALIA,** ON AN EXPEDITION, BECAUSE MY DAD DITCHED US AND LEFT HER IN THE **LURCH.**
WE WERE GATHERING **NEW SPECIMENS.** WELL, THE **TEAM** WAS. I WAS JUST SUPPOSED TO BE **PLAYING** --
htt
-- BUT I **FOUND** ONE.
I KNEW I HAD TO **HOLD ON** TO IT --
-- GET IT BACK TO **CAMP** --
BENNY!
BEN!

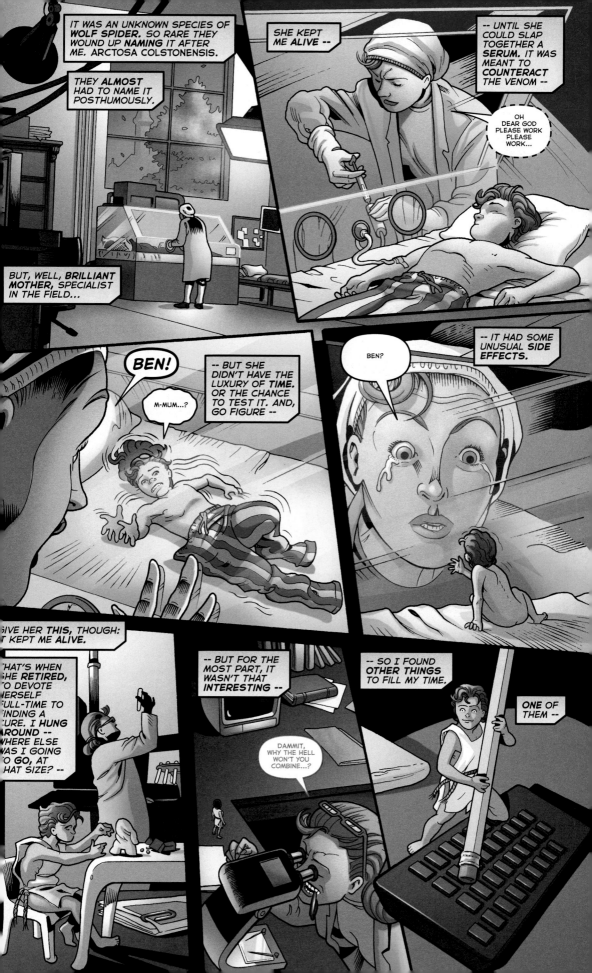

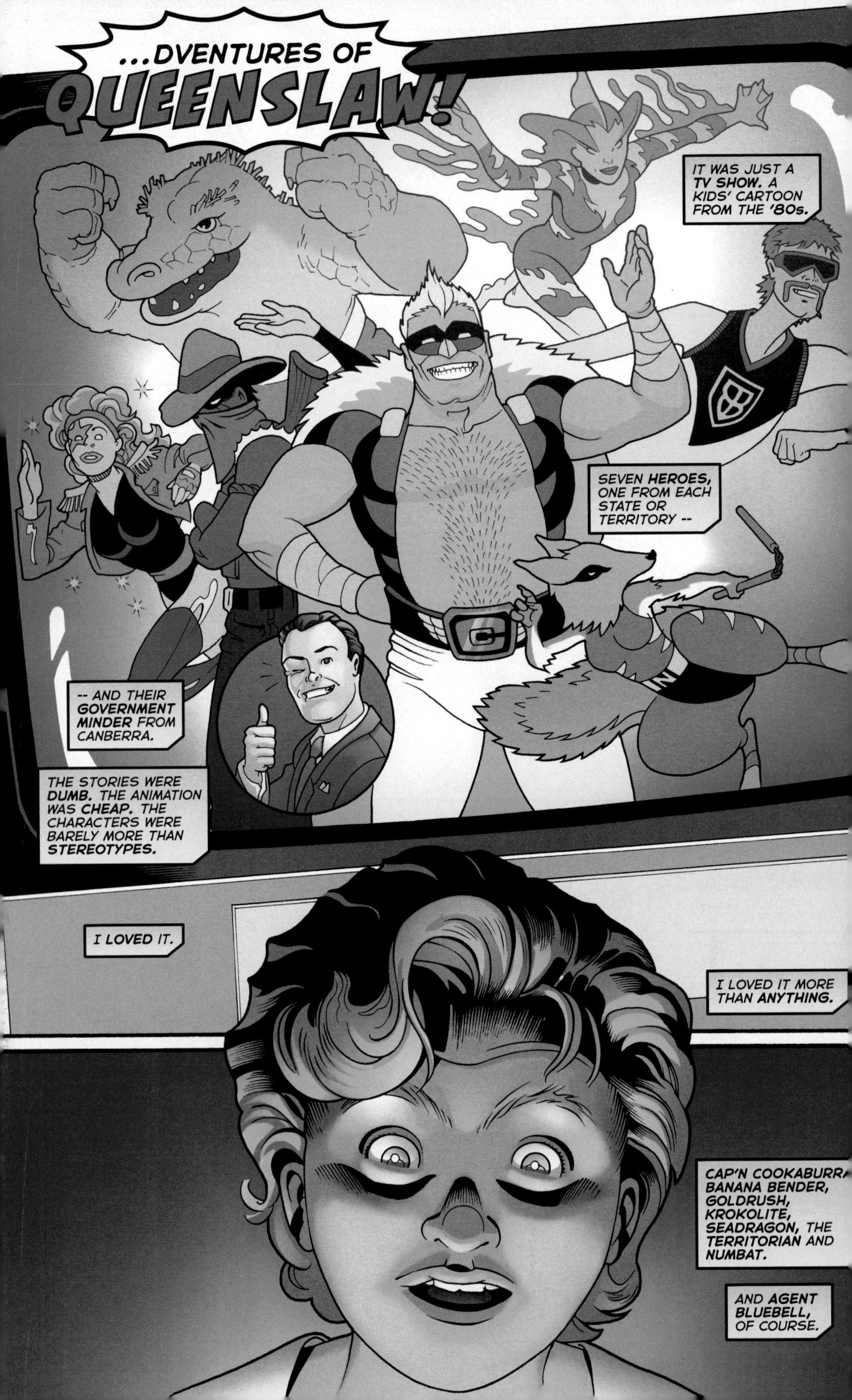
...DVENTURES OF QUEENSLAW!
IT WAS JUST A TV SHOW. A KIDS' CARTOON FROM THE '80s.
SEVEN HEROES, ONE FROM EACH STATE OR TERRITORY --
-- AND THEIR GOVERNMENT MINDER FROM CANBERRA.
THE STORIES WERE DUMB. THE ANIMATION WAS CHEAP. THE CHARACTERS WERE BARELY MORE THAN STEREOTYPES.
I LOVED IT.
I LOVED IT MORE THAN ANYTHING.
CAP'N COOKABURRA, BANANA BENDER, GOLDRUSH, KROKOLITE, SEADRAGON, THE TERRITORIAN AND NUMBAT.
AND AGENT BLUEBELL, OF COURSE.

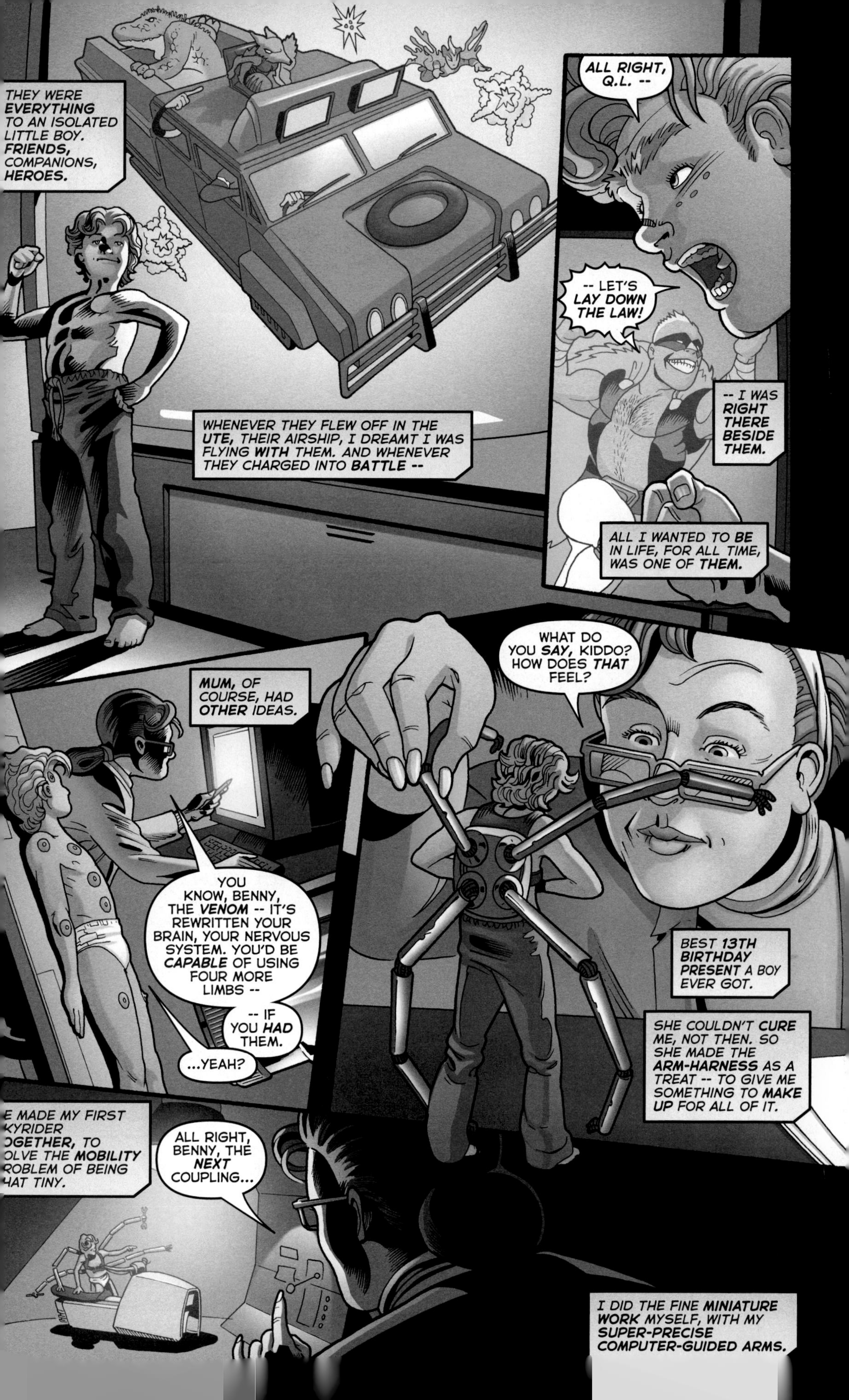

THEY WERE EVERYTHING TO AN ISOLATED LITTLE BOY. FRIENDS, COMPANIONS, HEROES.
WHENEVER THEY FLEW OFF IN THE UTE, THEIR AIRSHIP, I DREAMT I WAS FLYING WITH THEM. AND WHENEVER THEY CHARGED INTO BATTLE --
ALL RIGHT, Q.L. --
-- LET'S LAY DOWN THE LAW!
-- I WAS RIGHT THERE BESIDE THEM.
ALL I WANTED TO BE IN LIFE, FOR ALL TIME, WAS ONE OF THEM.
MUM, OF COURSE, HAD OTHER IDEAS.
YOU KNOW, BENNY, THE VENOM -- IT'S REWRITTEN YOUR BRAIN, YOUR NERVOUS SYSTEM. YOU'D BE CAPABLE OF USING FOUR MORE LIMBS --
-- IF YOU HAD THEM.
...YEAH?
WHAT DO YOU SAY, KIDDO? HOW DOES THAT FEEL?
BEST 13TH BIRTHDAY PRESENT A BOY EVER GOT.
SHE COULDN'T CURE ME, NOT THEN. SO SHE MADE THE ARM-HARNESS AS A TREAT -- TO GIVE ME SOMETHING TO MAKE UP FOR ALL OF IT.
E MADE MY FIRST KYRIDER OGETHER, TO OLVE THE MOBILITY ROBLEM OF BEING HAT TINY.
ALL RIGHT, BENNY, THE NEXT COUPLING...
I DID THE FINE MINIATURE WORK MYSELF, WITH MY SUPER-PRECISE COMPUTER-GUIDED ARMS.

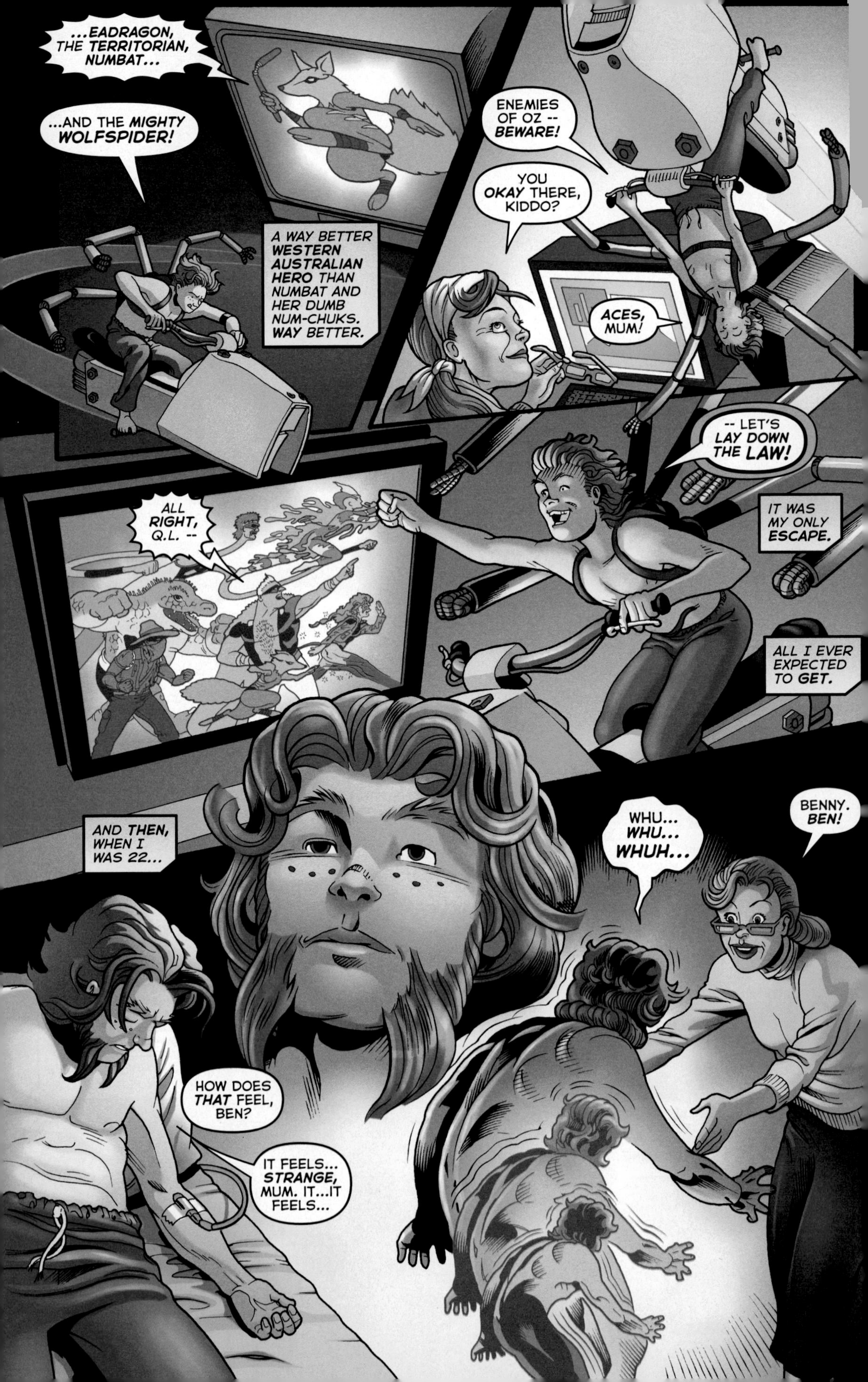
...EADRAGON, THE TERRITORIAN, NUMBAT...
...AND THE MIGHTY WOLFSPIDER!
A WAY BETTER WESTERN AUSTRALIAN HERO THAN NUMBAT AND HER DUMB NUM-CHUKS. WAY BETTER.
ENEMIES OF OZ -- BEWARE!
YOU OKAY THERE, KIDDO?
ACES, MUM!
ALL RIGHT, Q.L. --
-- LET'S LAY DOWN THE LAW!
IT WAS MY ONLY ESCAPE.
ALL I EVER EXPECTED TO GET.
AND THEN, WHEN I WAS 22...
WHU... WHU... WHUH...
BENNY. BEN!
HOW DOES THAT FEEL, BEN?
IT FEELS... STRANGE, MUM. IT...IT FEELS...

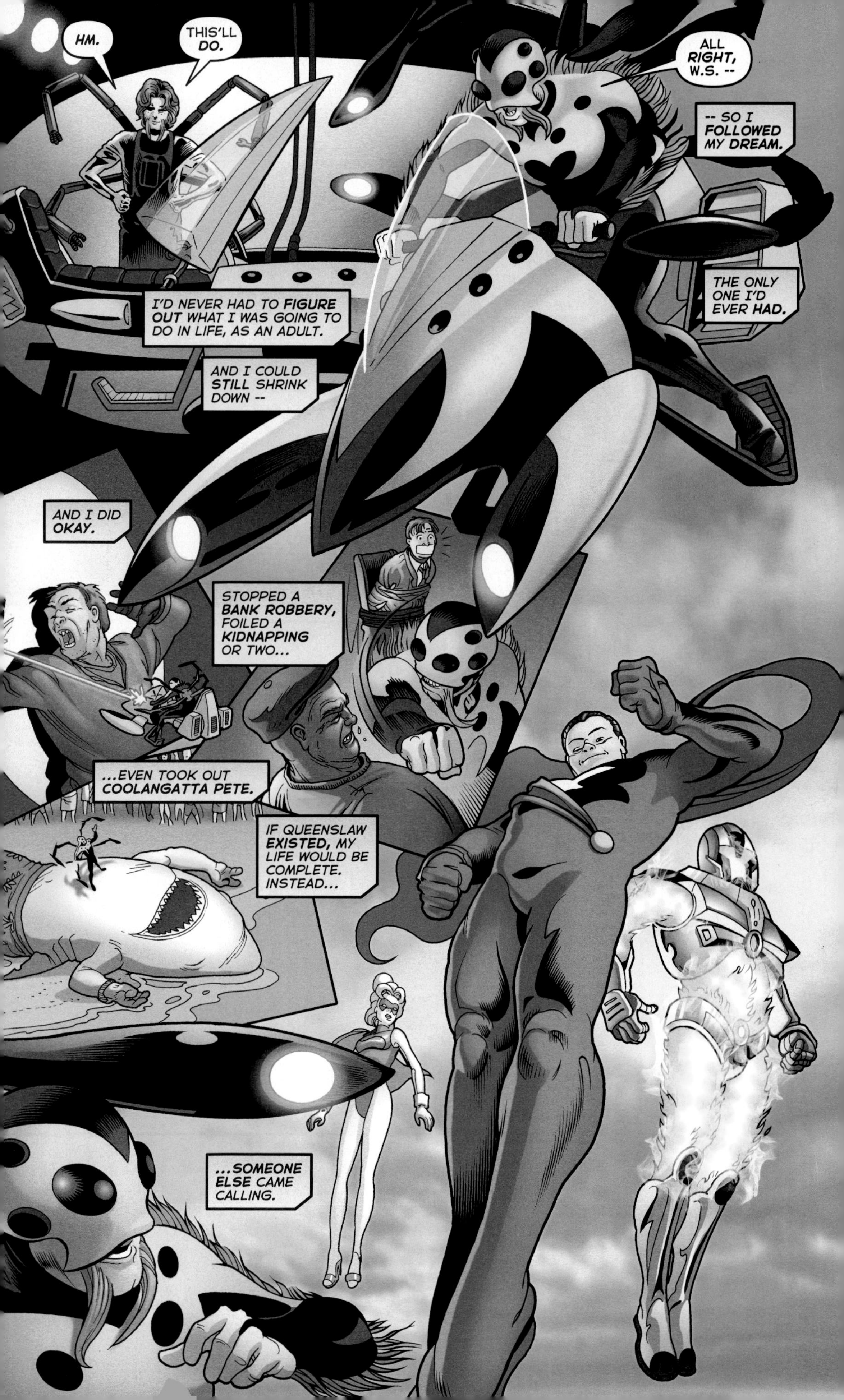
HM.
THIS'LL DO.
ALL RIGHT, W.S. --
-- SO I FOLLOWED MY DREAM.
THE ONLY ONE I'D EVER HAD.
I'D NEVER HAD TO FIGURE OUT WHAT I WAS GOING TO DO IN LIFE, AS AN ADULT.
AND I COULD STILL SHRINK DOWN --
AND I DID OKAY.
STOPPED A BANK ROBBERY, FOILED A KIDNAPPING OR TWO...
...EVEN TOOK OUT COOLANGATTA PETE.
IF QUEENSLAW EXISTED, MY LIFE WOULD BE COMPLETE. INSTEAD...
...SOMEONE ELSE CAME CALLING.

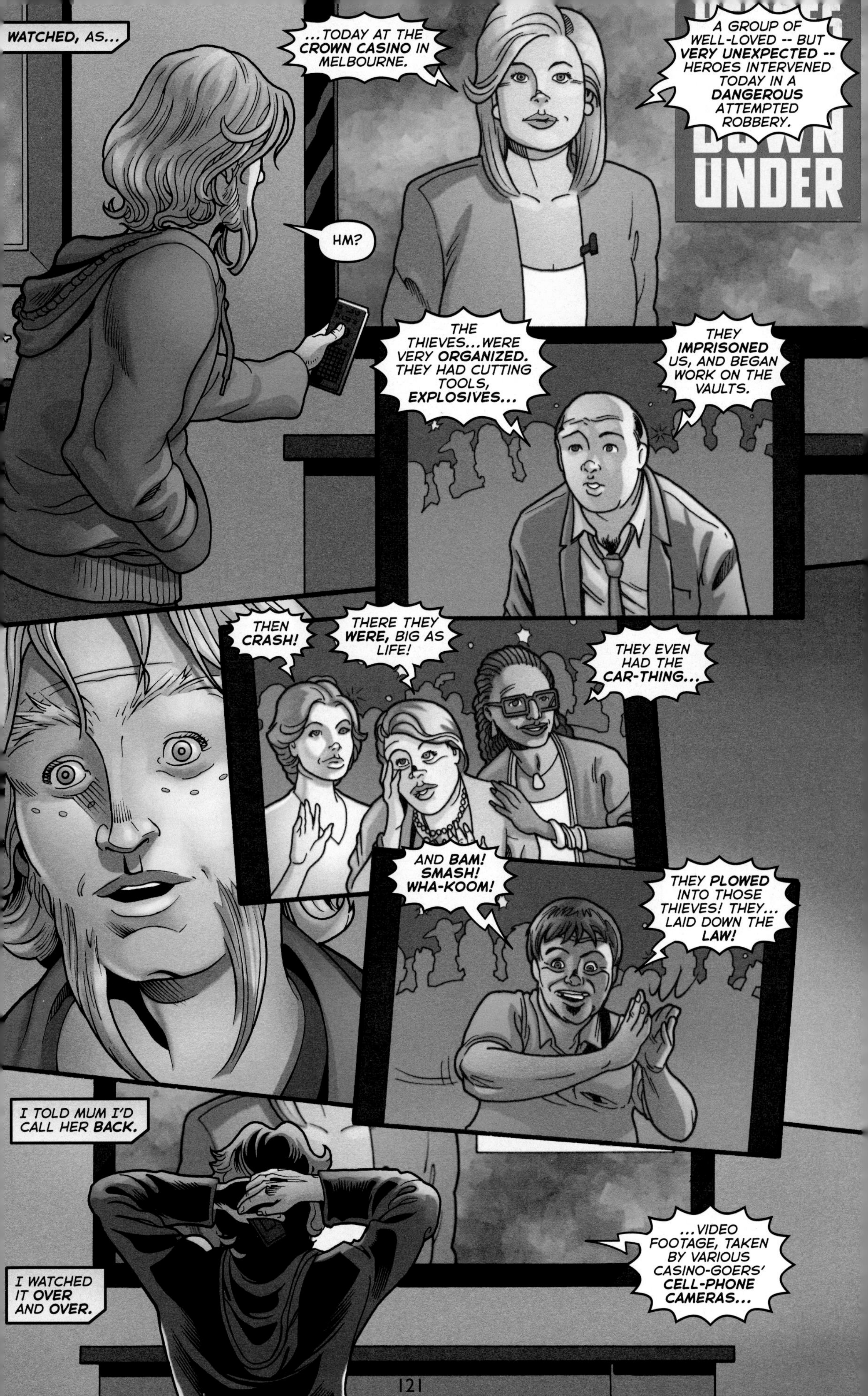
WATCHED, AS...
...TODAY AT THE CROWN CASINO IN MELBOURNE.
A GROUP OF WELL-LOVED -- BUT VERY UNEXPECTED -- HEROES INTERVENED TODAY IN A DANGEROUS ATTEMPTED ROBBERY.
UNDER
HM?
THE THIEVES...WERE VERY ORGANIZED. THEY HAD CUTTING TOOLS, EXPLOSIVES...
THEY IMPRISONED US, AND BEGAN WORK ON THE VAULTS.
THEN CRASH!
THERE THEY WERE, BIG AS LIFE!
THEY EVEN HAD THE CAR-THING...
AND BAM! SMASH! WHA-KOOM!
THEY PLOWED INTO THOSE THIEVES! THEY... LAID DOWN THE LAW!
I TOLD MUM I'D CALL HER BACK.
I WATCHED IT OVER AND OVER.
...VIDEO FOOTAGE, TAKEN BY VARIOUS CASINO-GOERS' CELL-PHONE CAMERAS...

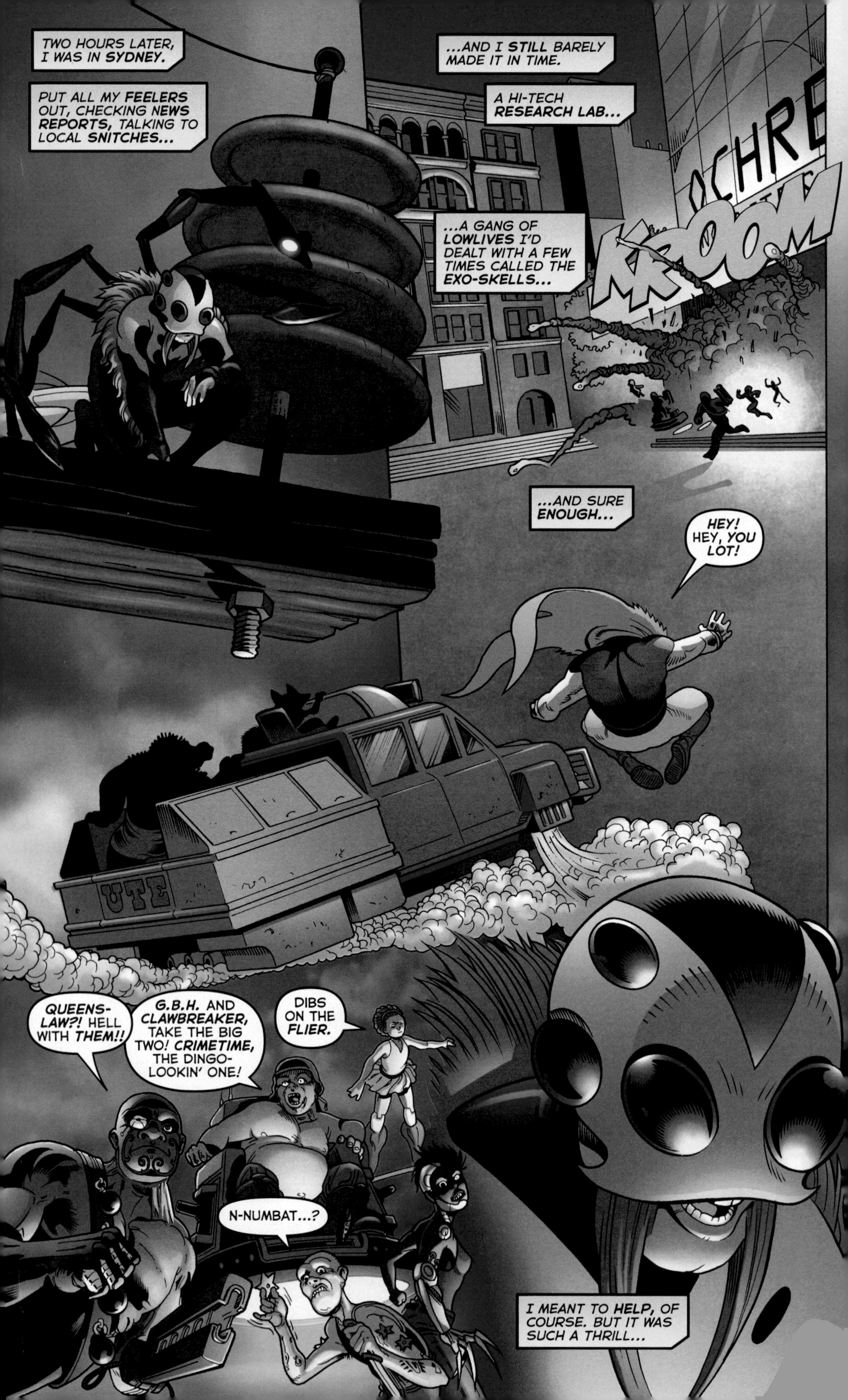
TWO HOURS LATER, I WAS IN SYDNEY.
PUT ALL MY FEELERS OUT, CHECKING NEWS REPORTS, TALKING TO LOCAL SNITCHES...
...AND I STILL BARELY MADE IT IN TIME.
A HI-TECH RESEARCH LAB...
OCHRE
...A GANG OF LOWLIVES I'D DEALT WITH A FEW TIMES CALLED THE EXO-SKELLS...
KRROOM
...AND SURE ENOUGH...
HEY! HEY, YOU LOT!
UTE
QUEENS-LAW?! HELL WITH THEM!!
G.B.H. AND CLAWBREAKER, TAKE THE BIG TWO! CRIMETIME, THE DINGO-LOOKIN' ONE!
DIBS ON THE FLIER.
N-NUMBAT...?
I MEANT TO HELP, OF COURSE. BUT IT WAS SUCH A THRILL...

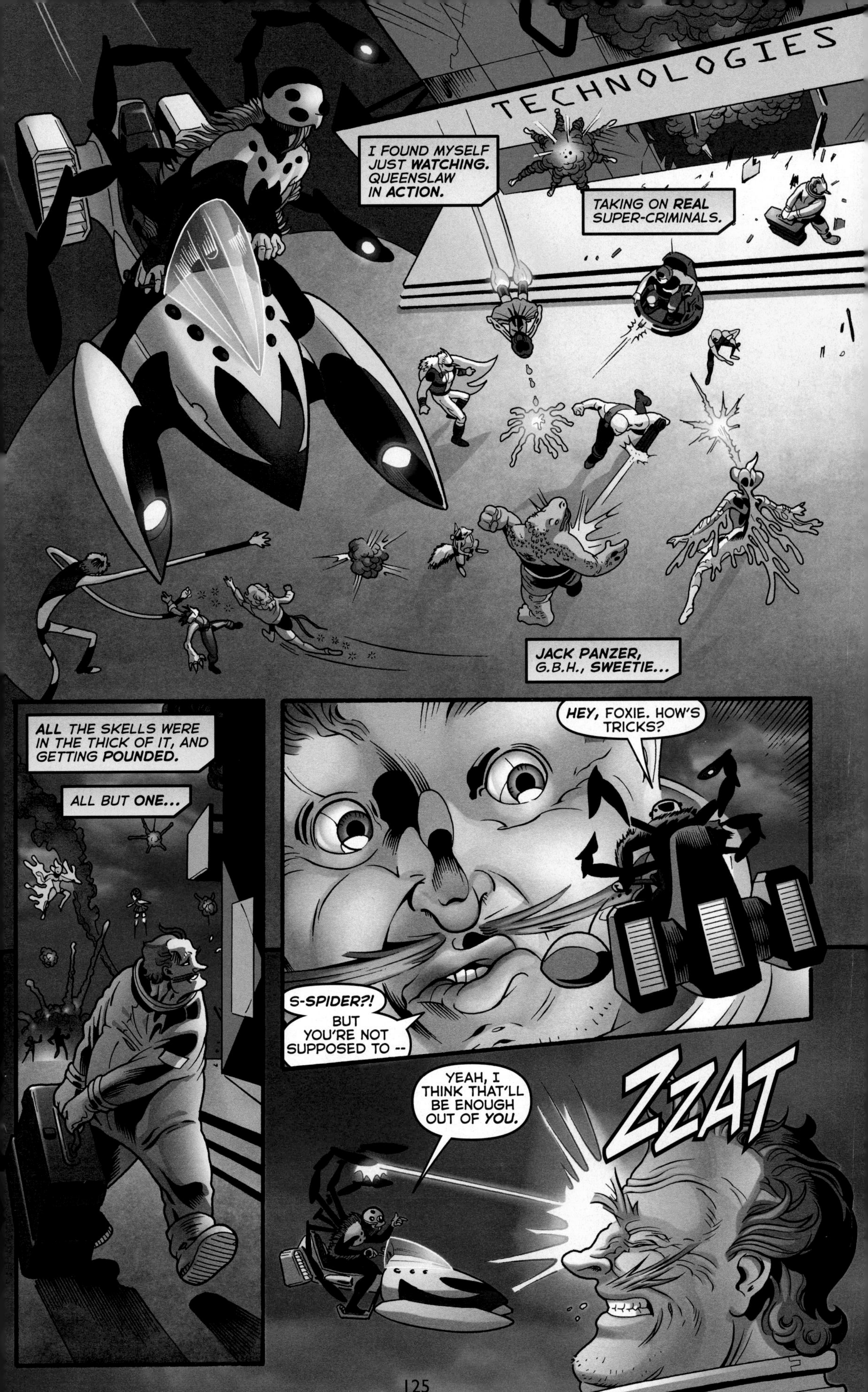
TECHNOLOGIES
I FOUND MYSELF JUST WATCHING. QUEENSLAW IN ACTION.
TAKING ON REAL SUPER-CRIMINALS.
JACK PANZER, G.B.H., SWEETIE...
ALL THE SKELLS WERE IN THE THICK OF IT, AND GETTING POUNDED.
ALL BUT ONE...
HEY, FOXIE. HOW'S TRICKS?
S-SPIDER?!
BUT YOU'RE NOT SUPPOSED TO --
YEAH, I THINK THAT'LL BE ENOUGH OUT OF YOU.
ZZAT

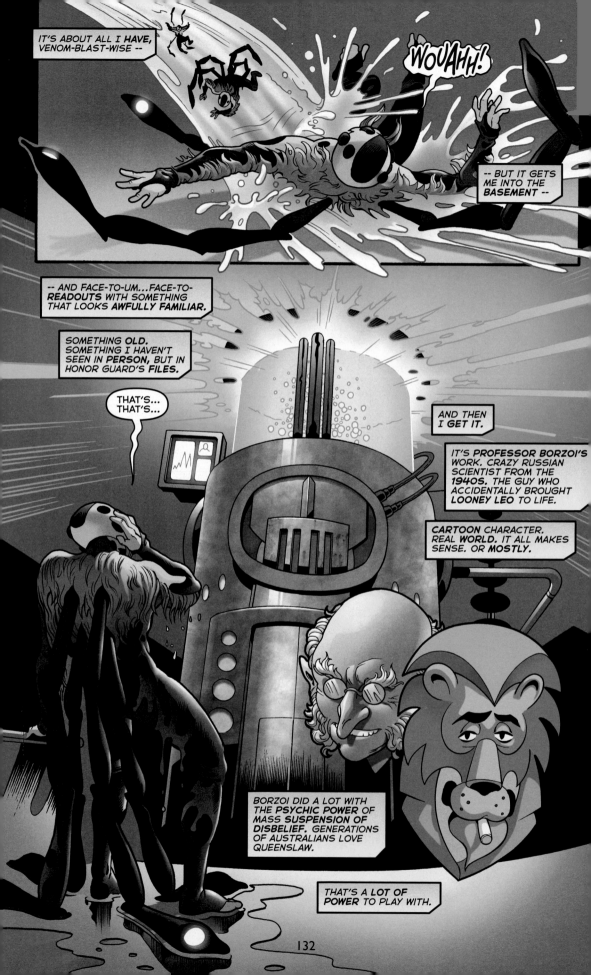

IT'S ABOUT ALL I HAVE, VENOM-BLAST-WISE --

WOUAHH!

-- BUT IT GETS ME INTO THE BASEMENT --

-- AND FACE-TO-UM...FACE-TO-READOUTS WITH SOMETHING THAT LOOKS AWFULLY FAMILIAR.

SOMETHING OLD. SOMETHING I HAVEN'T SEEN IN PERSON, BUT IN HONOR GUARD'S FILES.

THAT'S... THAT'S...

AND THEN I GET IT.

IT'S PROFESSOR BORZOI'S WORK. CRAZY RUSSIAN SCIENTIST FROM THE 1940S. THE GUY WHO ACCIDENTALLY BROUGHT LOONEY LEO TO LIFE.

CARTOON CHARACTER. REAL WORLD. IT ALL MAKES SENSE. OR MOSTLY.

BORZOI DID A LOT WITH THE PSYCHIC POWER OF MASS SUSPENSION OF DISBELIEF. GENERATIONS OF AUSTRALIANS LOVE QUEENSLAW.

THAT'S A LOT OF POWER TO PLAY WITH.

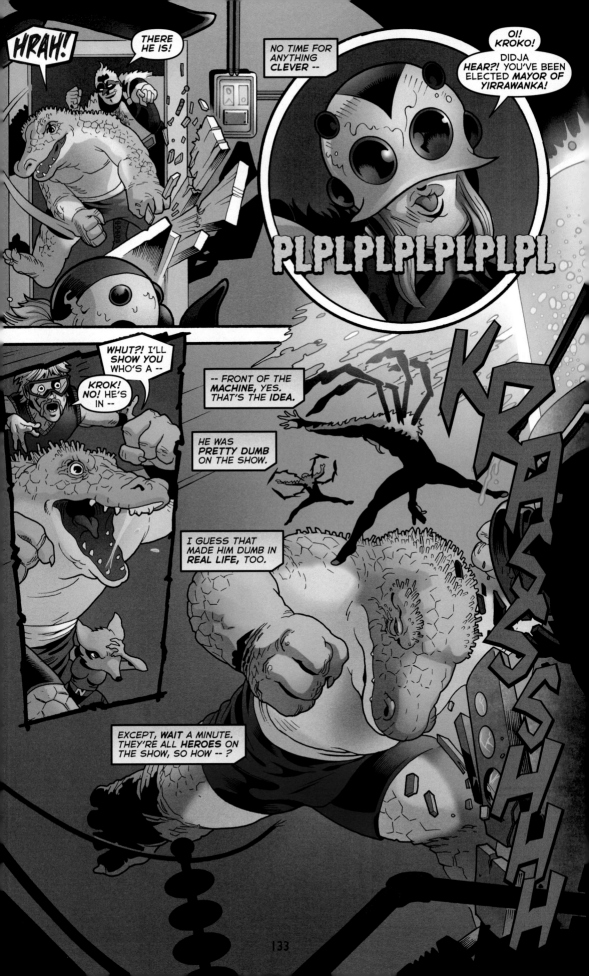

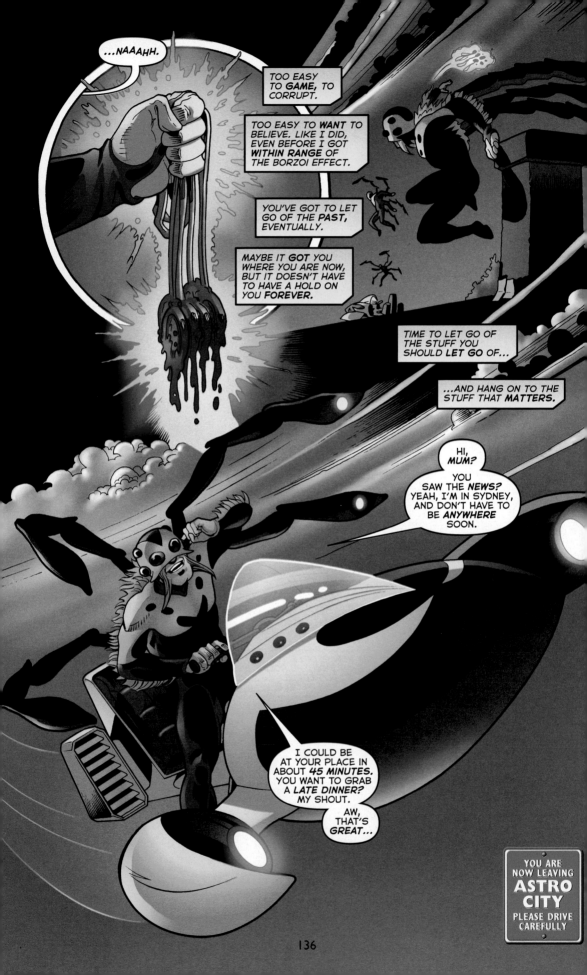

...NAAAHH.

TOO EASY TO **GAME**, TO CORRUPT.

TOO EASY TO **WANT** TO BELIEVE. LIKE I DID, EVEN BEFORE I GOT **WITHIN RANGE** OF THE BORZOI EFFECT.

YOU'VE GOT TO LET GO OF THE **PAST**, EVENTUALLY.

MAYBE IT **GOT** YOU WHERE YOU ARE NOW, BUT IT DOESN'T HAVE TO HAVE A HOLD ON YOU **FOREVER**.

TIME TO LET GO OF THE STUFF YOU SHOULD **LET GO** OF...

...AND HANG ON TO THE STUFF THAT **MATTERS**.

HI, **MUM?**

YOU SAW THE **NEWS?** YEAH, I'M IN SYDNEY, AND DON'T HAVE TO BE **ANYWHERE** SOON.

I COULD BE AT YOUR PLACE IN ABOUT **45 MINUTES.** YOU WANT TO GRAB A **LATE DINNER?** MY SHOUT.

AW, THAT'S **GREAT**...

YOU ARE NOW LEAVING
ASTRO CITY
PLEASE DRIVE CAREFULLY

136

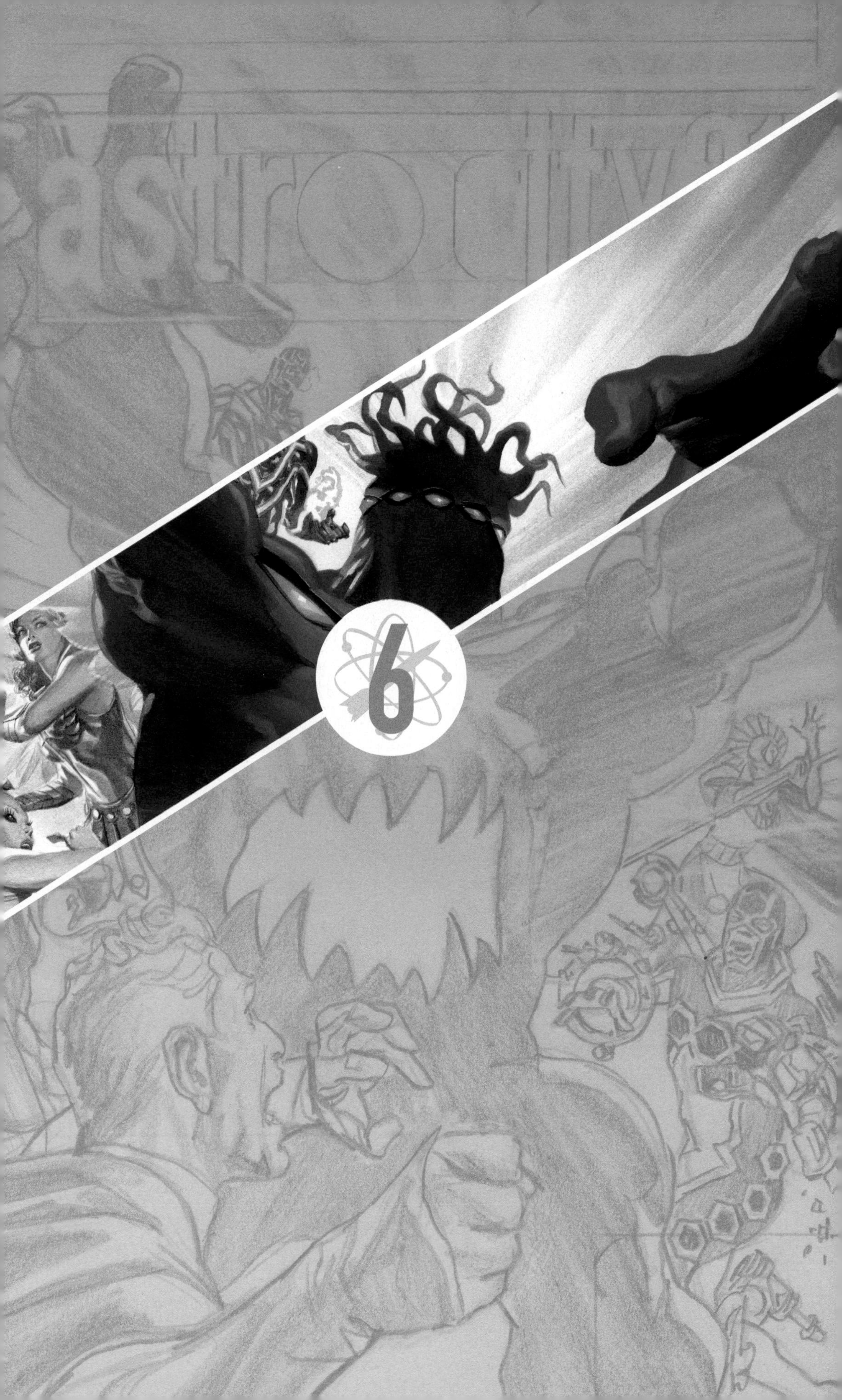
6

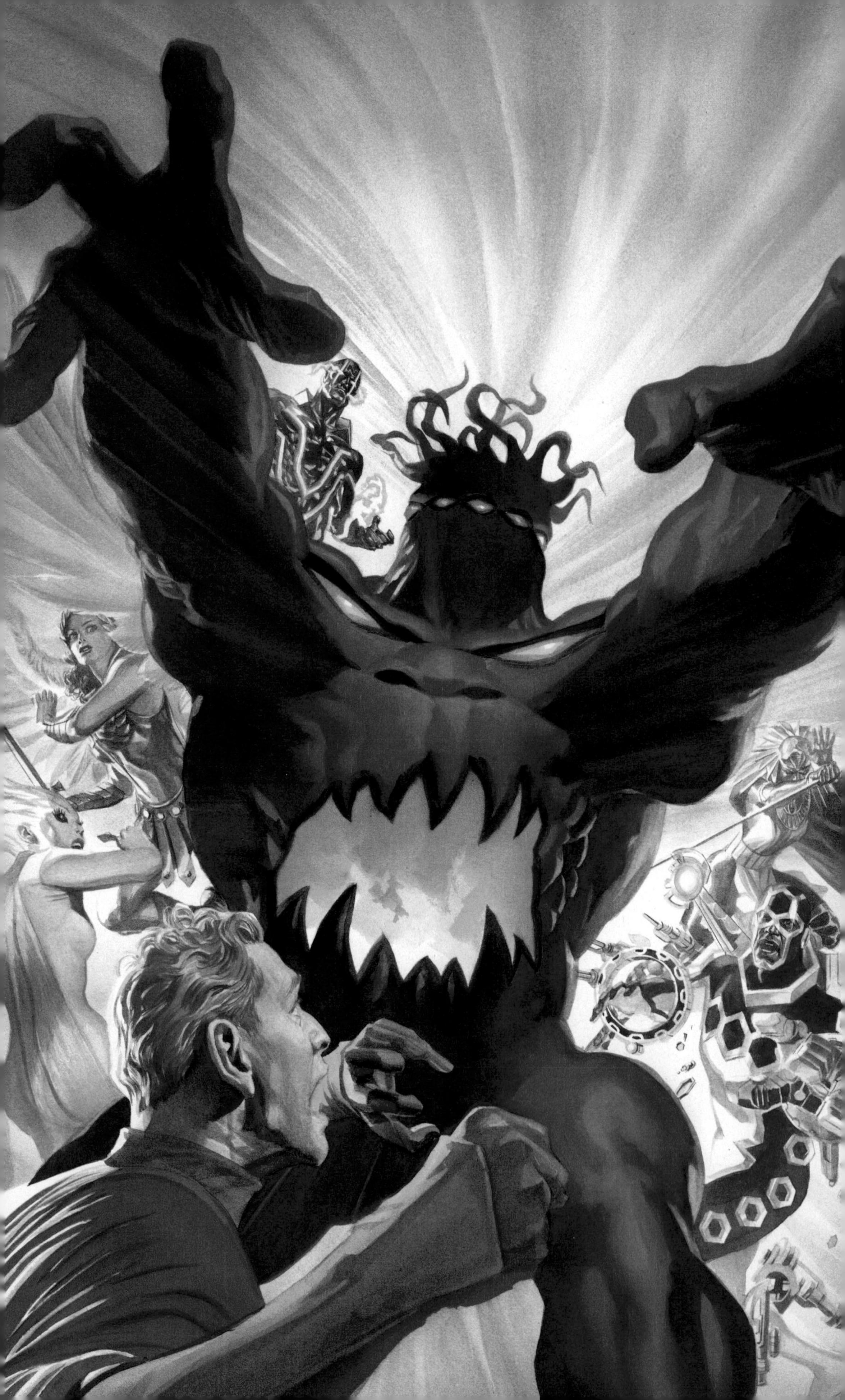

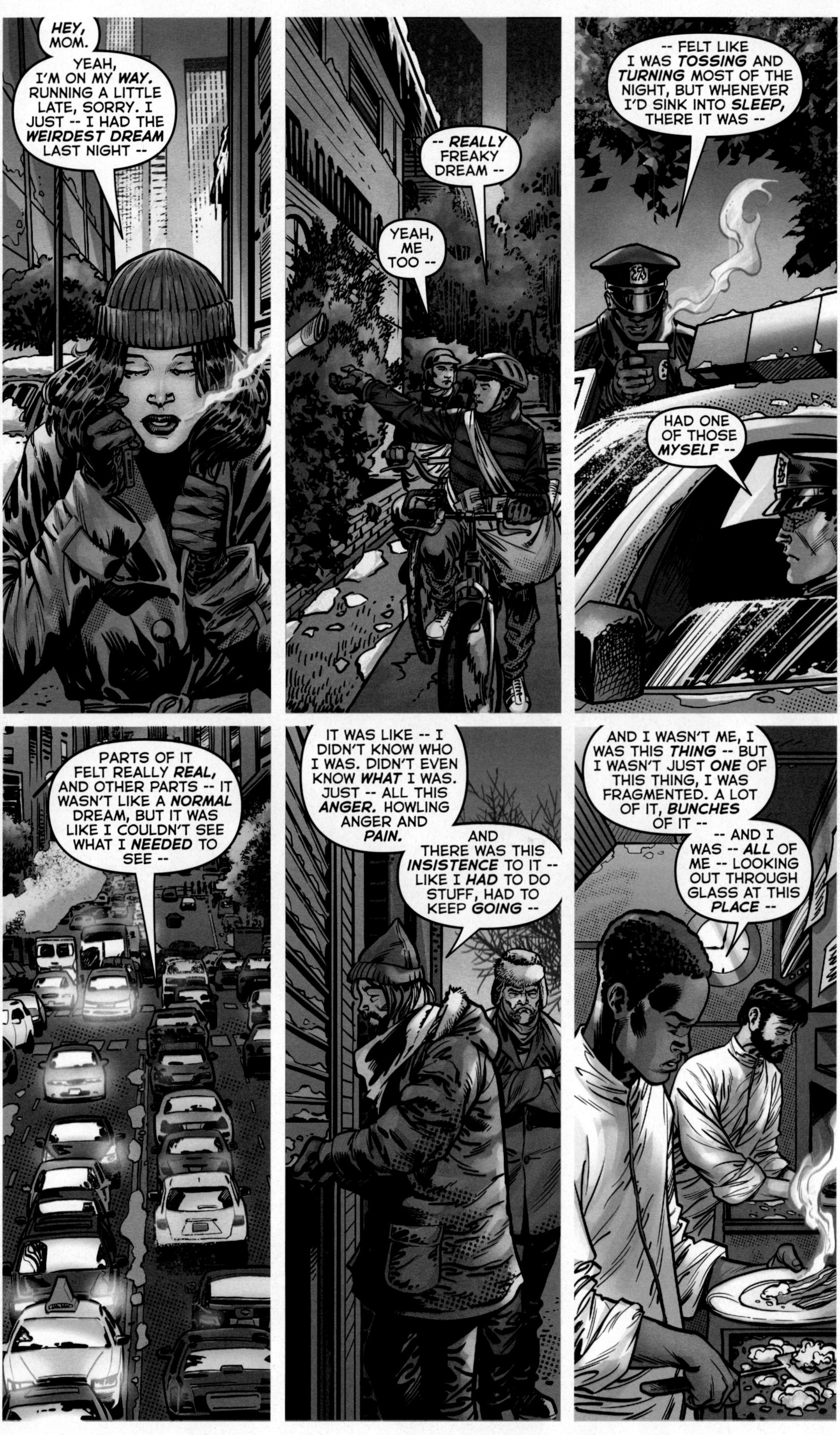
HEY, MOM.
YEAH, I'M ON MY WAY. RUNNING A LITTLE LATE, SORRY. I JUST -- I HAD THE WEIRDEST DREAM LAST NIGHT --
-- REALLY FREAKY DREAM --
YEAH, ME TOO --
-- FELT LIKE I WAS TOSSING AND TURNING MOST OF THE NIGHT, BUT WHENEVER I'D SINK INTO SLEEP, THERE IT WAS --
HAD ONE OF THOSE MYSELF --
PARTS OF IT FELT REALLY REAL, AND OTHER PARTS -- IT WASN'T LIKE A NORMAL DREAM, BUT IT WAS LIKE I COULDN'T SEE WHAT I NEEDED TO SEE --
IT WAS LIKE -- I DIDN'T KNOW WHO I WAS. DIDN'T EVEN KNOW WHAT I WAS. JUST -- ALL THIS ANGER. HOWLING ANGER AND PAIN.
AND THERE WAS THIS INSISTENCE TO IT -- LIKE I HAD TO DO STUFF, HAD TO KEEP GOING --
AND I WASN'T ME, I WAS THIS THING -- BUT I WASN'T JUST ONE OF THIS THING, I WAS FRAGMENTED. A LOT OF IT, BUNCHES OF IT --
-- AND I WAS -- ALL OF ME -- LOOKING OUT THROUGH GLASS AT THIS PLACE --

-- SOME SORT OF SCIENCE-FICTION PLACE --

IT WAS FIRST FAMILY HEADQUARTERS, I WENT ON A TOUR ONE TIME --

Hm? WHAT'S -- ?

AND ONE OF THE OLD GUYS WAS THERE. NOT THE SCIENTIST, THE OTHER OLD GUY --

BRAM BAM BAM BAM BRAM BAM BAM

-- AND WHATEVER I WAS, I HAD ALL THIS POWER, SUDDEN NEW POWER --

GUS? HEY, GUS!

SOMETHING SCREWY ABOUT THE LIVING NIGHTMARES WE SIPHONED OUTTA SAMARITAN'S BLOOD-STREAM! YOU SAID THEY'D STAY QUIET, BUT --

KSSH

KSHH

LORP

VORP

LLORP

AND THEN --

I WAS BACK TOGETHER AGAIN. ALL THE PIECES, THE FRAGMENTS, THEY COMBINED INTO ONE --

GUS! GUS, QUICK! MOVE YOUR WRINKLED OLD BUTT --

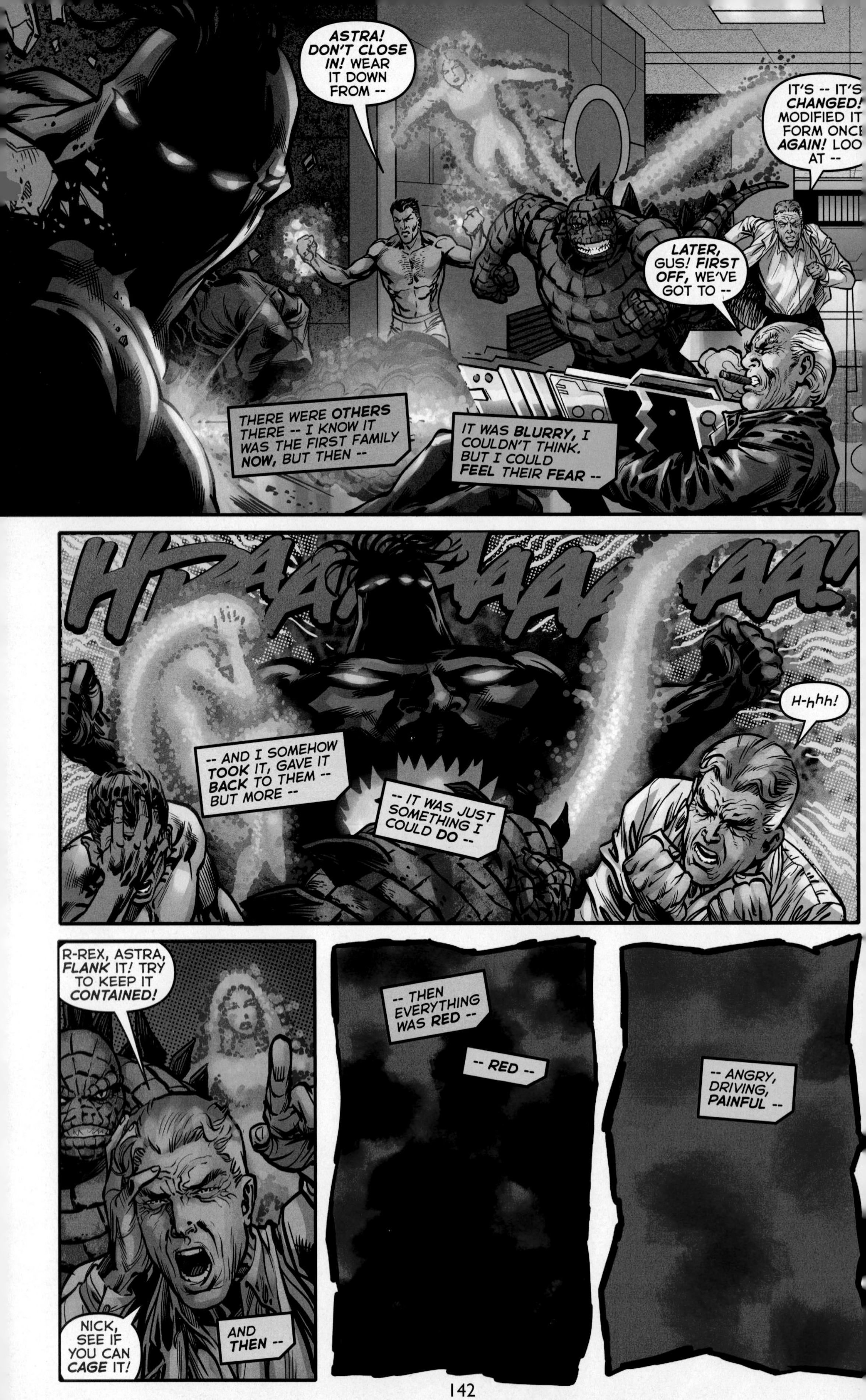
ASTRA! DON'T CLOSE IN! WEAR IT DOWN FROM --
IT'S -- IT'S CHANGED! MODIFIED IT FORM ONCE AGAIN! LOO AT --
LATER, GUS! FIRST OFF, WE'VE GOT TO --
THERE WERE OTHERS THERE -- I KNOW IT WAS THE FIRST FAMILY NOW, BUT THEN --
IT WAS BLURRY, I COULDN'T THINK. BUT I COULD FEEL THEIR FEAR --
HRAAAAAAAA!
H-hhh!
-- AND I SOMEHOW TOOK IT, GAVE IT BACK TO THEM -- BUT MORE --
-- IT WAS JUST SOMETHING I COULD DO --
R-REX, ASTRA, FLANK IT! TRY TO KEEP IT CONTAINED!
NICK, SEE IF YOU CAN CAGE IT!
AND THEN --
-- THEN EVERYTHING WAS RED --
-- RED --
-- ANGRY, DRIVING, PAINFUL --

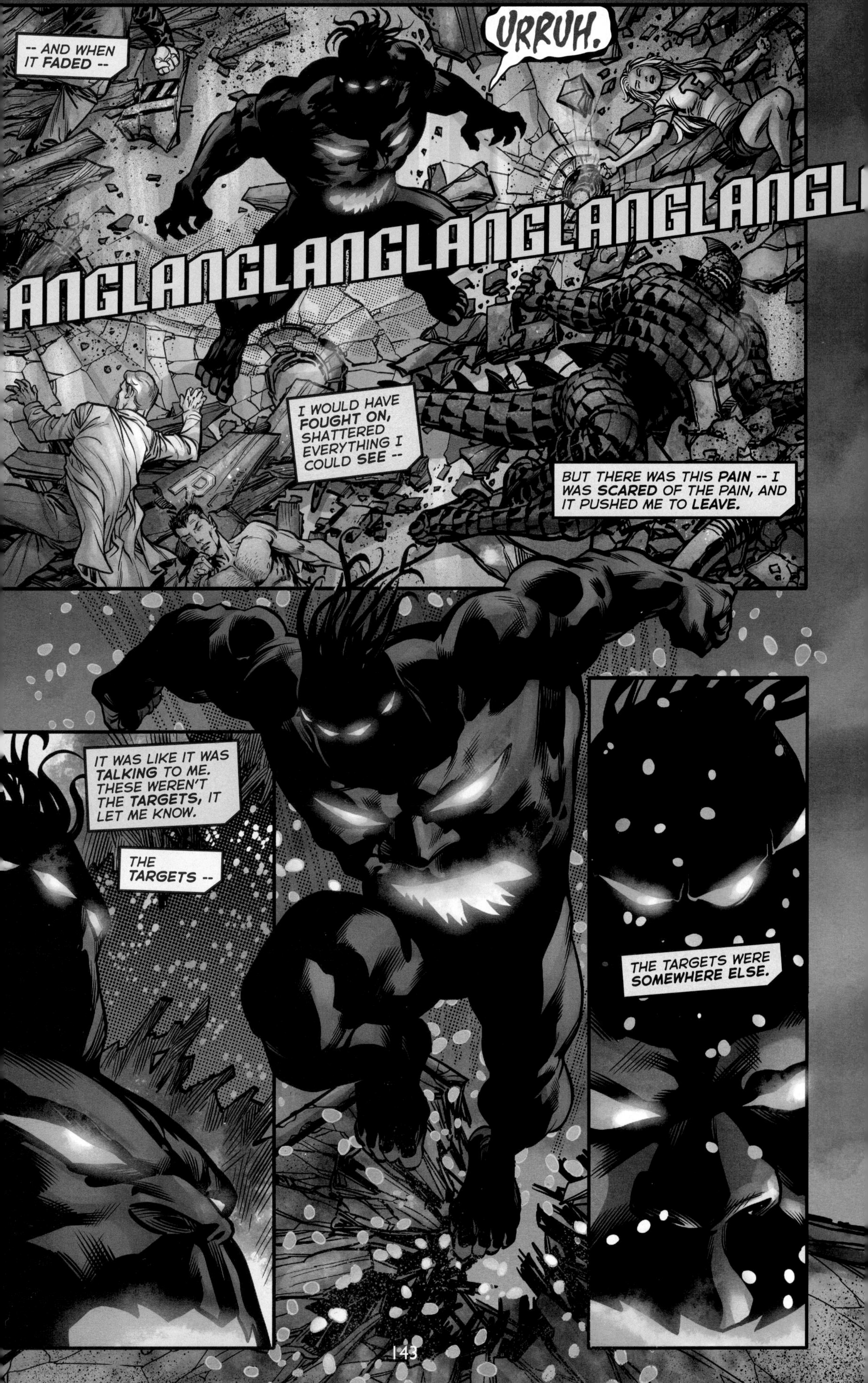
-- AND WHEN IT FADED --
URRUH.
ANGLANGLANGLANGLANGLANGLANGL
I WOULD HAVE FOUGHT ON, SHATTERED EVERYTHING I COULD SEE --
BUT THERE WAS THIS PAIN -- I WAS SCARED OF THE PAIN, AND IT PUSHED ME TO LEAVE.
IT WAS LIKE IT WAS TALKING TO ME. THESE WEREN'T THE TARGETS, IT LET ME KNOW.
THE TARGETS --
THE TARGETS WERE SOMEWHERE ELSE.

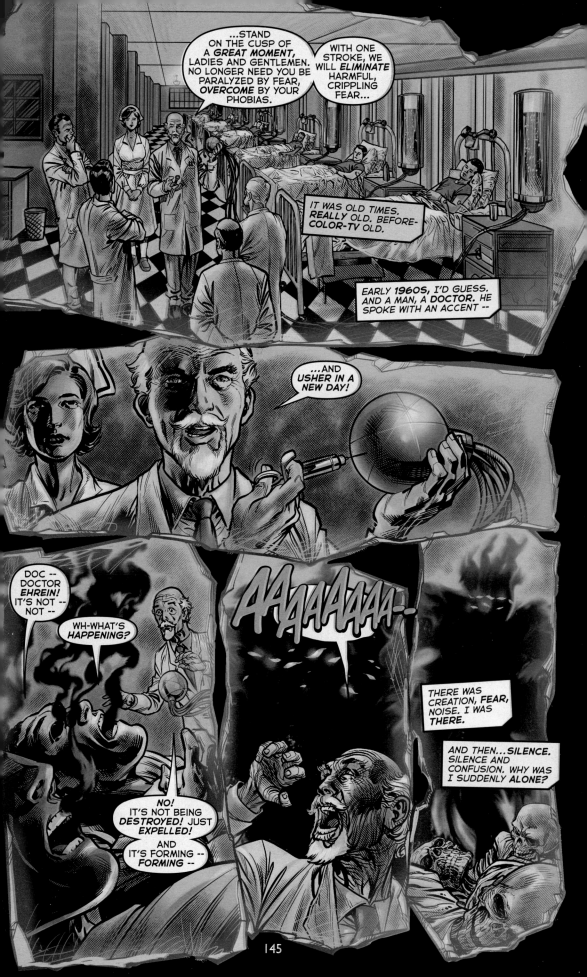

145

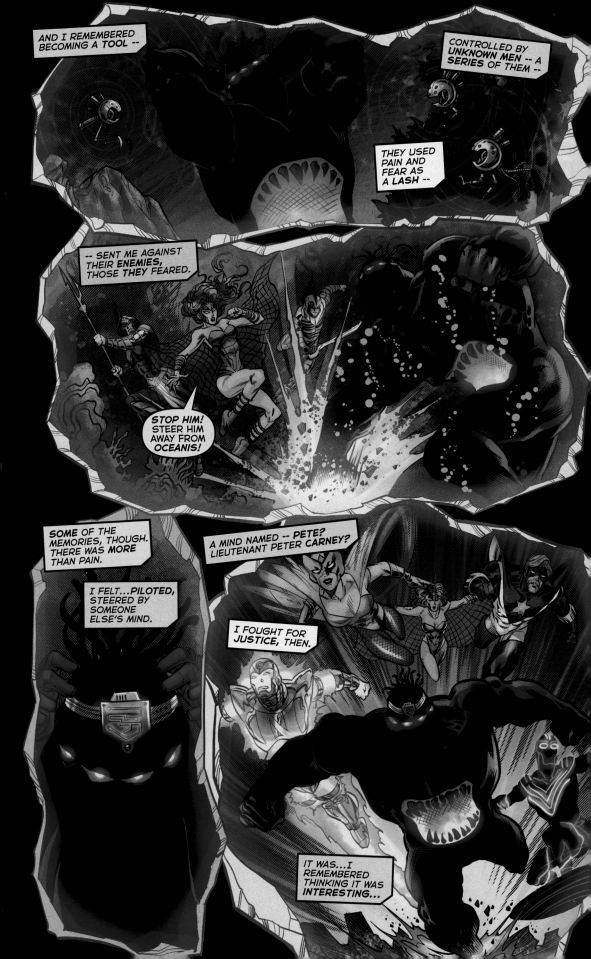

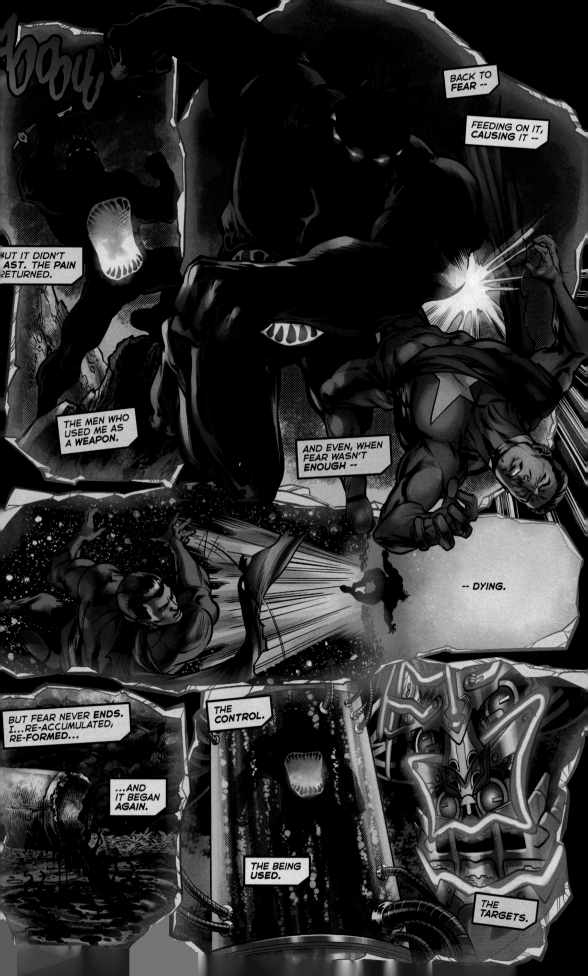

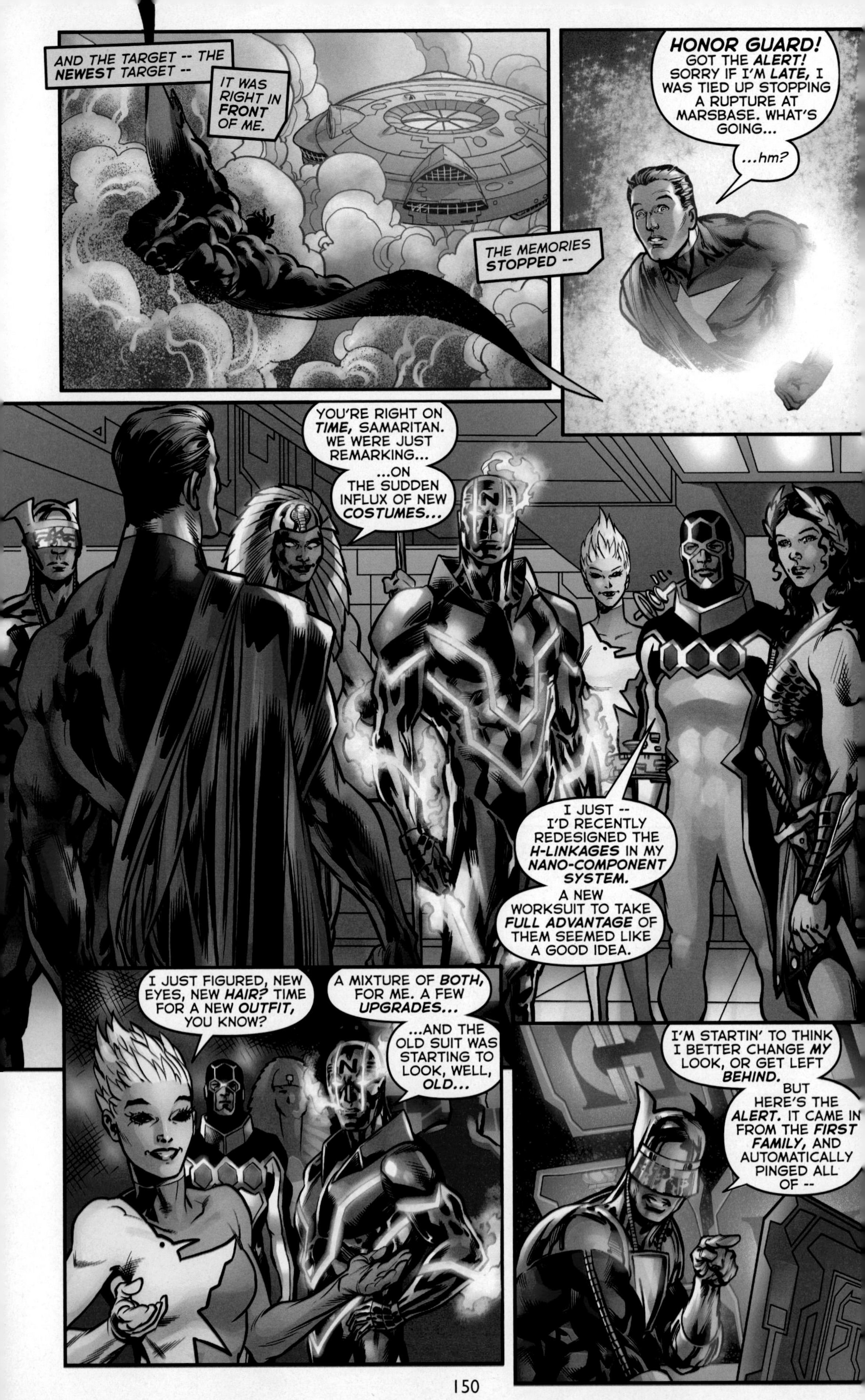
AND THE TARGET -- THE NEWEST TARGET --
IT WAS RIGHT IN FRONT OF ME.
THE MEMORIES STOPPED --
HONOR GUARD! GOT THE ALERT! SORRY IF I'M LATE, I WAS TIED UP STOPPING A RUPTURE AT MARSBASE. WHAT'S GOING...
...hm?
YOU'RE RIGHT ON TIME, SAMARITAN. WE WERE JUST REMARKING...
...ON THE SUDDEN INFLUX OF NEW COSTUMES...
I JUST -- I'D RECENTLY REDESIGNED THE H-LINKAGES IN MY NANO-COMPONENT SYSTEM.
A NEW WORKSUIT TO TAKE FULL ADVANTAGE OF THEM SEEMED LIKE A GOOD IDEA.
I JUST FIGURED, NEW EYES, NEW HAIR? TIME FOR A NEW OUTFIT, YOU KNOW?
A MIXTURE OF BOTH, FOR ME. A FEW UPGRADES...
...AND THE OLD SUIT WAS STARTING TO LOOK, WELL, OLD...
I'M STARTIN' TO THINK I BETTER CHANGE MY LOOK, OR GET LEFT BEHIND.
BUT HERE'S THE ALERT. IT CAME IN FROM THE FIRST FAMILY, AND AUTOMATICALLY PINGED ALL OF --

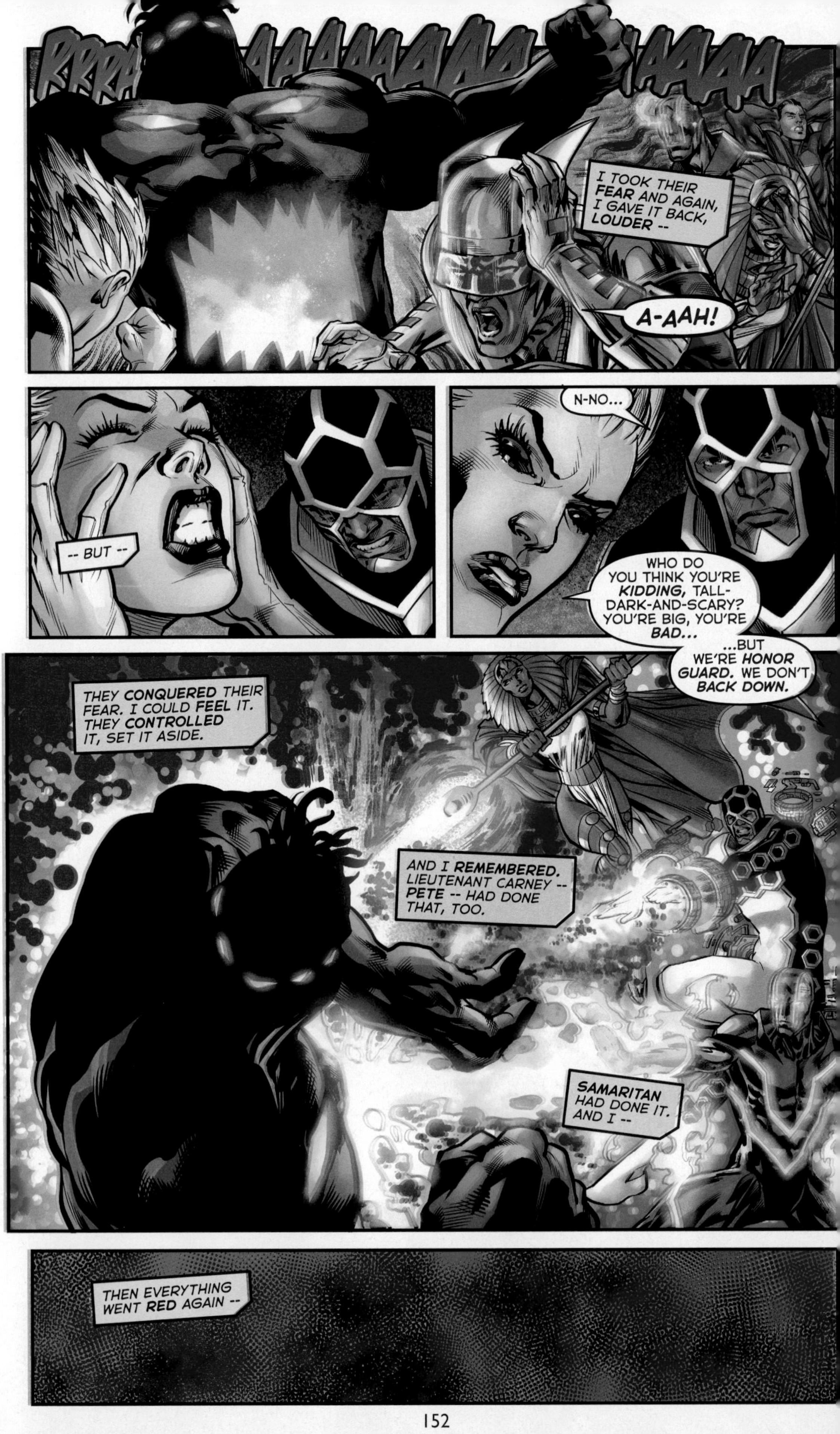
RRRAAAAAAAAAAAAAAAA
I TOOK THEIR FEAR AND AGAIN, I GAVE IT BACK, LOUDER --
A-AAH!
-- BUT --
N-NO...
WHO DO YOU THINK YOU'RE KIDDING, TALL-DARK-AND-SCARY? YOU'RE BIG, YOU'RE BAD...
...BUT WE'RE HONOR GUARD. WE DON'T BACK DOWN.
THEY CONQUERED THEIR FEAR. I COULD FEEL IT. THEY CONTROLLED IT, SET IT ASIDE.
AND I REMEMBERED. LIEUTENANT CARNEY -- PETE -- HAD DONE THAT, TOO.
SAMARITAN HAD DONE IT. AND I --
THEN EVERYTHING WENT RED AGAIN --

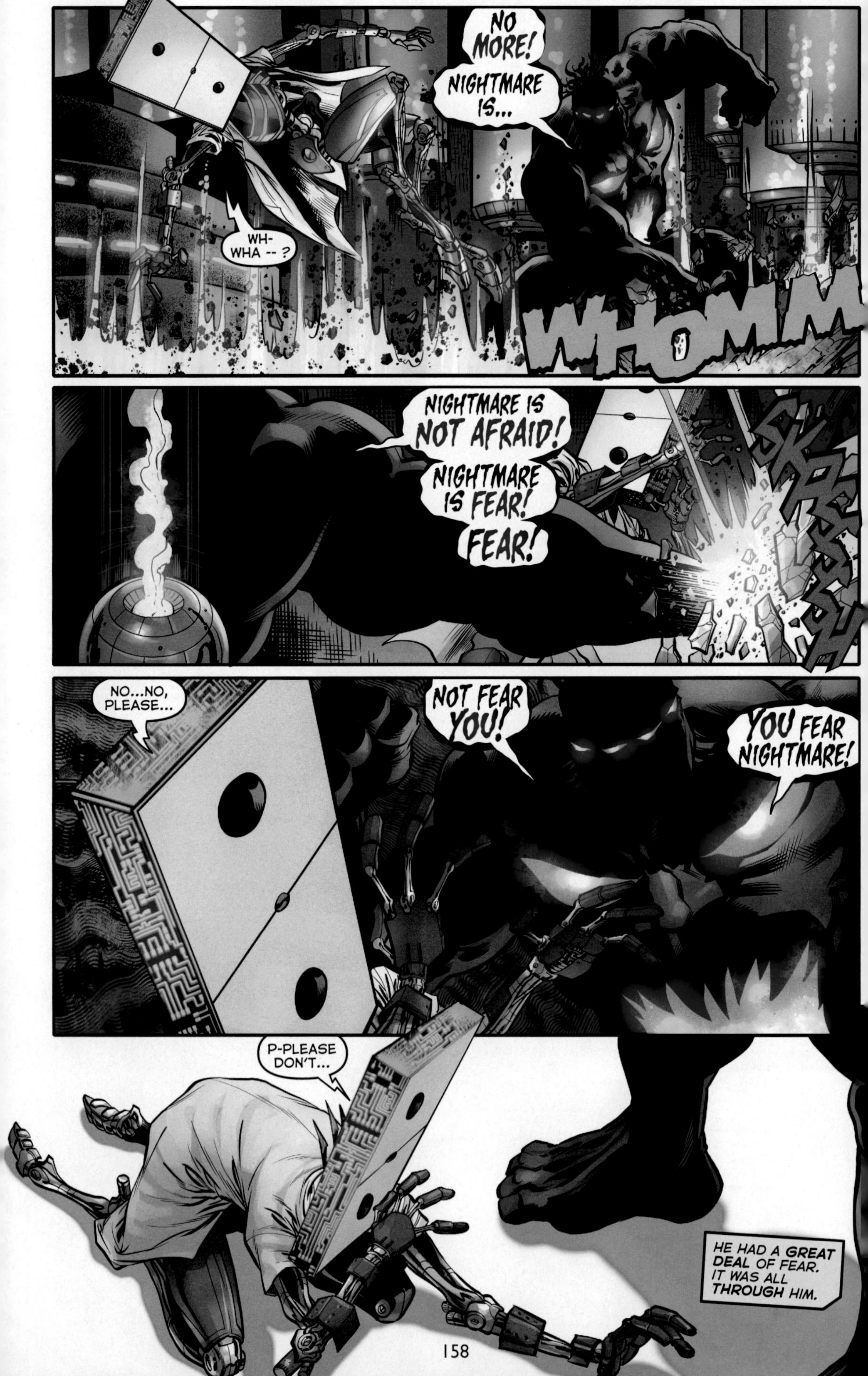
NO MORE!
NIGHTMARE IS...
WH- WHA -- ?
WHOMM
NIGHTMARE IS NOT AFRAID!
NIGHTMARE IS FEAR!
FEAR!
NO...NO, PLEASE...
NOT FEAR YOU!
YOU FEAR NIGHTMARE!
P-PLEASE DON'T...
HE HAD A GREAT DEAL OF FEAR. IT WAS ALL THROUGH HIM.

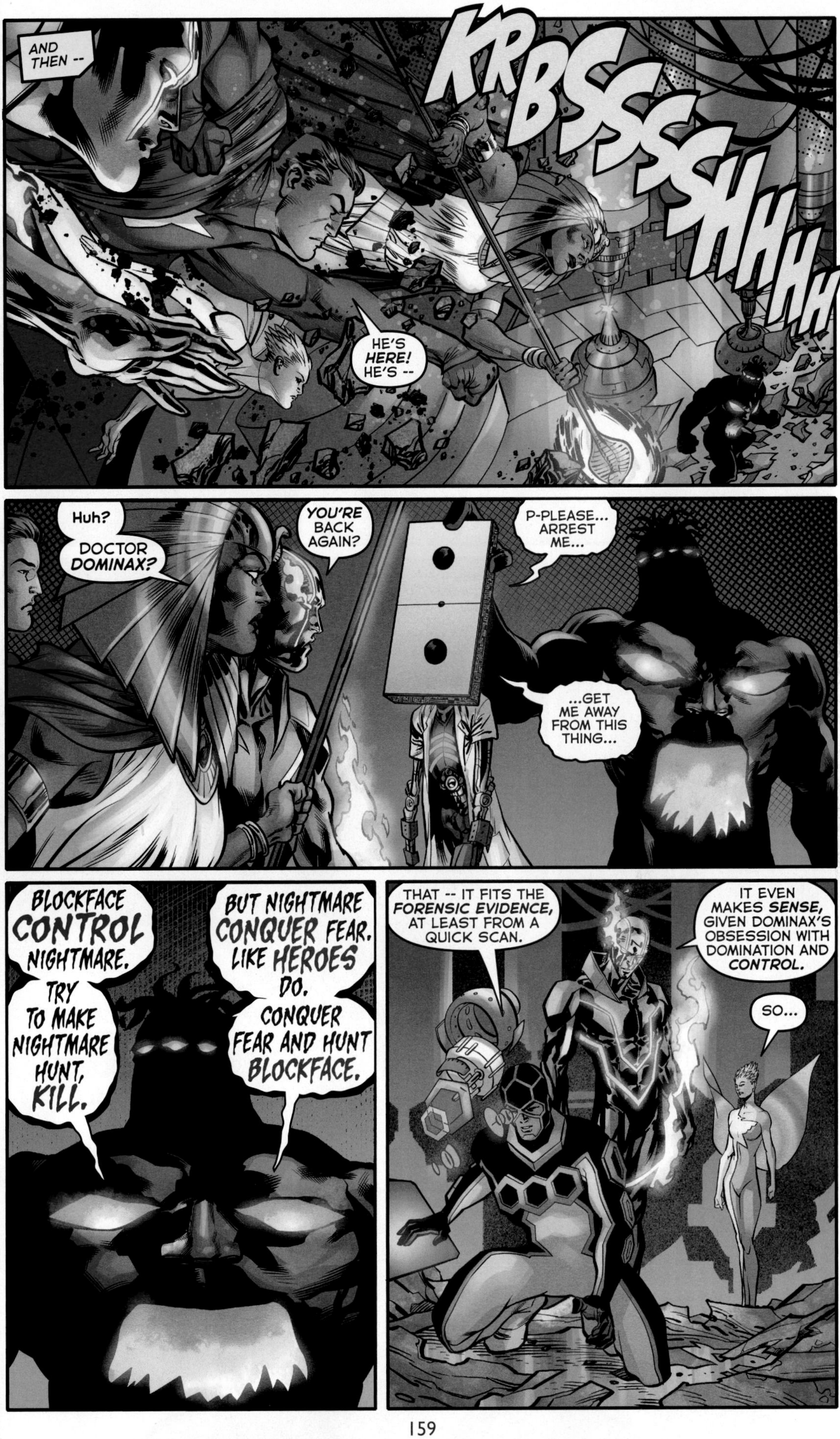
AND THEN --
KRBSSSHHHHH
HE'S HERE! HE'S --
Huh? DOCTOR DOMINAX?
YOU'RE BACK AGAIN?
P-PLEASE... ARREST ME...
...GET ME AWAY FROM THIS THING...
BLOCKFACE CONTROL NIGHTMARE.
TRY TO MAKE NIGHTMARE HUNT, KILL.
BUT NIGHTMARE CONQUER FEAR. LIKE HEROES DO.
CONQUER FEAR AND HUNT BLOCKFACE.
THAT -- IT FITS THE FORENSIC EVIDENCE, AT LEAST FROM A QUICK SCAN.
IT EVEN MAKES SENSE, GIVEN DOMINAX'S OBSESSION WITH DOMINATION AND CONTROL.
SO...

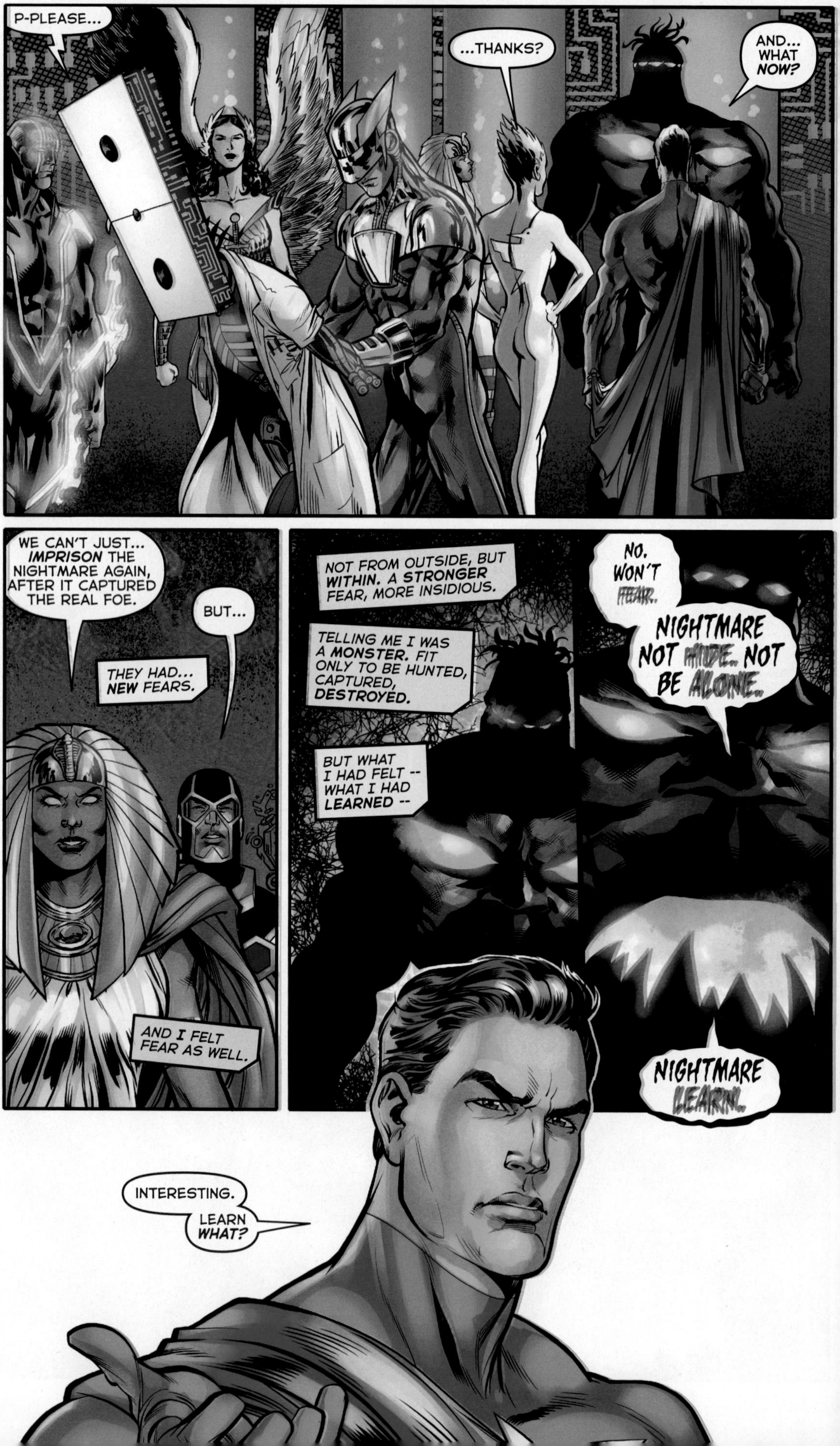
P-PLEASE...
...THANKS?
AND... WHAT NOW?
WE CAN'T JUST... IMPRISON THE NIGHTMARE AGAIN, AFTER IT CAPTURED THE REAL FOE.
BUT...
THEY HAD... NEW FEARS.
AND I FELT FEAR AS WELL.
NOT FROM OUTSIDE, BUT WITHIN. A STRONGER FEAR, MORE INSIDIOUS.
TELLING ME I WAS A MONSTER. FIT ONLY TO BE HUNTED, CAPTURED, DESTROYED.
BUT WHAT I HAD FELT -- WHAT I HAD LEARNED --
NO. WON'T FEAR.
NIGHTMARE NOT HIDE. NOT BE ALONE.
NIGHTMARE LEARN.
INTERESTING.
LEARN WHAT?

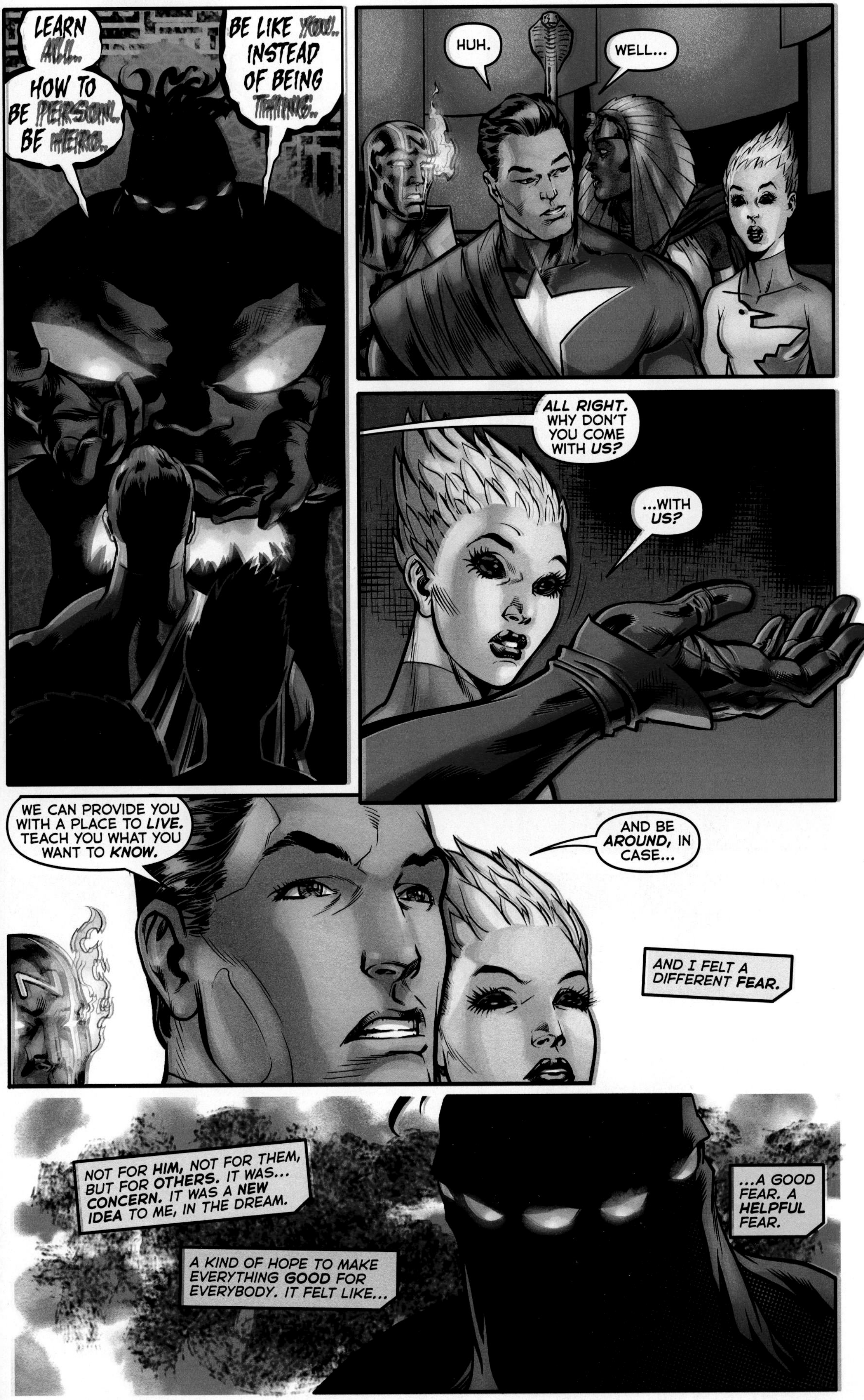
LEARN ALL..
HOW TO BE PERSON.. BE HERO..
BE LIKE YOU.. INSTEAD OF BEING THING..
HUH.
WELL...
ALL RIGHT. WHY DON'T YOU COME WITH US?
...WITH US?
WE CAN PROVIDE YOU WITH A PLACE TO LIVE. TEACH YOU WHAT YOU WANT TO KNOW.
AND BE AROUND, IN CASE...
AND I FELT A DIFFERENT FEAR.
NOT FOR HIM, NOT FOR THEM, BUT FOR OTHERS. IT WAS... CONCERN. IT WAS A NEW IDEA TO ME, IN THE DREAM.
A KIND OF HOPE TO MAKE EVERYTHING GOOD FOR EVERYBODY. IT FELT LIKE...
...A GOOD FEAR. A HELPFUL FEAR.

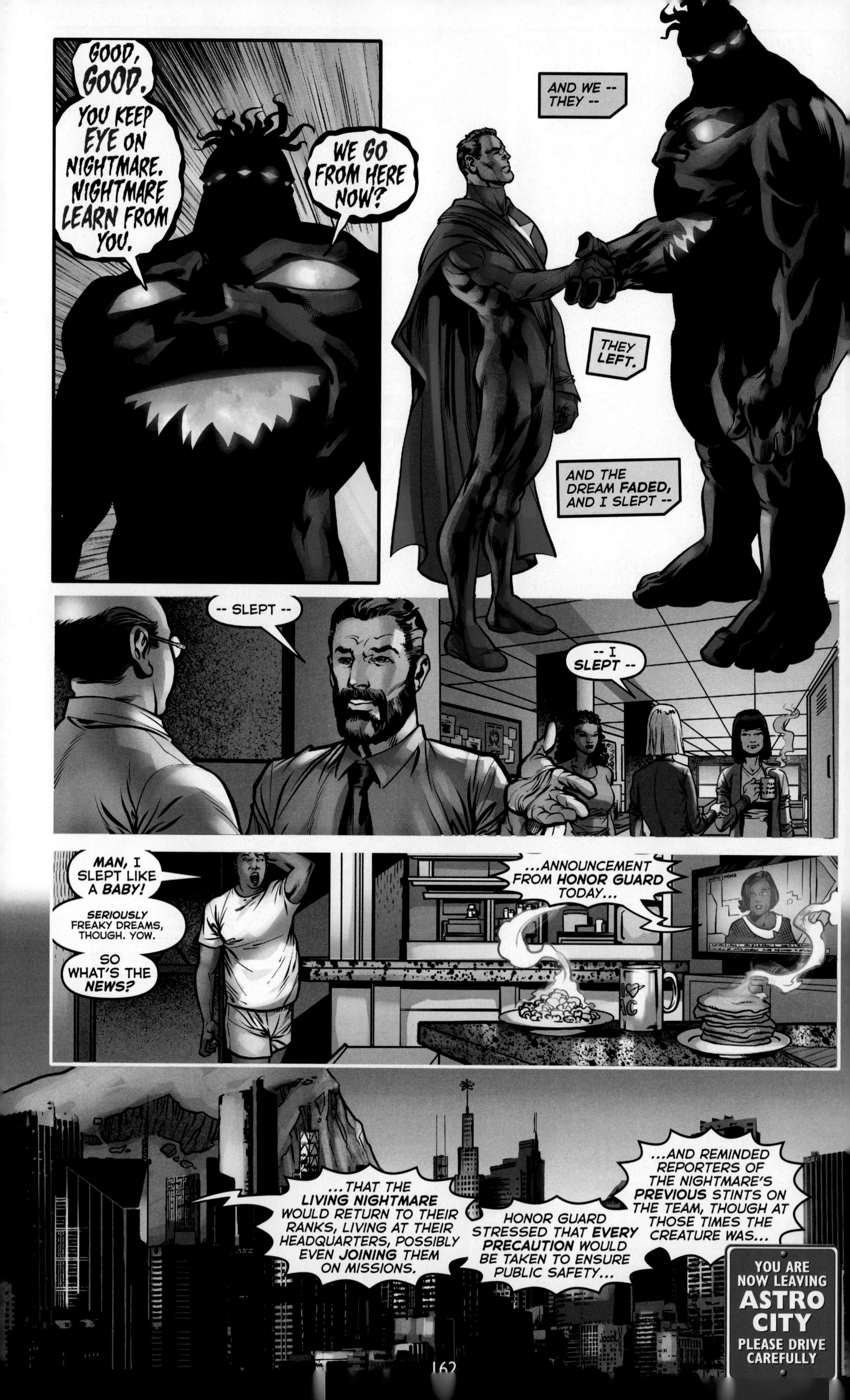
GOOD, GOOD.
YOU KEEP EYE ON NIGHTMARE. NIGHTMARE LEARN FROM YOU.
WE GO FROM HERE NOW?
AND WE -- THEY --
THEY LEFT.
AND THE DREAM FADED, AND I SLEPT --
-- SLEPT --
-- I SLEPT --
MAN, I SLEPT LIKE A BABY!
SERIOUSLY FREAKY DREAMS, THOUGH. YOW.
SO WHAT'S THE NEWS?
...ANNOUNCEMENT FROM HONOR GUARD TODAY...
...THAT THE LIVING NIGHTMARE WOULD RETURN TO THEIR RANKS, LIVING AT THEIR HEADQUARTERS, POSSIBLY EVEN JOINING THEM ON MISSIONS.
HONOR GUARD STRESSED THAT EVERY PRECAUTION WOULD BE TAKEN TO ENSURE PUBLIC SAFETY...
...AND REMINDED REPORTERS OF THE NIGHTMARE'S PREVIOUS STINTS ON THE TEAM, THOUGH AT THOSE TIMES THE CREATURE WAS...
YOU ARE NOW LEAVING ASTRO CITY PLEASE DRIVE CAREFULLY

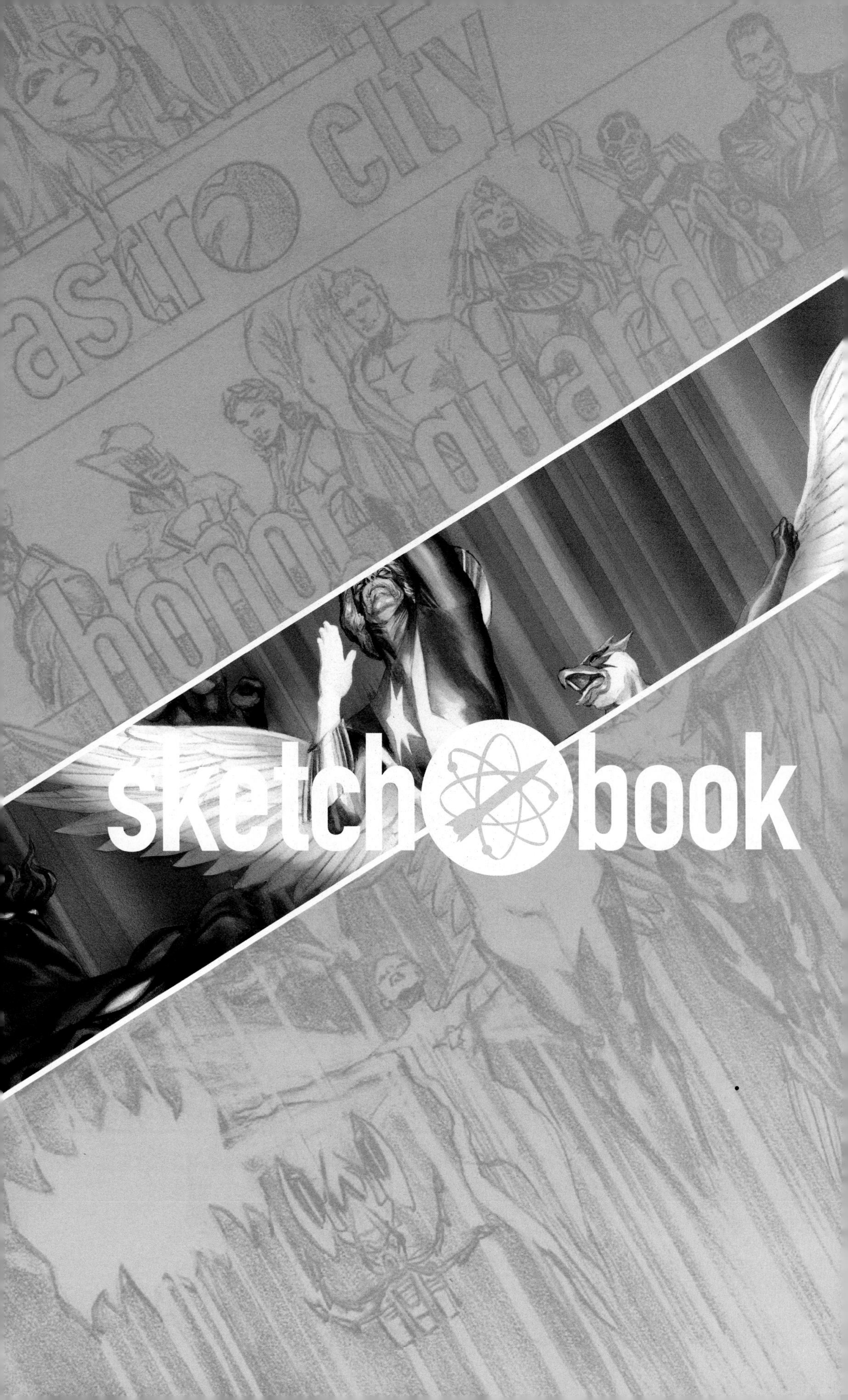
astro city
sketchbook

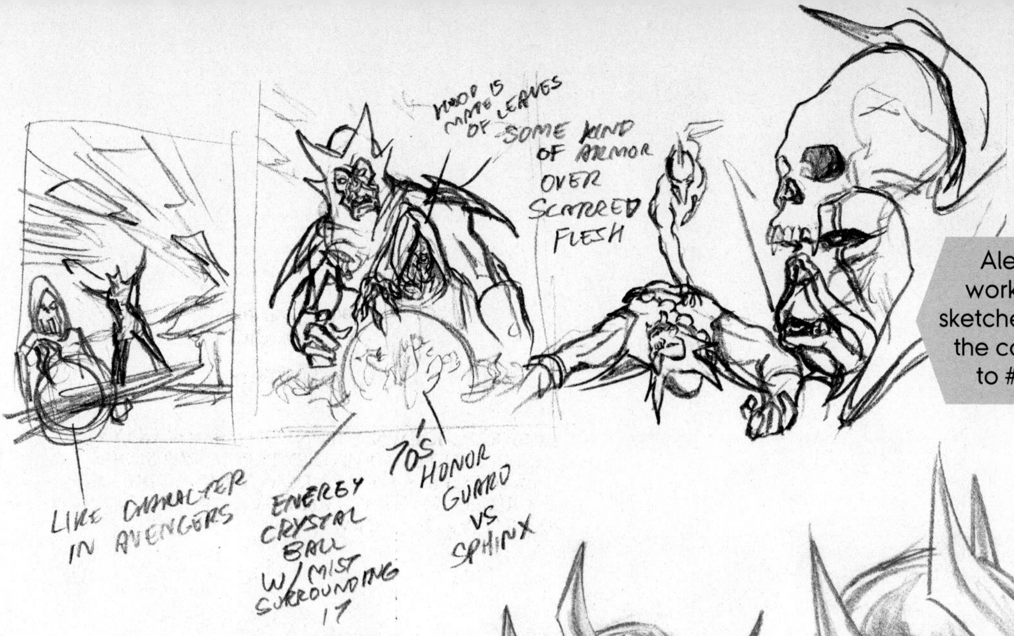
HOOD IS MADE LEAVES OF SOME KIND OF ARMOR OVER SCARRED FLESH
LIKE CHARACTER IN AVENGERS
ENERGY CRYSTAL BALL W/ MIST SURROUNDING 17
70's HONOR GUARD VS SPHINX

Alex's working sketches for the cover to #17.

For Krigari Ironhand, we needed a look that could go through "evolutions" as Krigari himself did—from desperate, naked survivor to barbarian reaver to the ruler of a worlds-spanning empire and commander of a star fleet.

krigari

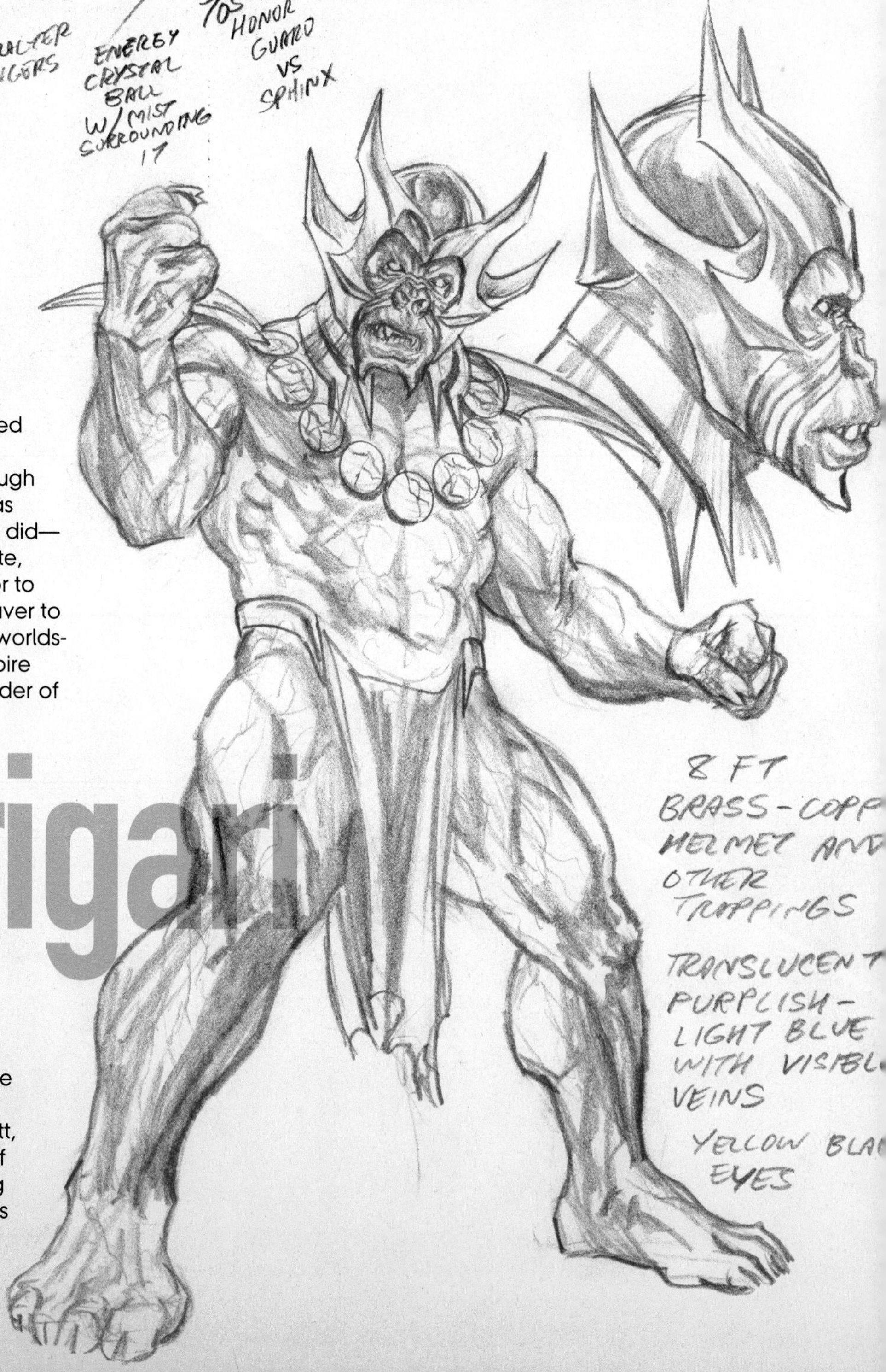
8 FT
BRASS-COPP
HELMET AND
OTHER TRAPPINGS
TRANSLUCENT
PURPLISH-
LIGHT BLUE
WITH VISIBL
VEINS
YELLOW BLA
EYES

Alex started, roughly, with an ape-like figure, and built a versatile design that Tom Grummett, the penciler of #17, could ring changes on as needed.

druin

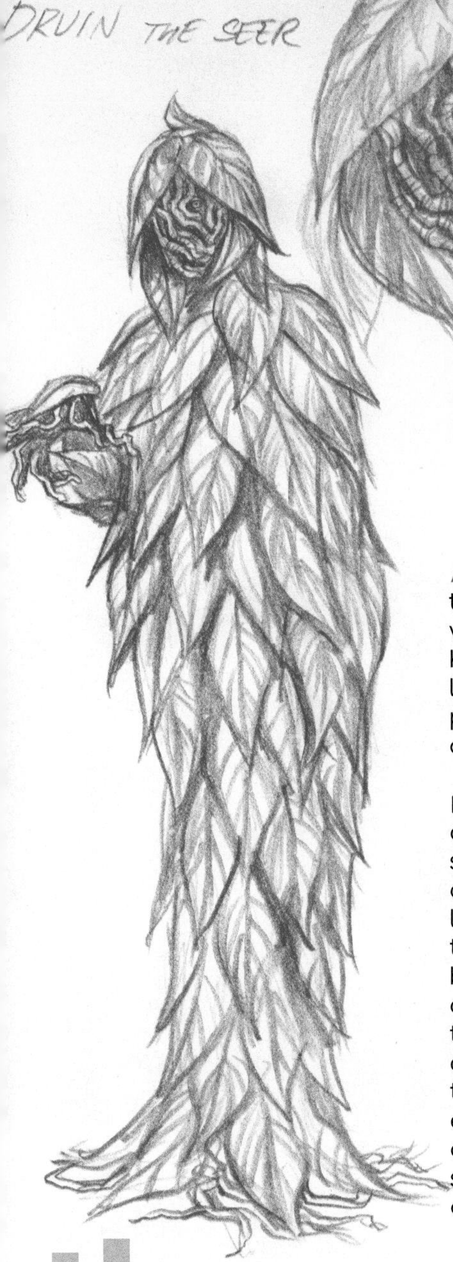

DRUIN THE SEER

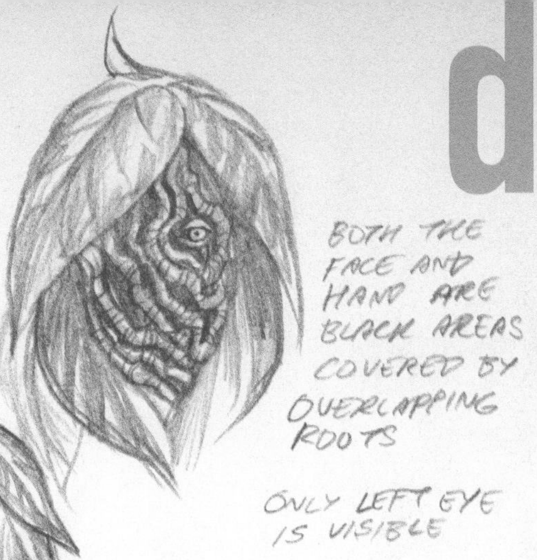

BOTH THE FACE AND HAND ARE BLACK AREAS COVERED BY OVERLAPPING ROOTS
ONLY LEFT EYE IS VISIBLE

For Druin the Seer, we wanted to contrast strongly with Krigari—a design rooted in flora, rather than fauna (in keeping with his secret), that looked creepy and mysterious rather than physically menacing. The roots covering his face worked particularly well.

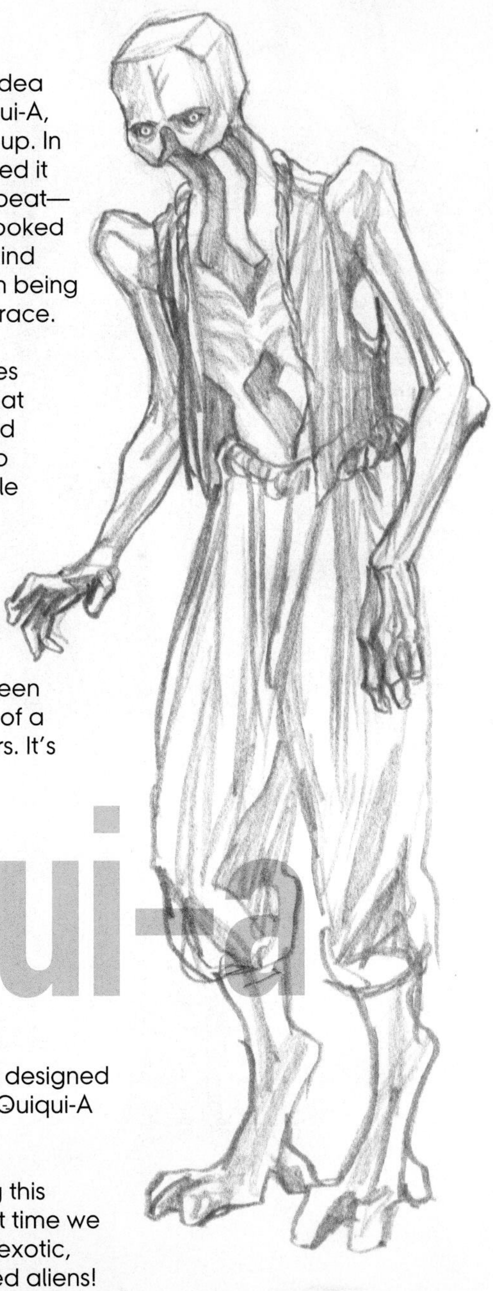

Alex had an idea for the Quiqui-A, and drew it up. In the end, we decided it was a little too offbeat—Kurt suggested it looked like they'd have mind powers rather than being a simple agrarian race.

(One of the oddities of ASTRO CITY is that sometimes our lead characters need to look like forgettable throwaway background characters, and the background characters need to look distinctive enough to have been an important part of a series cast for years. It's a balancing act.)

the quiqui-a

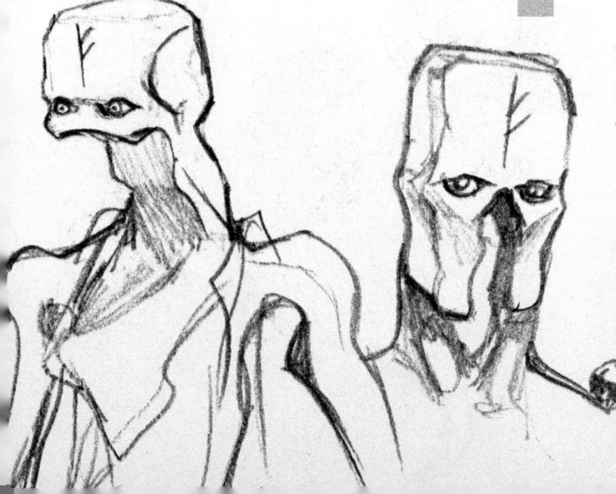

So Tom Grummett designed a simpler-looking Quiqui-A for the story...

...but we're saving this design for the next time we need some more exotic, mentally-advanced aliens!

Our interstellar hero, Starfighter, had looked slick and cosmic in his 1970s-era appearances, but now we needed him to look and feel old and weathered, like an aging gunfighter...

SONS OF ANARCHY LOOK

DUE ON THE 15th!

WIZENED OLD WIZARD VERSION OF SAURA
PONY TAIL
SAM NEILL

SHE'S OLDER TOO
52

BANGBOOM
BACKGROUND
FLYING CREATURES
VEGETATION

starfighter

For the next generation of Starfighters, Kurt gave Jesús Merino rough descriptions, and Jesús worked magic with them.

For Jarranatha, we wanted the feel of 1930s pulp science fiction, so Alex designed us some dangerous-looking male aliens...

jarranatha

...and exotic-looking, alluring women who don't seem to wear much. He specifically wanted Illula to have some Rubenesque heft to her, to go against the skinny fashion-model type, and give her an earthy, hearty look. And Kurt liked the idea that she might have been an archetypal pulp princess in her youth, but she'd filled out with age, even as Starfighter had kind of dried up.

ASTRO CITY #22 A

PRINCE DEVEN —

JAGUAR MEN —

khapak iqun

By our second issue with Jesús, we were a lot more comfortable throwing character design work at him.

And whether it was noble princes, murderous cat-men or exotic settings, he made it all look great.

GIANT STONE MEN (KIRBY-STYLE!)

Alex's working sketches for the cover to #22.